WESTMAR COLLEGE LI

P9-CRI-005

EXPERIENCE AS ART

SUNY Series in Philosophy
Robert C. Neville, Editor

Experience As Art
Aesthetics in Everyday Life

Joseph H. Kupfer

DEPARTMENT OF PHILOSOPHY
IOWA STATE UNIVERSITY

State University of New York Press   Albany

BH
301
.E8
K86
1983

For my students

Published by State University of New York Press, Albany

© 1983 State University of New York

All rights reserved

Printed in the United States of America

No part of this book may be used or reproduced in any manner whatsoever without written permission except in the case of brief quotations embodied in critical articles and reviews.

For information, address State University of New York Press, State University Plaza, Albany, N.Y., 12246

Library of Congress Cataloging in Publication Data
Kupfer, Joseph H.
   Experience as art.

   1. Experience.   2. Aesthetics.   I. Title.
BH301.E8K86   1983   111'.85   82-19258
ISBN 0-87395-692-3
ISBN 0-87395-693-1 (pbk.)

10 9 8 7 6 5 4 3 2 1

102190

Contents

Acknowledgments

I WOULD LIKE to thank my good friend and colleague, John Elrod, who encouraged me to write this book and advised me wisely in its preparation. I also benefitted from Iowa State University's generosity in providing me with a leave of absence during which a first draft was written. That first draft was substantially reworked in response to two trenchant critics: my wife, who urged me to be more concrete and colloquial; and John McDermott, whose insight into the project's potential was matched only by his patience in counselling me how to realize it.

Introduction

The serious matter is that philosophies have denied that common experience is capable of developing from within itself methods which will secure direction for itself and will create inherent standards of judgment and value.... [They have failed] to realize the value that intelligent search could reveal and mature among the things of ordinary experience. John Dewey*

Most of us readily acknowledge that art in particular and aesthetic values in general enhance the quality of life, making it more pleasant. Harmonious color combinations of food on our plates or well-proportioned eaves on our houses are certainly a nice added touch, but few think them as important as the nourishment or shelter we derive from them. It seems fair to say that we view aesthetic detail and form in everyday life as decorative lagnappe, far from the core of our interests and our urgent concerns. In books on "aesthetics" we expect and usually find discussions about art and the artistic properties of commonplace things like food combinations and housing architecture. They rarely address moral, social, or personal concerns. Appropriately enough, aesthetics has come to be regarded as the pretty accessory to the more momentous normative disciplines, not to be taken too seriously by the majority of philosophers.

In what follows, I depart from this common understanding, arguing that aesthetic values permeate everyday life and ought not to be thought of as the exclusive province of museums and concert halls. Now one way to show this is to emphasize how "artful" everyday objects such as clothing, furniture, utensils, apples, and sunsets may be. This is to demonstrate how much like works of art working artifacts or natural objects in our environment are. But while it's a

---

*Experience and Nature (New York: Dover, 1958), p. 38.

1

worthwhile task, this is not the approach that will be taken here. Rather, art and the "artful" are to be subordinated to the overarching perspective that aesthetic relations and qualities inform our personal and social development in very powerful ways, and they exert this influence through their presence in our daily undertakings, such as making decisions, playing and working with others, or engaging in sexual activities.

What is here emphasized, then, is the basic importance and pervasiveness of the aesthetic in various spheres of life, not just in the obviously artistic. This approach runs counter to the popular view which tends to place aesthetic ingredients in the everyday on the periphery of human interests. To loosen the grip of such a tendency of thought I try to exhibit the importance of the aesthetic within everyday activities by focusing on certain normative themes. These themes are not themselves "aesthetic" in the traditional sense in which "expression," "representation," or "meaning" are. Rather, such moral and social themes as personal development, responsibility, and community are worked out through the varieties of aesthetic experience. My interest in aesthetics is therefore part of a larger concern for the quality of the ins and outs of so-called ordinary experience. For it is in and out of our ordinary commerce with the world that the "good life" is led. This is not, then, a book "in" aesthetics in the usual sense, but an aesthetic investigation of the human interests and activities which comprise daily living.

Discussions of artistic theories of expression, beauty, representation, and the like are important, as are analyses of critical discourse about such matters. But this sort of work in aesthetics does not deal very much with the everyday material out of which art grows, with all its beauty and expression. We need to move the philosophical discussion back to the workaday world lest our analyses and theories, arguments and counterproposals, speak only to intellectual formulations of experience and not the experience itself. This book is an attempt to deal more directly with the impact of aesthetic experience in our everyday living, looking to the substance of everyday life, as the epigram from Dewey suggests, for direction and standards.

We can learn the significance of the aesthetic in our lives by "intelligent search among the things of ordinary experience"; at the same time we can learn the significance of its absence. The latter is necessary to understanding the subtle failure of contemporary American life. There is a felt but largely unarticulated aesthetic deprivation which underlies more and more of our daily dissatisfaction. This deprivation is brought to light by calling attention to the part aesthetic experience plays in the education of the individual and in his or her capacities for social participation.

It is precisely because the educational and miseducational power of the environmental aesthetic goes unheeded that so many of us feel disaffected and estranged in the midst of material abundance. We have only to look at the failure of "urban renewal," at classroom violence and intergenerational alienation for examples of the steep price we are paying for this neglect. Human growth requires a variety of aesthetic relations in the everyday environment. In examining these relations we will follow a dialectical procedure. By taking up such concerns as death and sex, the full scope and force of the aesthetic emerges; by setting forth a general conception of the aesthetic, we take a perspective from which to criticize everyday practices and institutions. Each facet is subsequently enlarged by the other. Our understanding of the aesthetic is completed through our inquiry into the everyday; and our grasp of the problematic nature of daily life is deepened by our aesthetic approach. In taking this approach, "aesthetic experience" occupies a central place.

The investigation here of everyday interests and activities turns upon a belief in the fundamental importance of aesthetic experience. It is "intrinsically" valuable or valued, worth having because of its inherent qualities and relations. While works of art are probably the most reliable and familiar sources of these experiences, they are by no means the exclusive or even most crucial loci for them. As this book tries to demonstrate, a variety of everyday interests and activities can (and should) be rich in aesthetic values. A basketball game is more enjoyable when appreciated as an aesthetic whole, with its changing rhythms, its sudden grace, and its dramatic tensions finally, decisively, resolved. And classroom life is more rewarding when students experience their learnings as the climax of spirited but directed give and take. To the extent that these daily activities are charged with aesthetic qualities and relations, we experience them as fulfilling and are fulfilled.

But the burden of this book is to show how the aesthetic dimensions of everyday life are "extrinsically" valuable, instrumental in developing people into more deliberate, autonomous community members. This is to look at aesthetic experience as educational in its broad, original sense: futhering the overall intellectual, emotional, physical, and social growth of the individual. Rather than summarize a conception of aesthetic experience that unfolds in a leisurely way throughout the book, it might be more helpful here to illustrate how aesthetic qualities and relations can perform this educational role in some particular everyday experiences. In this way, our preliminary sketch of the constituents of aesthetic experience will also introduce the book's pedagogical orientation.

The way we are educated by the constituents of aesthetic experience is illustrated in the nature of our sexual relationships. Are they defined by the dominance by one person necessitating the other's passivity? If so, then an important aesthetic dimension is missing: the balance within the individual between doing and taking in, between activity and receptivity. In aesthetically complete sex, our active and receptive sides are balanced because they are in phase with our partner's, each *responding* to the other. Good conversations evidence this active/passive mesh. It distinguishes them from lectures in which we either speak or are spoken to. What is especially important is the way responsivity in sexual behavior can dispose us to think, feel, and act in other, different situations. A friend of mine wrote that a man makes love the way he talks. One-sidedness in sexuality, lack of aesthetic "balance," disposes us to be unresponsive in nonsexual activities: either actively dominating or submissively passive. We see this in the way people work and play, drive and dance, as well as talk with one another. However, aesthetically complete sex contributes to our social growth by exemplifying relations characteristic of aesthetic experience per se. Realizing these relations in our daily practice helps promote the corresponding habits which make for fruitful human interaction in a range of contexts, for a variety of purposes.

In aesthetic experience, we respond to what is presented to us by discriminating among its constitutents so as to integrate them into a unified whole. The whole is formed out of the interaction among its parts. While these parts are distinct, making distinctive contributions, their relations with one another and their place in the whole is decisive for their meaning and value. In the aesthetic ideal, they enhance and deepen each other's significance: one word's connotation enriching another's meaning, this musical phrase heightening that one's effect, the shape of a roof setting off the window's lines. The parts are interdependent, forming a kind of community.

Or rather, we draw them into community. Because this unified outcome demands our sensitivities and integrative powers, aesthetic experience unobtrusively encourages us to participate in the formation of community. Since this activity is intrinsically rewarding, moreover, we receive subtle education in the joy to be found in an ordering, integrative life. Aesthetic experience thus provides a kind of playful practice in "community organization" in which we learn to work our contribution into the fabric of what another presents to us. This is exemplified socially in the ideal of the aesthetic classroom.

In the aesthetically formed classroom, the discussion grows out of the participation of the students. The contributions of each are modified by the responses of the others. In the ideal situation, the teacher does not exclusively bear the burden of orchestrating the interplay of ideas; rather, the students themselves aim for the most comprehensive, complete understanding of the subject matter at hand. This occurs when each strives to bring out the best in the others, the way contestants in sports can bring out the best in each other through the intensity of their competitive efforts. "Competition" among students, then, is not the attempt to defeat or outmaneuver one another, but an effort to draw out and elaborate upon the merit in one another's thought. A student "bests" another by making better his original contribution to the class: as in aesthetic experience per se, in which the parts deepen and strengthen one another.

In this way the class activity can itself constitute an aesthetic experience for students and teacher. The student (part) and the class discussion (whole) bring each other to completion. The ordering of thought within each student and the development of the discussion among them mutually progress and are mutually dependent. As a result of helping shape and direct such discussion, the students learn something beyond information or technical skill. They learn how to carry on inquiry with others: how to offer opinions, criticize and defend them; question, argue, and rethink ideas in a community of thought. They learn how to discriminate among the welter of facts and to organize them within an overarching conceptual scheme. Their thinking, in fact, becomes more comprehensive as they see how to overcome objections or sticking points and to account for more material. The conflicting and combining of opinion through which this takes place, moreover, is experienced as an aesthetic process when the class forms a community of inquiry.

But most education and miseducation occurs informally in the broad influence of our social environment. The institutions which define our society—family, work, politics, art, and so forth—have an enormous impact on what we become. When these institutions are aesthetically impoverished, the individual's form-making capacities go unnurtured. He or she is unable to form aesthetic relations in work, with other people, or in more direct attempts at artistry. Today we are witnessing the emergence of an individual who pursues aesthetic experience but whose constructive, organizing capacities have not been socially educated. A detached, self-conscious kind of violence becomes a natural course for this person when he or she tries to make the environment yield aesthetic value. "Ultra-Violence" is violence sought for its aesthetic qualities: the sensations obtained from the forceful destruction of people. In this perverse marriage between the aesthetic and the violent, the individual delights in the blood and screams of a human being broken up into so many no-longer-human parts. The ill-formed environment spawns an individual incapable of *forming,* creating anything in his or her life. The de-formed love of the aesthetic, therefore, turns for satisfaction to the sensations of violent destruction.

Everyday life requires thinking about what to do. Where sex, sport, or classroom life are specific undertakings, decision-making itself as a distinct activity cuts across all that we entertain with forethought. It occupies an organizing place, "above" particular concerns, so that when we think about decision-making as a distinct subject we are considering *ways* of proceeding with all the other business of life. To decide how to deliberate and make decisions is therefore a meta-decision, with ripple effects on all that we decide to do. Aesthetic experience, I argue, offers a standard, in fact, the best by which to evaluate our everyday decision-making. By imaginatively running through the consequences of possible action plans, we see and feel them yielding coherent or jarring sequences of events, patterns of interaction. We imaginatively experience them as wearing or stimulating, repetitive or diversified, dead-ended or evolving. Such aesthetic deliberation, what Dewey calls "dramatic rehearsal," also places *us* in the anticipated situations: Do they help prepare us for future, unexpected action because of their demands on us? Are we free to invent and improvise within the unfolding scheme? When we imaginatively project ourselves into the concrete implications of a plan of action, we can evaluate it aesthetically, according to whether or not it forms an integrated, continuous whole out of a diversity of interests and actions.

Without aesthetic qualities and relations in our daily lives, it is difficult to avoid succumbing to some form of fragmentation. In decision-making itself we too easily slide into the method of calculation in which the pleasures and pains, costs and benefits of each available option are weighed and summed. But no overall aesthetic "picture" of how we will live as a result of these decisions emerges, no sense of the continuities or discontinuities we will bring upon ourselves. Employing dramatic rehearsal, on the other hand, keeps before us the ideal of each episode of our life, as providing immediate value as well as helping shape it into an aesthetic whole. I urge, in the concluding chapter, that our conception of death has a consummatory part to play since it provides the ultimate limit to our life's time. By confronting death as our temporal end, we can better see our life as developing toward completion.

In its way, the organization and procedure of *Experience as Art* attempt to reflect the nature of the aesthetic. Just as aesthetic experience is complex, made up of diverse elements, so do we here explore the varieties of aesthetic significance in everyday life. Sport, sex, violence, and the like provide the diversity while the aesthetic focus on the individual's growth and well-being unifies the discussion. Each topic, then, can be seen as an ingredient in a heterogeneous whole, clarified and extended by its relationships with the others. Just as aesthetic experience per se requires the active contribution of the observer, so too is the individual reader called upon to bring the specifics of his or her life to these various discussions. The circumstances and makeup of the reader's experience must determine how the different aesthetic possibilities here articulated are finally understood.

The aim of the book is to call into question our ordinary experience, enlivening in the reader a sense of its aesthetic potential, implications, and—finally—its incompleteness. The temporal incompleteness threatened by death; the social incompleteness risked in sex and uncovered in violence; and the cognitive incompleteness necessary to learning. The felt quality, the *aisthesis* of such everyday incompleteness, must be ultimately substantiated by the reader. I begin with a discussion of the aesthetics of learning in part because this sense of lack is most acutely defined in the processes of intellectual growth. In part, too, because this opening chapter sets forth the book's major themes in a distinctly pedagogical arena and style—self-consciously investigating everyday experience for its educational promise. The role of the aesthetic in educating our human capacities in the formal classroom setting is writ small, eventually magnified in our unmindful daily traffic with the social world. What we do, and especially how we do it, is rarely indifferent with respect to what we become. Examining *how* learning in the classroom is aesthetically informed should establish a mode for investigating the less explicit but often more profound everyday pedagogical influences at work in our lives.

Philosophy is ever and again called upon to defend and explain itself. Its critical bite combines with an esoteric cast to make it suspect not only to the person on the street but to the vast body of nonphilosophic "professionals" as well. Even people who indulge it look with a cold eye (like Callicles) on those who devote much time, let alone their lives, to its study. There seems to me no better way for philosophy to defend or explain itself than by throwing some light on our everyday experiences, the episodes often deemed important by us but rarely held up to rigorous examination. This book argues that philosophy can make a special contribution to everyday life by taking up personal, social, and political questions aesthetically. In the last analysis, these essays in applied aesthetics may afford a practical apology for philosophy by demonstrating its grip on the noticeably unphilosophical but decidedly crucial ways we live.

Chapter One
Educating Aesthetically

HERE SHOULD BE little doubt that public education in America is in the midst of a crisis. Evidence that our grand democratic experiment is crumbling is as palpable as the harried and defeated look of our teachers. For one thing, there has been a dramatic decline in literacy and overall scholastic achievement during the last decade. Our Sputnik-inspired spurt in educational programs has been fizzling, and expectations by and for students have shrunk to fit their lack of academic accomplishment; we teach astonishingly less mathematics, science, and foreign language than is taught, for example, in secondary schools in the Soviet Union.

Complementing this academic decline is a crescendo of violence, truancy, and general apathy in the schools—not just in the "inner city" (read: minority ghettos) but in the suburbia of the middle class. Teachers take courses in self-defense, and attention that should be given to serious students is siphoned off by disciplinary demands. From the standpoint of a democracy in which a concerned and participating electorate is essential, what we see is frightening. We are breeding an uncaring, disturbed, semiliterate future citizenry.

It may be naive to diagnose this crisis in academic terms, but part of the problem seems to be a scholastic program and process which ignores students' interests. Certainly, there are various nonacademic sources of this problem: inadequate funding, a subculture of poverty and drugs, extreme ethnic heterogeneity, and the like. But it would be equally facile to dismiss what actually goes on in the classroom as irrelevant to the present state of education. Classroom rhythm, organization of subject matter, and method of presentation must engage the students by speaking to their nonscholastic interests and questions.

Much contemporary classroom teaching, however, is indifferent to

9

the students' everyday experience, making classwork ineffective because, I shall argue, it is unaesthetic. Information and technical skills, for example, are imparted as ends-in-themselves rather than as ingredients in a process of human development. Irrespective of any connection with their daily concerns, the curriculum preestablishes the bodies of information and the levels of skill mastery that the students are to acquire or achieve. In fact, the two are seen as going hand-in-hand: The skills are the means by which the isolated bits of information are to be processed.

But in isolation from the students' everyday experience, interests, and perceptions, bodies of information and technical abilities lack meaning. Meaning must be "added on" to the information that is stored, *awaiting* occasion for relevance, and similarly with techniques; unless acquired as ways of "making sense" of what is in fact *experienced* as perplexing, neither will be understood. Successful application of mathematical formulae, for instance, will seem like so much magic.

Instead, we must pay heed to *how* information and technical skills are acquired. In aesthetic learning, they are introduced to meet a student's felt need, a need growing out of the student's investigation of something of interest. A technique or skill is ideally acquired when the student is called upon to *do* something by his inquiry; he feels the need to determine the length of the line derivable, for example, by Pythagoras' theorem. The same holds for information or data acquisition. Instead of memorizing such things as the royal succession in England or the capitals of all of the states in the United States as so much material to be ingested, students should discover them in the course of remedying a felt lack of understanding.

1. Teacher As Midwife

More often than anyone else in history, Socrates is held up as the paradigm of the great teacher—one who, not so incidentally, heeded the aesthetic character of teaching and learning. He describes his teaching activity as midwifery, by means of which those associated with him may find in themselves "many fair things" and bring them forth, giving birth to worthwhile thoughts as a result of rigorous discussion with Socrates. His job, however, is more difficult than the literal midwife's because ". . . women do not, like my patients, bring forth at one time real children and at another mere images which it is difficult to distinguish from the real."[1] Some of the student's opinions will be true, others merely plausible images of the real. Before assessing or inviting others to assess the student's intellectual off-spring, however, the teacher must first assist in the birth, which may require inducing pangs of labor. Now this conception of teacher as midwife has been much used in pronouncements on the "art of teaching." But it does not seem to have been thought out; it sounds catchy but its implications have stayed hidden. To give meaning to the analogy, what we need is an account of the student's experience. In what follows, I shall offer an interpretation of this Socratic midwifery. While teachers will do other important things with students, this seems most distinctive of teaching, requiring a talent that perhaps cannot be learned or reduced to a set of plans.

We must begin with the student's ordinary life, as it is the seedbed for the ideas brought forth by the teacher's ministrations. The student, like all of us, attends to what is about him. The senses acquaint us all with a world of objects and events, so it is no wonder that we occupy ourselves with sense experience. Since the senses provide an ample supply of interesting events, we all naturally live the "life of the senses." But there is more to reality and learning than meets the eye. At least, such an assumption seems necessary if the midwife concep-tion is to be meaningful.

The hypothesis I shall explore is that there is another kind of "at-tending" that is latent in our sensuous experience. It goes unnoticed because we are preoccupied with what we see, touch, smell, and hear. Yet, all the time we are registering, unaware, an aspect of the sensuous world that is not itself sensed. We are "seeing" (with our mind's eye, so to speak) the intelligible side of reality, a side which is hidden in the sensible. This hidden intellectual apprehension is a sort of latent learning: an unnoticed, submerged "life of the intellect" which accom-panies the more obvious life of the senses. It is a kind of seeing "through" the objects of sense experience to their nonsensible rela-tions. By virtue of such latent learning, we become acquainted with such notions as sameness and necessity.

Why do we say that the tree we see today is the *same* (identical) tree our senses disclosed to us yesterday? The tree we see today has fewer leaves than the one we perceived yesterday, yet we do not doubt that it is identical with it. How do we know that the person we see today is the *same* person we saw last year? We think she is the same even though many perceivable things about her are different. We cannot, obviously, *perceive* the identity or sameness that we ascribe in the case of the tree or the person.

Similarly, "necessity" cannot be perceived in or between objects of sense. We never perceive the connection among sensible objects as necessary. There is no necessity in the fact that the dropped glass is followed by the sound of shattering or the feeling of wetness. It is possible for the dropping not to be followed by the shattering or wetness.[2] We can easily imagine the relation or order as other than the way the senses perceive them. How then do we ever form the notion of necessity?

The relations of sameness and necessity (among many others) are not themselves sensed, but rather are formed by the intellect in an unnoticed way. As we explicitly attend to sense objects, the intellect is implicitly making connections among them. The intellect abstracts certain features from sense experience and then, by some unknown process, forms general conceptions that apply to the objects sensed. This life of the intellect is obscured from us ". . . due to the natural outward direction of our attention through the senses." As a consequence, ". . . essential sides of the real, including the basic inactive [nonsensuous, intelligible] side, are left implicit, unattended to."[3]

Most of the time, most of us fail to attend to, let alone understand, our intellect's latent learning. What we "see" in this latent learning is the intelligible, nonsensuous side of reality. As we pass among the sensed objects of experience, the intellect glimpses relations among these objects. The job of the teacher as midwife is to provide an occasion for the student to recognize the presence of this unnoticed learning. The teacher must help make explicit what for so long has remained implicit in the student's mind. The student must be brought to attend to this hidden cognizing. This is why Socrates calls learning "re-cognizing": cognizing or seeing again, in a reflective way that calls for effort. In a sense, the teacher is instructing the student to "know himself" (another Socratic theme), to know explicitly what he has already cognized of the nonsensuous side of reality. This helps flesh out Heidegger's insight:

> This genuine learning is therefore an extremely peculiar taking, a taking where he who takes only takes what he actually already has. Teaching corresponds to *this* learning. Teaching is a giving, an offering; but what is offered in teaching is not the learnable, for the student is merely instructed to take for himself what he

already has. True learning only occurs where the taking of what one already has is a self-giving and is experienced as such.... The most difficult learning is to come to know all the way what we already know.[4]

It is important to note something in what Heidegger says that is easily overlooked: that learning is not merely a self-giving, but is *experienced* as such. When we do experience it as a self-giving, there is an aesthetic quality which would be missing were we simply to take on the ideas of another:[5] a sense of self-completeness, in which we have come home to ourselves. There is a special *aisthesis* to this return, that distinguishes it from simply remembering facts or the opinions of others. In aesthetic experience proper, we help form an integrated whole by "funding" present experience with the reservoir of our past. (This will be elaborated upon in Chapter III.) We call upon this reservoir to complete and give meaning to the present material. In aesthetic education, the present interaction (between student and material, or student and another individual) occasions a similar inward turn. The structure of this return and its special *aisthesis* will be clarified shortly in the discussion of the peculiar kind of love involved in it.

In the self-giving that is experienced as such, a division in the self is overcome. The "forgetfulness" brought about by the life of the senses is overcome in the active gathering up of what has been unobtrusively learned by the intellect. Yet that other, dominant life of the senses is not then ignored. On the contrary, the intelligible relations made explicit in learning give order to the sensible. And while that is quite another (Platonic) story, it is important to mention here that this provides the experience with still greater unity. The intelligible side of things is first drawn out of the sensible experience (in the intellect's latent learning) and then is returned to it, to make it understandable. This coming full circle adds to the aesthetic impact of self-giving. We give something to ourselves, i.e., come to know all the way what was "seen" by the intellect. We experience this *as* a self-giving, i.e., making the hidden explicit to ourselves by our own effort. And, finally, our full recognition of this intelligible side of reality enables us to organize and, ironically, "make sense" of the sensible. In the case of the identity of the perceived tree, for example, we must make explicit the intellect's latent conception of sameness. Out of that conception we formulate a principle of identity that accommodates perceived change in the object over time. Armed with such a principle, we could *say* why we believe that this is the same tree we saw yesterday. The principle would "make sense" of our perceptions.

Intellectually seeing, when it first took place in the past, was passively undergone; now it receives attention and is "activated." We actualize a potential hidden in our experience, just as we do in aesthetic experience proper when we fund the present material with our past. In this way, learning is aesthetically rich because the active and the passive are balanced in the uniting of the past with the present. When the student exclaims, "Now I see it!", he also senses that it is not for the first time. What was previously seen, but not said, is now brought into focus and speech by his own activity. What does the teacher do to assist in bringing the implicit learning into focus and speech? How does the teacher get the student to take himself past the life of the senses to the hidden life of the intellect?

As the metaphor suggests, labor pains can be brought on naturally or induced by the midwife-teacher. The pains signal the student's need and readiness for the intellectual effort to bring the indistinct learning into speech. The need is felt when the sensuous itself strikes us in a strange way, in fact when it strikes us as strange or perplexing. The ordinary seems unusual. Commonplace beliefs and perspectives which usually get us through our sensuous lives give way and are felt to be inadequate. In such moments we feel ourselves unguarded, open to suggestion and new possibilities. The awareness of the ordinary as appearing novel calls forth questions; we question the bases for our commonplace beliefs about the sensible world.

The identity or permanence of human beings, for example, may become problematic as we leaf through a photo album or read about an auto accident. In the first case, we notice how much people change physically, yet we persist in calling and considering old aunt Flo the "same" person. Conversely, the brain damage someone suffers in an auto accident seems to call into question our ordinary assumptions about human identity. In this case, the individual looks the same but can no longer think the way he used to. In what sense is he the same? In what sense do "normal," uninjured people remain the same as time goes by? These, and everyday instances like them, force us to conceptualize and evaluate the beliefs we ordinarily take for granted.

It is as if in such moments the latent seeing, hitherto unnoticed, now presses forward into the gap in our commonsensical thought. We voice as wonderment the feeling that our ordinary beliefs and assumptions are inadequate; we wonder why and how we ever manage to think of an individual as the "same" from day to day or year to year. We wonder at the bases for such everyday judgments as these. At such times, the teacher can assist the student to appropriate fully what has all the while been his as a partial possession. In this case, it is his latent learning of the concepts of sameness and permanence.

This is the "natural way" of labor pains, the pains that indicate the need for inquiry into what makes the sensuous intelligible. The teacher may also have to induce the labor pains, that is, lead the student to feel the inadequacy of his ordinary sensible experience and its assumptions. One way is through questions. While there are other ways, such as ironic speech and storytelling,[6] this is the method I shall treat in discussing the process of midwifery. Because of its unique connection with the life of the intellect, questioning reveals much about teaching as bringing the student to self-giving. By questioning, the teacher can lead the student to see the inadequacy of his understanding. Ideally, the student learns how to question on his own. But before he can shape questions for himself, the student must become aware of his own lack, his own ignorance.

Forming a question is not easy; it requires that we see *how* our understanding is limited. Good questions mark a course of investigation into what we do not yet know but are aware of as a likely place to look. The teacher can prepare the student for setting his own course by first leading the student to see where and how his knowledge is limited. He may question the ordinary way we deal with sensible objects: Why do things with different features have the same name? After all, rather different objects are called "trees." The teacher may call into question the assumptions upon which our ordinary beliefs about the sensible world rest: How is communication between people possible when we cannot be sure that one another's experiences correspond? How do we tell that images are dreams?

It is a healthy sign when students complain that they are upset, uneasy, or confused by questions. The natural process by which their ordinary sensible world is called into question has received a pedagogical boost. By asking good questions the teacher aims to help the student formulate his own. Questions are of singular importance because they express a relationship of the individual to himself. When self-formulated, therefore, the individual has put himself in this relation and is not simply thrust into it by the teacher. What sort of relation to oneself is this?

Questions open up a search or inquiry. They mark a way of orienting ourselves in a subject matter: an advance over mere confusion in which our perplexity is without shape or direction. This sort of orienting is also a way of orienting ourselves with respect to ourselves. Questions require a willingness to reconsider our experiences and opinions, and their bases. In questioning, we stand both negatively and positively oriented toward ourselves. We are ignorant, there is a gap in our understanding, but we are aware of it and have begun a remedial quest. In struggling to formulate a question appropriate to our perplexity, we come to see something of why we do not understand. We begin to get a hold on the hidden learning that has been going on unnoticed.

A good question gives a sense of tapping this hidden reserve of learning. The query gathers up this earlier learning and begins to make it explicit in speech. The quest is to make explicit what has been seen unreflectively by the intellect. This is why a good question leads us on to more questions. It tugs at some thread of our submerged learning, which in turn connects to other threads. In questioning the basis for identifying a person over time as the same individual, we might begin by noticing that physical alteration does not usually inhibit us from thinking that the person is indeed the same. This seems to suggest that personal identity depends upon something permanent in the mind or, more generally, the psyche. Yet here we might query: But the notion of personal identity seems to tolerate alterations in beliefs, attitudes, and emotional propensities. At the very least, we do not expect the same person to have the same thoughts or feelings all the time. We must then ask what in or about the psyche must remain unchanged and how unchanging that must be. Each question generates question-embedded responses.

As with aesthetic experience proper, questioning generates thought that reaches past itself. Although aesthetic experience is complete in itself, its richness suggests many directions and further possibilities. This is why a great novel, for example, can support a variety of competing, conflicting, as well as mutually enhancing, interpretations. This is also why works of art feed on one another, forming a tradition. Aesthetic experience takes us beyond our ordinary perception of things. It forces us deeper into ourselves in an attempt to gain a fuller view of the world. A good question is also aesthetic in quite literally composing the student's thought. As in aesthetic experience, it plumbs the individual's unarticulated depths of insight, except that here the purpose is primarily cognitive. In the quest for explicit understanding, for knowing "all the way," questions relate what already has become explicit to what still remains obscure. They bridge the gap between what we understand and what we do not, by developing a special sort of love. It is the teacher's job to quicken this love that all have, and make it a controlling influence in the student.

2. Love and Learning

Consideration of this special sort of love will fill out the midwife analogy and also explain why the student would be willing to make the effort to bring the underground life of reason into the clarity of speech. What kind of love is it that the teacher must enliven in the student? Clearly it must be a love that initiates and sustains a quest. It is a love that might be distinctive of us as humans bound up with what a human being is, but also with what he is not yet. In this respect, it reflects the way a question orients a person both negatively and positively toward himself. Negatively put, this love is a *lack* in us and a longing for what we lack. It is expressed mythically by Aristophanes in Plato's *Symposium* as the desire to find our missing halves, that which would complete us. And there is truth in this myth, that the love we are here concerned with is a longing for that which will make us whole as human beings. We experience ourselves as lacking and seek completeness. What is wrong with Aristophanes' story is that it presents what we lack as outside ourselves, another thing (a person) altogether.

This takes us to the positive aspect of this love that prompts learning. It is also a desire to beget, to bring forth what is within us. To be human is to have a love of producing and giving what is within. This aspect of self-love is suggested by Diotima in the *Symposium*. Now these two aspects seem to be opposites. The first is a lack or need; the second a fullness or bounty. As aspects of one love, lacking and having would seem to be irreconcilable. There is, however, a way the two could be aspects of one love: if the positive aspect, the bringing forth from within, fulfills the longing for completeness. We seek what we are not (yet), what we are missing, by producing from within ourselves. This is possible only if our incompleteness is not absolute, only if we "are" in some sense what we are not. Heidegger gets at this when he says that the student takes "what he already has." And this idea of being or having something incompletely, not yet all the way, is found in the preceding account of the life of the intellect.

What will complete us is the explicit understanding of the intelligible side of reality. It is already present in us as a latent intellectual way of seeing. Our desire to produce, then, can be met by making this latent learning explicit. The begetting aspect of love is realized when we attend to our hidden reserve of understanding. We "are" therefore what we will become by possessing knowledge in an obscure, incomplete way. The negative and positive aspects of love correspond to the two aspects of our latent learning. The negative side is the life of the intellect while still hidden from us, merely potential knowledge. This is experienced as a deprivation; its *aisthesis* is a longing for what will complete us (by completing our grasp of reality). The positive side is the desire and willingness to make the latent learning explicit. We take a joy in enlarging our understanding. This is experienced by us as a fullness; its *aisthesis* is a desire to beget, to bring forth something that we have to give.

Our longing for what will complete us can, therefore, be met in the same activity by which we produce from out of ourselves. We make ourselves more complete by making the hidden intellectual learning explicit in speech. This bringing out into a more stable, sharable knowledge makes us more complete as human beings.[7]

Insofar as our latent learning is not yet brought to the level of explicit understanding, we experience ourselves as incomplete. We are aware of our lack because the latent learning is not (yet) real knowledge. However, as that which is *potentially* knowledge, we experience our submerged intellectual seeing as a fullness. We are pregnant with thought, however inchaote or obscure. Like anything in the process of growth, our becoming is at once a lack and a presence. A sapling is not yet a mature tree, yet the tree is *potentially* present in its structure and functioning. But unlike other things that grow, we must take an active self-conscious part in our growth. Our latent learning comes to be knowledge only by our efforts. The desire to bring out what is hidden in our understanding of the world is a form of self-love. This is what motivates us to think and subsequently to realize our potential.

As suggested above, the intimation of this potential within us has a distinctive *aisthesis* or felt quality. It is this which the teacher must work to intensify in the student. Because of the strength of this self-love, the student makes the effort to form the questions which can bring the hidden learning to light. The *aisthesis* that attends our sense of inner potential develops as the labor pains issue in questions. When these receive satisfactory responses, there is a sense of aesthetic closure. A process begun in disturbance, carried forward in the shaping of questions, reaches temporary completion. But this is at the same time experienced as our own growth. The delight we take in seeing anything grow is intensified when it is ourselves, for then we are "inside," experiencing the growth from within as well as watching it from without.

Thus we experience a small sense of growth and aesthetic closure when we are able to answer the question concerning the way we tell the difference between dreams and real objects. Shaping our perplexity into a question in the first place, of course, carries with it a sense of development and movement-to-conclusion characteristic of aesthetic experience. We might bring the hidden life of the intellect forward in such a way as to notice that there is less congruity within the dream world than there is within the real one. Time and place shifts, for example, often do not make sense in the dream. Furthermore, there is usually a marked discontinuity between the dream world and the real one. We jump quickly from a desert chase to our beds with nary a trace of sand or sun. Arriving at such principles as these rounds out the process begun in labor pain, and carries a sense of aesthetic completeness. (The criteria that emerge in this case, moreover, are themselves aesthetic or aesthetically oriented: continuity and integration of experience.) Because the expansion and completing of our understanding comes about as a result of our own efforts, the sense of aesthetic completeness is deepened.

The growth, and its aesthetic quality, is experienced as self-promoted, a self-giving. We are involved with ourselves in a way strikingly like the way we are involved with external material in aesthetic experience. However, in this experience of learning, we are both agent *and object* of the activity. The development and organization of the thought material occurs through our own efforts, just as when artist or appreciator actively engages the material in aesthetic experience. Yet the object to be brought to fuller completion is here part of ourselves—our own thoughts correspond to the colors, sounds, or word meanings found in aesthetic experience proper. In learning, therefore, agent and object are united in us: *Our* activity is responsible for the development of *our* thought. As in aesthetic experience proper, we are distanced from ourselves. In forming and dealing with questions, we treat our hidden learning as something separate from who we are. We question and work on our own thought as though it were another's. Yet we are intimate with ourselves—as in aesthetic experience. The hidden life of the intellect did, after all, occur within us; making it explicit is, after all, making clear what we have seen, what has been our obscure possession all along. Because the aesthetic closure which occurs in learning is the consequence of our own activity, and is a closure in our own thinking, the unity of the experience is more pronounced than in other areas of aesthetic activity. We are decidedly unified as thinkers. Self-promoted self-completion is particularly elating.

3. Information and Techniques

What I have said so far about midwifery and love must seem rather remote from the daily activities and subject matter of the classroom. Surely classroom learning is concerned with acquiring information and mastering intellectual skills or techniques. It would seem that a midwife such as I have discussed is hardly needed for attaining these goals. Moreover, what has "self-giving" and the "life of the intellect" to do with getting straight on the facts of the Crimean War or the election of presidents in a democracy?

No one denies the need for data or factual information. It is that about which we think, and our opinions can be altered radically by the addition or subtraction of a piece of information. The rub lies in the *way* students acquire information. Is it in "pieces" like so many computer "bits"? As the use of computers has grown, so too has the vocabulary. Students and teachers alike seem to speak of knowledge as so much information acquisition, regardless of how the acquisition takes place. Because our thinking unthinkingly follows vocabulary, we conceive of thought as information-processing. This makes it easy to transmit information in isolation from what it *means*—almost as an end in itself.[8] And this is actually detrimental to real learning or thinking.

Too often the teacher puts a premium on the students' ability to reproduce a body of information in a particular subject. The subject matter is regarded by teacher and student as complete in itself: something to be "gotten through" or "across." So, little effort is made to relate it to the students' interests and desires. The pupil "... acquires a technical body of information without ability to trace its connections with the objects and operations with which he is familiar."[9]

This, of course, points to the way students *should* acquire information: in connection with what moves them to inquire and think. The motivation occurs when the life of the senses is perplexing and the intellect's latent learning must be called upon. Instead of memorizing the major exports of Brazil or the Periodic Table of the Elements as material to be ingested, students can discover these things in the course of making an inquiry, an inquiry begun *because* they experience a lack of understanding. Information is thereby acquired in a meaningful way. There is then no problem of "attaching" meaning to it. It is not simply stored away awaiting an occasion for relevance, but is connected to interest and fitted into a network of related facts from the start. The acquisition of factual information in the midst of a quest will not result in a mere piling up of unconnected bits of information. The data will be organized within the area of inquiry, meaningful since it is part of an intellectual self-giving.

* * *

The mastery of intellectual technique is obviously also important in education. We operate more effectively and efficiently when we are skilled in mathematics, science, reading, spelling, and the like. But too often a value is placed on the technical facility for its own sake and it, too, is taught without care that the student understand what is going on. Education comes to be identified with skill mastery in addition to information-processing. Indeed, the two become nicely intertwined. Intellectual skills are the means or methods by which the information is "processed." The student is not likely to understand how the skill or technique works, what its purpose is, or how it relates to any subject matter, however, unless it is learned in response to his labor pains. Is the technique acquired as a method which draws upon the student's hidden life of the intellect? When learned in this way, the skill is acquired as a tool by which the life of the intellect can make sense of the life of the senses. Learning technical skills must be situated in the daily life of the senses, grown perplexing—in *need* of intellectual manipulation.

Teaching science as a collection of technical exercises, for instance, separates it from its function in everyday life. Technique then has no bearing on the objects and concerns with which the student is at home. The techniques or methods of science should be exhibited as bringing order and control to the ordinary life of the senses. Otherwise, the methods will seem to apply only to unfamiliar, "technical" material. They will be isolated from real life along with the body of information to be transferred in the classroom.

Without connectedness to ordinary interests and subject matter, the array of technical mastery will be without meaning. Each skill will become a specialized routine, rattling around unavailable for effective use. This is pointedly illustrated in the case of reading, in which the technique can be without "meaning" in the strictly literal sense as well as the more general one indicated so far.

> It is customary for teachers to urge children to read with expression, so as to bring out the meaning. But if they originally learned the sensory-motor technique of reading—the ability to identify forms and reproduce the sounds they stand for—by methods which did not call for attention to meaning, a mechanical habit was established which makes it difficult to read subsequently with intelligence.... Meaning cannot be tied on at will.[10]

The student will attend to "meaning" when the subject matter is one into which he has begun inquiry. As an activity to further the self-giving, to help formulate a question or find an answer to one, reading is necessarily meaningful. As this indicates, the *way* techniques are mastered determines whether they will facilitate or obstruct subsequent learning and performance. When cut off from the purposeful task of sustained questioning, techniques and skills are isolated from other abilities. This is because general capacities of observation, analysis, and generalizing are not increased; the isolated skill does not broaden such powers. Speaking of spelling, Dewey notes:

> . . . the more he confines himself to noticing and fixating the forms of words, irrespective of connections with other things [meanings, context of use, derivation], the less likely is he to acquire an ability which can be used for anything *except* the mere noting of verbal visual forms.... The connections which are employed in other observations . . . are deliberately eliminated when the pupil is exercised merely upon forms and letters of words.[11]

These last claims connect up this way. When technique is taught without reference to intellectual purpose, without inquiry into a subject matter, then its context of acquisition is narrow. When the context of acquisition is narrow, the abilities cultivated by the technique are specialized. When specialized, they do not admit of incorporation into other techniques or adaptation to new situations. It is difficult to integrate different techniques when they are acquired without being situated in a common experience or pursuit.

A correlate of learning techniques or methods in this way is a lack of understanding how or why they get the results they do. How many of us applied mathematical formulae or methods and then greeted the resulting answers as so much magical success? We saw *that* the technique worked but not how. Missing were the links of connection which make applying technique meaningful. When a student does understand how and why a technique works, it is because his latent learning has been made explicit. He grasps intellectually the whole situation in which the technique figures. Nonsensible concepts such as square root, exponent, and proportional variation, define the context within which the formulaic method works. Unless these concepts are integrated in an understanding of the whole mathematical "situation," the method or technique will seem mysterious and will be applied without understanding.

The isolated way of imparting technical mastery is unaesthetic in that it disjoins the technique from the individual's particular interests and questions. Because it does not grow out of the student's perception and appreciation of everyday connections, the perception and appreciation are restricted. In aesthetic education, however, the student's capacities are expanded because technique is situated in his overall intellectual labors. The technique must be situated in the student's ordinary experience if it is to be learned aesthetically and not as a fragment. The situatedness of technical learning implies that the student employs the technique when called upon by his inquiry to *do* something. It is part of a response to a question arising within the student's purposeful activity.[12]

The technique or method should be introduced by the teacher to satisfy a student's felt need. In the midst of a problem that he finds interesting, the student should experiment with techniques that seem promising. They are therefore meaningful from the moment of introduction; the student sees their connection with subject matter, function, and value. " . . . One has a knowledge of mathematical conceptions only when he sees the problems in which they function and their specific utility in dealing with [these problems]."[13]

When the student directly experiences the payoff from the technique in results in which he is interested, an "episode of inquiry" is completed. The sense of aesthetic closure washes back upon the technique. It is appreciated as an integral part of a process with distinctive contours and culmination. It is integrated into an aesthetically whole process in which problematic beginnings reach satisfactory conclusion. Since it is crucial to the achievement of this aesthetic closure, the technique is valued in connection with the other human powers with which it has meshed.

Aesthetic integration of technique includes its role in effecting continuity in the student's thinking. Applying the technique not only enables the student to deal with the present material, but furthers the thought which follows. The skill or technique helps continuity in thinking by utilizing previous thought "... for some other stage, until ... the end ... which ... summarizes and finishes off the process."[14] In this way, for example, might inventory-taking be preparatory to book-balancing, which in turn furthers budget-projection. The idea is for technique to take its place in a whole in which each event contributes to the occurrence and worth of others. Techniques so enmeshed take their place in an aesthetically satisfying process. The "summarizing and finishing off" of the intellectual episode of inquiry, then, has a consummatory quality characteristic of aesthetic experience proper.

So far our discussion is still once removed from the ins and outs of actual classroom life. The teacher is a midwife who situates information acquisition and technique mastery in the student's labor to give birth to a hitherto dormant understanding. But what are the implications of this for the student's participation in the classroom?

4. Platonic Dialogue As Aesthetic Model

I propose examining the dramatic form of the Platonic dialogue[15] because I believe that Plato has the most to teach us about the aesthetics of education. He forms his instruction aesthetically—as a dialogue, and so might be expected to reveal something important about the aesthetics of education in that form. In drawing out the implications for the classroom, I will pay particular attention to the relationship of the dialogue's meaning to its characters and reader. Both the characters' and the reader's participation in the dialogue have something to say about the nature of student participation in the classroom.

The first thing to notice about a dialogue is that it is neither a play nor an essay. Yet it resembles both. Like a play, a dialogue is composed of characters, their speech, and their (limited range of) actions. The characters show emotion, sometimes interrupt or break off with one another, and occasionally storm out of or burst into the discussion. The drama of the dialogue is crucial to its meaning and what it has to teach, but this does not make it a theatrical play. The characters' lives do not change as visibly or significantly as they do in a play, and the interest that brings them to talk together is always intellectual: to inquire into some topic of lasting human importance such as love, death, or justice. Bona fide plays are never (or ought never to be) so lopsidedly cognitive.

In this respect, then, a Platonic dialogue (hereafter "dialogue," for brevity) is like an essay or treatise. Positions are offered, arguments are proposed and modified to meet objections, examples are given, and analogies are drawn. It is too much like what goes on in a classroom or academic forum to be a "real" play, yet the fact that the positions and arguments are espoused by particular characters (hereafter "interlocutors" to indicate people in a dialogue) make it unlike a treatise on death or justice.

A. Agency

The reader of a dialogue cannot simply identify with or reject the author's viewpoint, since that viewpoint encompasses the whole: all the opinions and their objections, and the ensuing movement of the discussion. The reader is forced to contribute to the thinking of the dialogue since he cannot simply accept a particular position as the "right" one. Rather, he must work his way through the interplay of positions. What then emerges is also conditioned by what is revealed of the interlocutor's personalities. The reader must, then, interpret what is said in light of who is saying it.

Because no position offered in a dialogue is complete or unassailable, "... the reader's soul is constrained to search for the result and be set on the way on which it can find what it seeks."[16] In Plato's *Crito*, for example, Socrates claims both that citizens owe obedience to the state *and* that citizenship includes the responsibility for making free choices. The conflicting views cut to the core of the issue, forcing the reader to search for a means of resolving or synthesizing their opposition. The result is that the reader must actively think through the views and bring the interlocutors' personalities together with their argumentation.

This is what I claim for aesthetic classroom education. The student must be brought to *feel* the need for his own active involvement, to feel the deficiency when he merely "takes what is offered" by another. Thus, the first lesson Plato teaches is the necessity of making the student feel the need for his active engagement. This is beautifully mirrored in the agency of the dialogue's interlocutors.

A dialogue is perhaps unique in developing "... language as a discussion in which man's agency is explicitly incorporated."[17] The discussion of justice in the *Republic*, for instance, begins with the initiating, originating acts of its participants: Socrates goes to observe a strange festival; two others force him to discuss politics. The importance of the characters as agents who originate conversation is thereby strengthened by the *way* this dialogue (and others) itself originates. Moreover, the dramatic form displays the effectiveness of agency "... through spontaneous speech and then more deeply through the interplay of personality, temperament, and context which this makes possible."[18] In the aesthetic classroom, students initiate discussion and the teacher is mindful of the part the students' personalities play in what they say. Student expression and interaction is dramatic, not simply intellectual.

By treating discussion as the expression of human agency, Plato emphasizes precisely what is needed in an aesthetically nurturing social environment: the creative power of individuals coming together to determine matters of common concern. (The next chapter explores the lack of such agency in contemporary society and its significance for distinctively contemporary forms of violence.) The dialogue also offers a double reminder of the place of agency in aesthetic experience. Not only is exercise of the *reader's* creative powers needed to appreciate the dialogue, but the *interlocutors'* agency within the dialogue is essential to its aesthetic depth and unity. This suggests that the agency of the student in the classroom must be taken into account and fostered in order for education to be aesthetic.

There is more to agency, whether an interlocutor's or a student's, than the isolated use of intellect; the individual's desires, emotions, purposes, and particular situation enter in as well. The dialogue shows how an individual's thinking is entwined with these nonintellectual elements of the psyche.[19] To return to the beginning of the *Republic:* There we hear Cephalus offer his conception of justice, a conception which is rooted to his concrete situation. His view that justice is debt-repayment grows out of his emotional response to his old age. He fears dying with a blemish on his earthly record and so wishes to "square accounts" with his associates. He is also glad of the release old age brings from the hold of strong appetites, since powerful appetites can make it difficult to keep accounts even. The appetites can get in the way of repaying debts since the latter may require giving up appetitive satisfaction. Moreover, an unappetitive individual is less likely to incur debts in the first place. In Cephalus, we see how the agent's particular situation shapes his conception of justice: absence of debt aided by release from the power of appetites.

If we take the lesson of the dialogue seriously, then the teacher must deal with the particular concerns students bring to class discussion. Locating the student's thought within the emotions and desires germane to his situation is crucial to showing the student the limitations or deficiencies of his thinking. A complete account of justice, for example, must take in more than the cancelling of debts and the cessation of appetite symptomatic of someone in Cephalus' situation. The class, like interlocutors in the dialogue, can explore the *implications* of the student's thought for a more complete understanding, one that extends past his particular situation. Cephalus' loss of appetite, for instance, can be extended to other stages of life and related more deeply to the concept of justice. What is one to do who still has strong appetites, who is not released by old age or infirmity from their power? One suggestion is that self-control will be needed. The loss of appetite found in Cephalus' life points to a more universal feature of justice. It requires freedom from rule by desire. For those with strong desires, therefore, effort at self-control will be needed.

Awareness of the individuality of the student's agency enables the teacher to develop and extend his original thought. Consider white male students in discussions on the justice of reverse discrimination: hiring minorities, such as women and blacks, over white male job applicants. White male students tend to speak out of their individual, practical concern. They worry about the implications for themselves of favoring minorities in the business world. Consequently, many reject reverse discrimination as a legal working out of justice. After all, the white males are the ones who will be (reversely) discriminated against in the name of justice. These concerns must be taken into account if the opinions that express them are to help the class to an adequate understanding of justice in the business world.

In a dialogue, the weakness of an interlocutor's conception is revealed by exposing the limitations of his viewpoint. The particularity of his view is shown rooted in the particularity of his situation.[20] In the case of the white male student, the teacher needs to introduce a larger perspective in order to expose the limitedness of his viewpoint. But more is needed. The larger perspective must be *felt* as more adequate by the white male student. The classroom must be extended imaginatively into the real world; the white male student must imagine himself in a different situation, feeling different concerns. Enlarged perspective is needed not only to alter the student's thinking, but to solidify it.

Even if the white male student publicly concedes (grudgingly?) the weakness of his position, it does not follow that his thinking has really been enlarged or developed. The dialogue shows how intellectual agreement alone is not enough for true education. Enlargement of perspective must engage the whole student, his emotion and appetite as well as intellect. Emotion and appetite must be made congruent with the conclusions of reason, otherwise they will overturn these conclusions at the first provocation. An aesthetic means must be found to bring the appetites and emotions into line with the work of reason. Thus, Socrates offers a myth at the end of the *Republic* which indicates how a comprehensive psychological ordering is essential to the ordering and development of thinking.

The myth illustrates the aesthetic interplay among reason, appetite, and emotion. Socrates presents it in order to stabilize the thinking and psychological ordering of reason, appetite, and emotion begun in the interlocutors earlier in the dialogue. The myth is a philosophical work of art and does not give the interlocutors something they "in no sense understood before," but enables "a more complete possession of what was partially grasped."[21] The strength of emotion or appetite is liable to upset the focus that reason brings to questions of lasting importance, in this case, justice. Our understanding can become blurred by fear or greed, for example. Similarly might a student's assent to what is agreed upon in class become obscured later in emotional and appetitive response to everyday concerns. The myth tries to give the interlocutors and reader experience in ruling emotion and appetite with reason. Without going into too much detail, let us examine how this myth tries to bring emotion and appetite into line with the tentatively held opinions of reason.

The myth tells of an afterlife in which people are given the opportunity to choose the kind of life they wish to live in their next stay on earth. Like gods, the people exercise *total agency* in selecting the lives that seem most attractive. The selection occurs after the people have seen the suffering of those punished for the kind of life just led on earth. The prudent take this into account in selecting their next kind of life. Some, however, choose imprudently, such as one man whose gluttonous appetite induces him to choose the life of a tyrant. He later reconsiders, lamenting his shortsighted decision. The myth forces the interlocutors and reader to respond to the *whole* of time and to the threat of death. As with the white male student in the classroom who considers the justice of reverse discrimination, the interlocutors in the *Republic* are not going to respond completely to argument alone. A dramatic means is necessary to engage their emotions and appetites. This particular myth makes emotion and appetite oppose their own excesses; they see the need to limit themselves. Fear of suffering as a result of yielding to greed or gluttony, for example, curbs the influence of these strong emotions and appetites. The philosophical art presents us with an image of choosing in which our agency as whole people, not just intellects, is called upon to respond: imagination giving us a grip on our lives as an aesthetic whole.

The interlocutors and reader see that some thought must be taken to the whole span of life. They see and feel it, moreover, with their *whole* psyches. Similarly, the white male student must give some thought to the whole of *society*. Considerations of justice refer to all of society's members. A dramatic means might enlarge his social view to convey the interdependence of the different segments of society. The white male members of society suffer, for example, because of the loss of productivity due to the subjugation of women. Rather than extending the temporal perspective of the *individual* into the future, as the myth does, an imaginative means might vivify the discriminatory treatment which took place in the society's past. Social discrimination could also be likened to stealing: the products of slaves' labor being stolen from them and subsequently "inherited" by contemporary white society.[22]

The Platonic suggestion is that the ordering of thought, which might seem to be the sole concern of education, requires a more general ordering of the whole psyche. It is not enough for a student to give his assent to a position in language of the intellect alone. The emotions and appetites must concur in the intellect's verdict. In the question of the justice of reverse discrimination, fear for one's own loss must give way to concern for those who have been wronged and the functioning of society as a whole. The student's imagination must be enlisted if he is to be drawn out of his particular situation. Works of art such as myths are simply the most obvious way to do this.

B. Aesthetic Discussion

What sort of classroom life is most conducive to ordering the students' thinking and psyches? To begin, the teacher must steer the class clear of two extremes—license and constriction, each of which leaves its respective imprint on the students.

By license I have in mind the classroom that is a-buzz but without direction. So much importance is placed on student "participation" that students are popping off without paying much attention to what one another are saying. Issues are not joined; still less are conclusions reached. At best, topics are thrown out for discussion and the students jump from one to the next, attaining little depth. I consider this licentious because it amounts to students saying what they feel or wish without regard for a standard which directs what they say. There is no regard for the limits imposed either by the subject matter or the input of others. The licentious classroom encourages the student to yield to the promptings of emotion or desire. His thinking becomes capricious curiosity. Consequently, he receives little practice in either intellectual or overall psychological ordering. This style of classroom teaching seems to have sprung up as an over-reaction to the earlier constricted classroom in which students had almost no role in what took place.

In this latter extreme the teacher simply puts the students through their paces. Whether or not rote learning actually takes place, a routine prevails in which the students are always responding to the teacher and following his lead. In this constricted extreme, students rarely address one another, rarely initiate or alter the course of discussion. All responses pass through the teacher; he alone determines what takes place.

The teacher-as-lecturer is but the most obvious form classroom constriction takes. All forms of it operate and affect the student in the same way. "Covering material," narrowly directing thought, and defining what is valuable for the student, are achieved at the expense of student-generated discussion or thinking. Constriction prevents growth and initiative. The student's reason is not given practice in developing itself. Consequently, what psychological order exists is imposed from without, from the teacher, as the student's reason is constrained to follow outside influence.

If the first licentious extreme overemphasizes the student's spontaneous expression, the latter extreme strangles it. In the first, all is means to no end. In the constricted classroom, on the other hand, achieving prescribed ends leaves the student with no independent means. Nothing novel can develop since the students are not allowed real interaction; the teacher's "plan" functions as a blueprint totally delimiting what will be thought or said.

Aesthetic experience involves a balance between doing and undergoing, between activity and receptivity. The first extreme actually exaggerates the "doing" side of aesthetic experience. The student is all activity, with little receptivity to outside energies. The second extreme simply reverses the emphasis. The student is made passive recipient of information and technique. What doing there is that takes place is mere following of thought, not initiating, collaborating, or reformulating it. If either the doing or undergoing side of participation is eliminated, then *a fortiori* the two cannot be maintained in balance. No chance for aesthetic classroom interaction exists when the student is all-doing or all-undergoing.

As with all extremes, we tend toward them because the "mean" is difficult to achieve. How much easier it seems for the teacher to attain pedagogical objectives by simply handing them out, telling the students what is what or what to do. It seems easier, also, to get students to talk if no one is too worried about what is said, ordering it, or taking it somewhere. And as with extremes in other areas, classroom license and constriction can alternate with one another; days or periods of lecturing, for example, can alternate with free-wheeling sessions. A semblance of the ideal is presented by such alternating. But students probably become bored in both extremes, even though alternation might stave boredom off for a time. Failure to go anywhere or accomplish much must make undirected discussion empty, just as passive reception dulls attention. To focus discussion, however, is no easy task.

Aesthetic discussion is "free," possessing the spontaneous excitement of students generating ideas found in license, but with the control and direction predominant in constriction. It represents a practical synthesis of opposed approaches. The students' speech is not self-contained, the expression of merely private thought as it is in the licentious class. The control, on the other hand, is not imposed from without. It comes from students paying attention to what others say. Just as "a dialogue develops through the mutual modification of the originative contributions of its participants,"[23] so is the class discussion determined by the modification of the students' contributions. The participants in discussion, moreover, are themselves modified in the course of the reshaping of their intellectual contributions.

Within the contours of aesthetic interaction, the psychological ordering of the students takes place. The students' thought and psyches become ordered as their contributions become integrated. The order within the student and the meshing of the discussion depend upon each other. The more the students' psyches are ordered, the better able are they to contribute to what others are saying. Conversely, as the class discussion increasingly ties together, the students' own ideas, feelings, and desires should harmonize. The student (part) and the class discussion (whole) bring each other to completion in aesthetic interaction with the result that class activity ideally constitutes an aesthetic experience for the student. An aesthetic experience develops from the movement and ordering of the class discussion as a whole, together with the corresponding psychological and intellectual ordering within the student.[24]

In aesthetic interaction the student responds to what others say rather than pursues an exclusively private line of thought. Issues are joined, criticisms exchanged. Taking part in discussion entails reciprocity; each opines expecting response, and criticizes as one who has been and will be criticized. Each speaks to others as a listener, and listens as a speaker. As indicated above, the aesthetic classroom actually has two "objects" being aesthetically formed: the discussion of subject matter, and the psyches of the participants. Each is modified by the other in the course of discussion, but the fundamental concern of education is with the psychological community. The development of the students' powers in a community of inquiry is more important than the specific content of the discussion. What is of importance, then, is *how* the content is discussed; how the discussion unfolds is crucial to the development of the student. Again, the Platonic dialogue is revealing.

C. Comprehensive Thinking

A dialogue grows, and the way it grows discloses further aesthetic aspects of classroom experience. Arguments and opinions are elaborated by the interlocutors. Questions and objections are then raised, and in the ensuing attempt to take account of these questions and objections the thought moves on. Positions are patched up or given up for alternatives as suggestions are made for revisions or substitutions. Positions and arguments thus grow out of what precedes and in turn are succeeded by new or modified thought. In the most aesthetically rich dialogues, succeeding positions are ever more inclusive, comprehending what has preceded. Almost like an onion, layers of thought enclose one another as the interlocutors work toward ever more complete understandings of the subject. The inadequacies of a view force the speakers to go beyond or beneath it, to ever more fundamental matters. Thus, difficulties in the conceptions of justice offered early in the *Republic* prompt a deeper discussion of human nature or the soul.

The beauty of a dialogue is that it does not simply pluck a problem out of thin air and begin considering opinions or arguments. The issues are situated in the interlocutors' lives; therefore, opinion-giving and argument grow out of their interested interaction, just as they would in the ideal classroom. Interlocutors or students opine together. Out of the conflict among their opinions arise argument, agreement, and accommodation. To draw out the aesthetic lesson for classroom teaching, it is important to distinguish between compromise and synthesis as ways of overcoming the inevitable and desirable conflicts in viewpoint.

On many issues students are divided. Sometimes the division falls neatly into opposing viewpoints, or at least sharply contrasting positions. When this occurs it is rarely the case that one of the viewpoints is defensible and the other unsupportable; each usually has some credibility and supporters. The typical constructive classroom response is to try to effect a "compromise" between the two positions. The term "between" is a clue to the nature of compromise, for it indicates a position which falls within the intellectual space separating the antagonistic viewpoints. By taking a little from each, by bending each in the direction of the other, they can "meet each other half way" (or thereabouts) at a new position. This would seem to be a nice balance between independence and capitulation. The students are not "giving up" their original viewpoints by "giving ground" in the subsequent compromise. They do not desert their position, yet they are heeding their peers' advocacy of an opposing view, its criticisms and alternatives.

To some extent this is certainly true. But what is missing is a resolution of the conflict whereby each view brings the opposed viewpoint within its own scope. In compromise, it is true, the opposed viewpoint is heeded, but from outside one's own, in a linear, quantitative sort of way. In compromise, no alteration *within* the originally opposed views occurs, no change in the concepts that *define* the positions. A dispute over political governance or ruling with illustrate the difference between compromise and "synthesis" in education.

Students usually disagree over a state's "right" to rule its people. On the one side are those who see the need for obedience to a central political authority. Without it, they argue, people's lives and welfare would be jeopardized; it would be difficult to get organization needed for concerted action. Let us call this the view of "Statists." On the other side, students argue that the individual is the ultimate authority and should obey only his own "conscience," will, or desires. No one has the right to tell the individual what to do; he is obliged to obey no one.[25] Let us call this the view of "Individualists." Now obviously these characterizations are extreme and somewhat simplified; however, they not only come close to real divergencies in people's thinking, but they serve well to illustrate the way such divergencies are often compromised.

Compromising such opposition involves getting concessions from each side. The Statists concede that the state does not have the right to command obedience on everything, every aspect of the people's lives. The state should not be totalitarian. The Individualists concede that centralized political authority is sometimes needed, to avert disasters or (as a consequence of their basic claim) to prevent infringement on those very individual rights so cherished. In compromising, each side gives ground to the other, agreeing that while the individual's authority is crucial, the state does not have the right to command obedience in *certain areas* or under certain conditions.

Notice that the compromise affects only the *sphere* of rule, not its nature. Where the Statists' viewpoint originally saw political authority over a rather large area of life (perhaps, in principle, unlimited), the Individualists' saw it over *none*. Each gives ground to the other. The Statists narrow the scope of the state's right, the Individualists expand it. But neither really questions or alters its *conception* of "ruling" or "authority." At bottom, they share a conception of ruling as commanding. The state either has the right to tell people what to do or it does not; the people are obliged to obey or they are not. The ruler is distinct from the subjects. This command view of political authority is not altered in the compromise, only its sphere of legitimate application.

In synthesis, however, each position is changed within. The new position goes beneath the concepts which define the original opposition in order to produce a more inclusive, encompassing viewpoint.[26] In the compromise proposed above, the authority of the individual and the state are simply given separate spheres to oversee. In a genuine synthesis, however, the very concept of authority or ruling is altered. Rather than segregate the authority of the individual in a private sphere, it could be *incorporated* into the very way political rule in the state takes place. We then cease to view ruling as one group telling another what to do. Ruling ceases to mean a command-obedience relationship between separate groups.

Rather, a conception of "self-rule" can bring the originally opposed views more closely together in a more inclusive one. In such a conception, those designated as "government" are responsible for proposing policy, posing alternatives, providing information to the people, and so forth. But government is not identical with the *state*. The individuals themselves, exercising their individual authority together, arrive at the decisions in which the state's authority or rule consists. They are obliged to obey their *own* collective decisions because the procedure by which these decisions are arrived at respects the authority of each equally.[27]

The purpose of this foray into political philosophy is to give content to the claim that in synthesizing opposing viewpoints a *new* conception emerges. It incorporates the opposing viewpoints but in a way which alters their original terms.[28] This synthesis incorporates the Statist idea of obeying political authority with the Individualist stand on the irreducible authority of the individual. To do more than compromise between the two positions, however, more than the scope or quantity of political authority has to be adjusted. The very *nature* of political authority must be rethought. The synthesized conception of self-rule blends the Individualists' and Statists' positions. The authority of the state is made a function of the authority of the individual. I am not saying that compromise is bad (in the classroom or in everyday negotiations) or that the sort of synthesis presented here is always attainable. I am saying that there are important differences between the two and that synthesis is educationally superior.

It is superior on two related aesthetic dimensions: the rethinking of fundamental conceptions; the achievement of a more inclusive position. In aesthetic experience, reworking and reconstituting original material yields a whole in which original oppositions in the material are comprehensively integrated. Synthesis provides the student with a richer aesthetic experience in the classroom. Compromise is like a not wholly satisfactory resolution of thematic conflict in a play or musical composition. It is better than the uneasy coexistence of irresolution, but lacks the closure essential to aesthetic experience. What are the details of the reconstruction and comprehensiveness which occur in classroom synthesis?

First of all, the interaction of the students enters *into* the new position. The cooperation is a reconstruction of conceptions, not simply an adding to or subtracting from what has already been conceived. The Individualists' view penetrates *into* the Statists' in the synthesis of self-rule. The authority of the state is defined as an exercise of the individuals' authority. Similarly, the Statists' view enters *into* the Individualists'. State authority is a responsibility of the individual. This interaction is deeper and more demanding than that required for compromise.

The difference between compromise and synthesis is like the

difference between two ways of building a house. In the first way, two people build two different parts of a house and then join them together. Each part is essentially unchanged as it is made to abut the next. In the second, "synthetic" way, the two people reassemble and modify what they have separately made in light of what the other has built. The design of the building comes from a cooperative redoing of both segments so that the work of each penetrates into that of the other. This is like synthesizing opposed positions by working out a new conceptual design. Moreover, synthesis yields a stronger because more encompassing position.

In compromise, the rift between the originally opposed views is not truly overcome. In exactly the same terms it reappears. In our example, it reappears as, "How broad should be the scope of political authority over the individual?" "What criteria will be used to determine the bounds of the state's rights over the individual?"[29]

The questions that arise after synthesis, however, are *new* (the way the parts of a work of art are given new significance by virtue of their aesthetic relationships and situation within the whole work). The new questions call for rethinking basic concepts and conceiving new ones. Synthesizing expands the students' perspective on what is at issue. It moves them to call upon fresh resources or old resources in fresh ways. It requires connecting the new-made concepts with others, reorganizing and developing a conceptual scheme. Doing this cooperatively produces a more complex, deepened unity among the class participants themselves.

Each student is more modified by the activity and personality of the others in synthesis. Each lets the other's contribution as an agent affect who he is and what he thinks. Since it is a synthesis, the modification is reciprocal and growing. Each incorporates the other's input in developing the new position. Because a new position carries with it emotional and appetitive meaning—it has significance for what we feel and want—students mutually modify their whole selves, not just their thinking. The aesthetic whole thus formed is the most interesting one possible, since it is the most complex; synthesis is more complex than compromise by being more inclusive through the forging of new conceptions. Synthesis should, therefore, always be attempted before compromise is settled for.

* * *

The nature of the classroom activity carries forward into its result: The student learns how to *do* something. He learns how to think aesthetically in communal conversation. As a result of participating in something resembling a Platonic dialogue, he is psychologically ordered in fundamental ways. Of course, the student also acquires information, becomes adept at intellectual skills or techniques, and no doubt carries around a set of general beliefs—more or less justified. He has learned that some technical approaches to problems are more fruitful than others; in the course of trying them he comes to hold some and reject other beliefs about the world. But I wish to stress something more encompassing that the student learns how to do; this more encompassing ability enables him to acquire information, skills, and beliefs in the future.

The result of aesthetic classroom activity is that the student learns how to carry on inquiry with others. He learns how to take part in conversation:[30] how to opine, question, argue, and criticize with others. It is genuine learning because it involves appreciation for those activities which have come to constitute aesthetic experiences. While this sounds simple enough, it is nevertheless not easy to accomplish. It requires that the student be able to hold fast to what he thinks and wants to say, while following the flow of the discussion. It requires that the student keep yet two more poles in balance.

On the one hand, the student must speak his mind and be willing to defend what he says. His conviction is needed, otherwise he plays an empty intellectual game. At the same time, he must be open to criticism and the modification or abandonment of his original position which criticism can compel. This requires something like a "detached commitment"; detachment from our opinion insures that our commitment will not make us obdurate.

We must offer our opinion or criticism with a willingness to see it through and not shrink from criticism. Yet openness to criticism implies that sound argument and incisive objections can win us over, gently. We might say that the student who has learned to talk harmoniously with others avoids the extremes of stubbornness and spinelessness. Consequently, he must have enough faith in his beliefs to risk exposing them to the very scrutiny that can overturn them.

This is most likely to occur when the students are committed to working out the best possible position.[31] This overarching goal requires the combining of steadfastness with openness. It can elicit this combination since only by putting forth one's opinions can the best, most comprehensive view emerge—but only in the context of amenability to objection.

The best position or understanding will emerge from the class in which each brings out the best in the other. This parallels the way contestants in sports bring out the best in each other through their competitive efforts. "Competition" among students is, then, not the attempt to defeat or humiliate one another, but the effort to draw out the merit of one another's thought. Competition becomes bringing one another further. A student "bests" another by bettering his thought, as in aesthetic experience proper, in which parts or moments enhance and deepen one another.

* * *

Learning is aesthetic from start to finish. From the wonderment which signals the onset of inquiry to its satisfactory culmination, the educational process is delineated by aesthetic qualities and relations. It is no hyperbole to say that learning proceeds dramatically. This is why a discussion of education in the classroom so appropriately turns to Plato, a philosopher whose own teaching takes the shape of pedagogical dramas. In articulating the aesthetic dimensions of classroom education, I have looked to Plato for both his definitive, lively examples as well as his more elusive theories. Where Socrates and the dialogue afford rich images of the teacher and classroom, Plato's theories of love and learning disclose how the student's aesthetic experience comes to be.

Beginning with the metaphor of the Socratic midwife, we see how the teacher does not stuff facts and skills into the student so much as encourage a markedly aesthetic process to unfold. The student must respond to a felt lack or inadequacy in his understanding by making explicit a cognitive repository only dimly, incompletely grasped. Eventually this self-giving may culminate as an educational episode, rounding off an aesthetic experience.

The student's awakening dissatisfaction with his present understanding and subsequent search for what will overcome it occur within the context of classroom interaction. Here the form of the Platonic dialogue itself proves instructive. The concreteness of the dialogue's interlocutors mirrors the students' particular desires, emotions, and unreflectively held opinions. Ignoring the individuality of the class members must prove as fatal to the pedagogical enterprise as would overlooking the way they interact with one another. Here the dialogue teaches us that two organizing processes must proceed apiece: one is the organization of the public discussion, the "subject" being examined, and the other is the ordering of the individual students' psyches. This classroom discussion, in fact, is the temporary social context in which the ordering of opinion, emotion, and desire takes place, and this ordering, in turn, is crucial to the purposeful functioning of the student once out of the classroom and in the workaday world.

The workaday world, however, must continue educating the individual aesthetically. A sociocultural analogue of the classroom is needed to develop or even maintain the gains of formal education. Relations with other people, the physical and political environments, as well as the objects of work, must continue to engage the individual in aesthetic processes. By far the strongest influences in our overall educational development are found in the conditions which pervade our social world. Where the classroom provides a purposefully wrought, controlled context for ordering intelligence and self, our social environment willy-nilly now tests and furthers, then strains and frustrates this psychic ordering. There should be little doubt that without a social environment hospitable to the making of aesthetic relations, classroom advances will be undermined and shortcomings exaggerated.

In the next chapter we will see how just such inhospitability in our contemporary, anti-aesthetic environment accounts for strange new forms of violence. Because our sociocultural world is failing to enlarge upon the aesthetic education prescribed for the classroom, more and more individuals are becoming disordered and de-formed. Profound changes in the nature of personal violence, and not just its increased incidence, are traceable to this larger educational breakdown—but only if we attend to its aesthetic character.

Chapter Two
An Aesthetics of
Contemporary Violence

A LBERT DOTSON was angry. He had recently bought a 1979
Dodge Diplomat from Spitzer Motor City (located in Parma,
a suburb of Cleveland, Ohio) and it was not running very well.
Dotson was getting no satisfaction from John DiChiro, the salesman
who had also sold him a special warranty for his white two-door with
green roof. On Tuesday, August 5, 1980, Dotson complained to
DeChiro that it was unfair for him to have to spend $199.00 on the
engine to make it run "up to his standards." He wanted DiChiro to take
it back or fix it or do something. DiChiro pointed out that the warranty
did not cover the work he wanted done. Dotson came back Thursday
afternoon to complain about the car's front end and its blinkers. Seeing
John DiChiro, he pointed a finger at him and yelled: "You just watch
yourself. Because if I have to pay somebody, I'm going to get you."
DiChiro came over to him and suggested a front end alignment, for
$24.95. Dotson got into the car, raced the engine and screamed, "This
isn't going to cost me anything, right John?" and drove off. He returned
later, shortly after six o'clock, and asked DiChiro to listen to how
poorly the engine was running. Whatever the latter replied, it was not
what Albert Dotson wanted to hear. He ran around to his trunk, took
out a 12-gauge, pump-action shotgun, pumped it and began to load.
Running after a fleeing John DiChiro, Dotson shot him in the hip,
pumped, reloaded, and blew the back of DiChiro's head off. He was
quickly apprehended in his used car and said that he was sorry for
killing a man.[1]

If the Eighteenth Century was the Age of Reason and the Nineteenth
the Age of Industrialization, then perhaps ours is the Age of Violence.
The three periods may even be connected: contemporary violence the
result of over-mechanization and a fundamental failure of reason.

Certainly something has gone awry in a century during which two world wars and numerous "local" conflicts are echoed in the growth of everyday violence. Our daily lives seem soaked in it. It threatens to erupt within the most mundane transactions—a disgruntled customer shooting a used-car salesman. Classrooms resemble the Old West. And familial abuse of spouses and children certainly make questionable the idea of home as sanctuary. This should be more than enough to give us pause, yet our "make believe" world keeps pace with the real: television, movies, magazines, and sports are filled with the sights and sounds of violence.

But violence is not homogeneous, and the most disturbing types seem rather recent phenomena. Born out of a specific configuration of conditions in the Twentieth Century, they should be distinguished from the sort with which the world has long been familiar. This "traditional" violence is a "practical" sort of violence: chosen as one means over others (where others often exist) for such ends as money, career, power, revenge, or jealousy. Even war is usually a practical kind of violence, a means to territorial expansion or economic resources. Violence—the sudden, intense, forceful tearing down or apart of someone or something—is one alternative for people to get what they want, avoid what they dislike. Practical violence is just that, a violent alternative as a means to something sought.

Even practical violence, however, is different in our age. It is not just that there seems to be more of it, but it seems qualitatively different. The ends for which most practical violence is a means are now more private and more desperate. Social and political objectives motivate people less, their own needs more. Moreover, the alternatives to violence appear to have diminished, at least for many people. Put together, it means that more practical violence is committed to satisfy a private need, economic or emotional, for example, for which little nonviolent recourse is or seems to the individual to be available. Both the privacy and desperation of recent practical violence indicate its connection with especially contemporary forms. The first I would like to consider is "assertion-violence," violence whose main motive is the assertion of the self. While the same act may have aspects of both practical and assertion violence, as types they are different. Where practical violence is concerned chiefly with the product of the violent act (e.g., the elimination of a rival or the obtaining of funds), assertion violence focuses more on the act as a process. It is a process by which the individual tries to affirm himself as someone who matters in the world.

1. Assertion Violence

Self-assertion has become a growing basis for violence because more and more people feel powerless more and more of the time. Assertion violence is a flailing response to a lack of power. Everyday experience confirms our mushrooming sense of impotence. What can we do about food and fuel prices, traffic congestion, or our own unemployment? So a husband beats his wife because of job frustration, a motorist shoots someone who cuts in front of him or honks too loudly. Less and less of our lives seem amenable to our control. At best, most of us can make small adjustments in our small lives—granted that some of these matter a great deal. Whom we live with, how we raise our children, what we do for a living are important. But control over even these matters seems to be shrinking as our sphere of power diminishes in proportion to its amount. It is as if the shadow of the enormous politico economic machinery within which we move dims our very prospect for power.

Power, as I am using the term, is the ability and opportunity to change one's situation in the world. One has power to the extent that he has both the ability and opportunity to restructure and re-form the conditions that determine his life. Ability and opportunity must be distinguished from one another, since one may be able to alter his situation without the chance to do so, or have the chance but lack the ability. However, they are tightly intertwined; opportunity is needed to develop the ability to reshape one's environment and possessing the ability is a natural impetus to seek out the opportunities to do so. As the discussion proceeds, then, mention of one should suggest implications for the other.

Power signifies constructive possibilities for one's energies, and is precisely what is missing in more of our lives, in more areas of life. Without such possibilities we possess simply force—strength or energy—but not power. (Of course, lack of power can be due to deficiency in the individual's force or strength, but this does not produce violence.) The lack of power which is at the root of assertion violence stems from the social impossibility of energies reaching out into the world in a constructive way. In the summer of 1981, Europe found itself beset by waves of violence:

In West Germany they are known simply as "the no-future people"—a growing army of aimless, sometimes violent, inarticulate, usually jobless and often unemployable youngsters. . . .

Drifting casually from riot to riot, squatting in houses that don't belong to them. . . . "The violence is an expression of pure frustration," said Van Den Berg [Amsterdam social worker]... but in general it has little ideological content. . . . As one slogan daubed in Berlin put it, many young protestors are interested in 'self, not society'. . . .[2]

The individual's energies cannot make a difference in the shared public environment or the quality of his life. This is why he is without power, and without power he cannot become a controlled, ordered, deliberate person. The individual necessarily lacks the purposefulness of deliberate, controlled action unless he can use his force constructively. We shape our actions according to the purposes we hope to realize in the world. Without such purposes our actions lack direction and contour. There is no reason to deliberate about or control the direction of our energies if they cannot achieve our practical ends.

This is what happens in a classroom in which students cannot engage in purposeful participation; as noted in the preceding chapter, they either passively follow the teacher's lead or discharge their energies in directionless self-indulgence. Their interests and initiatives are either stifled or collide with one another's. So it is in the social world. When the individual's force cannot blossom in purposeful, constructive action, it either diminishes (through apathy or atrophy) or turns destructive. Whether in the classroom or society—the classroom writ large—the individual cannot develop self-control without the chance to perform deliberate, responsive actions. Desires, emotions, and thoughts cannot be organized without the aesthetic milieu in which force becomes power.

This order and self-control help constitute what I have been calling "agency" (see section 3, A, in preceding Chapter I). Among other things, agency is assumed when we hold people responsible for what they do; conversely, it is implicitly denied when we excuse people for momentary failures, such as a crime of passion, or for chronic incompetence, as in the incapacitation due to senility. Agency includes a certain level of command over one's impulses and desires, a certain level of discipline and reason characteristic of an "orderly" psyche. But such self-command and orderliness develop over time, through actions comprising the individual's daily responses to the world. These are more important than classroom life. Without the opportunity to develop agency in the social environment, "lessons" learned in the classroom—even the ideal, aesthetic classroom—will seem irrelevant to daily life. Work, family, social interaction, and the like will mock the classroom community, making life all the more frustrating for the individual.[3]

Assertion violence, then, is due to lack of genuine agency when the exercise of power in purposeful activity through which agency develops is missing from much of our lives. So far, these claims have been presented abstractly, with little connection to everyday life. The connection I wish to make is an aesthetic one. Assertion violence is the product of an anti-aesthetic society: a society in which more people more of the time are denied not simply power, but its exercise in the *establishment of aesthetic relations*. Areas within which people are powerless to structure such relations include the physical, occupational, social, artistic, and political aspects of life. The anti-aesthetic society denies its people the chance to take part in aesthetic relations in this wide range of spheres, yet these are the very forms of living necessary to order the psyche. Without them, the individual fails to participate in the aesthetic relations which foster agency. At one extreme, their lack starves all zest for identity and the individual becomes dulled, a passive conformist. At the other pole, aesthetic deprivation produces an emotionally charged psyche; violent emotions such as rage, anger, and frustration dominate the individual and are expressed in assertion violence.

But in neither case is the individual educated in the use of his or her energies and abilities. He is to one degree or another either enervated or emotionally roiled. Deprived of the power to initiate and develop aesthetic relations in a growing range of activities, the individual finds assertion violence an attractive way of proclaiming the self as a public factor. Destruction and disruption are ways for someone who sees little constructive opportunities in his life to make himself heard and felt.

A group of amiable artists and rock musicians came together a summer ago [1969] to plan a grand free outdoor festival of their joyful crafts in San Francisco, but a man who called himself Mother John appeared at their meetings and said he'd tear them apart, he'd burn them down. "I ain't rational and I'll wipe you out."[4]

* * *

Consider first the most obvious aesthetic aspect of everyday life, the physical environment. The arrangement of our streets and buildings, trees and traffic not only offers us sights and sounds, but determines how we move and interact with one another. Architecture, for example, is not simply something to look at, but is responsible for large segments of our work and home surroundings. As Robert Hughes points out in *The Shock of the New*, it is the "one art nobody can escape." And it has social consequences: "The fact that New Yorkers are piled up so unnaturally in overbearing buildings may explain the fact that they behave in ways that stress their impatience with normal manners."[5] But our architecture and its decoration are not just dwarfing or cramping, they are also dull and offensive both without and within: . . . "In a systematic fashion we are replacing the extraordinary wall mosaics of those [subway train] stations with strips of white tile, turning them into replicas of large public bathrooms."[6]

Perhaps nowhere is the destructive quality of our building and rebuilding felt so keenly as in our efforts at "urban renewal." "Urban renewal" is a double misnomer: It not only destroys the sense of neighborhood and the aesthetic qualities inherent in the perceptions of neighborhoods but it replaces neighborhood with materials and forms that have little connection with living in the city. There is no renewal of the senses, and what is built does not speak to the urban qualities of life.

> A neighborhood, a block, a tenement is not simply an external setting. Rather it is a complex field of relationships that form an ecological network, the strength of which is often beneath the surface. The human organism struggles for salvation, no matter how impoverished his context. He does this by building himself into his environment by means of establishing confidence in a number of relational ties. They may evolve 'landmarks'—a candy store, a playground, a house of worship, a merchant tradition, or perhaps vicarious participation in the passing scene.... With the cutting of these inexplicit yet deeply felt ties, people become estranged, and while thrashing about in search of a recognizable hold, they tend to reject a new and comparatively alien environment.[7]

The problem, however, is not simply an urban one. All of America is blanketed by highway and gas station, shopping mall and motel. Fast-food odors and the garish shacks from whence they issue are the decor of our senses. The list includes much more, but what we forget is that "...the objects which the senses confront and apprehend are the products of . . . a specific society, and the senses in turn are geared to their objects."[8] J. B. Jackson offers State Street in Chicago as an example of an environment which affords impoverished, even numbing, sense-experience.

When we walk along it our hearing and our instinctive feel for the proper interval between human bodies are affronted by the noise and the crowds; a monotonous dead-level surface is underfoot, and a monotonous geometric perspective stretches in either direction; monotonous facades rise on either side. The signs and window displays, often defended for the variety and visual stimulation they offer, are actually addressed to a totally different aspect of our vision; they are meant to be read and interpreted, rather than to be seen.[9]

Now obviously the quality and texture of environment is radically uneven in America, but the dull and dulling, ugly and cheap seem to be gaining. Most alarming and least obvious is their ultimate impact on the imagination. The senses provide the basic material for the imagination and most of us have little power to change our anti-aesthetic sensible surroundings. Tawdry and impoverished, these surroundings tend more and more to deprive our imaginations of good food. "The freedom of the imagination is thus restrained by the order of the sensibility..."[10] If I am correct, it is sadly fitting that Marcuse refers to typical sense experience as "mutilated": the mutilation occurring in assertion violence as the natural extension of mutilated perception.

The anti-aesthetic environment shows itself most pointedly in the ways in which it is inhospitable to the human body, failing to accommodate the body or to welcome its activity: "...We still have to provide satisfactory stimulation for the muscular sense; the urban landscape is full of immovable, untouchable objects."[11] In addition, the built environment seems to conspire to detach our bodies and senses from what is left of nature. We drive across a highwayed country or fly over it, but never engage the land or its people.

The evolution of the automobile is characterized by an increasing discontinuity of our bodies with that environment, as we became simply steerers of a powerful and largely unintelligible container. The development of a host of appliances and the advent of packaging still further removed us from intimate contact with the fundamental affairs of our daily life. Even our buildings are becoming containers, . . . more often repressing the opportunity for effective participation.[12]

The various physical environments in which we play, live, and work are anti-aesthetic, but so are the activities that take place within them. Consider work:

What makes work inherently rewarding or interesting? Several things come to mind: variety and choice of tasks; challenge that when met generates expanded ability; and control over the work situation. All of these elements yield development and integration of one's abilities. All of them demand and foster growth of one's powers in a purposeful way. In short, all contribute to agency.[13] They seem to be exactly what is missing from the work in which most Americans are engaged. Work seems so much routine, even for those with "good" jobs. Even corporate life, and not just assembly-line work, is characterized by lack of individual decision-making. Because the individual cannot see clearly what he has or has not accomplished, he can take no responsibility for success or failure;[14] he has no sense of his distinctive contribution. Since he cannot perceive the effects of his power, he is *virtually* powerless. Success or failure can have meaning only in terms of pay or promotion rather than in the quality of an independent, objective "product" or achievement. Amount of money or "height" in rank, however, are aesthetically empty—sheer quantity with neither form nor felt quality.

For many others, work is simply another place where their powerlessness is made obvious. Violence then becomes an apparent antidote for the powerlessness and routinization of work. Heywood Hale Broun quotes a minor league hockey player who values his institutionalized, and therefore socially acceptable, mode of assertion violence:

"The people you work for are always changing their minds, and after days of pulling out nails you've just driven in, you dream about getting on the ice and bashing a few guys. It's very relaxing. I know I've gone as far as I can in hockey, but I'll miss it. Who can I bash then?"[15]

—perhaps his wife, an inconsiderate motorist, or a drinking companion.

Disconnected from the fruits of his labors, today's worker is also cut off from his fellow workers. This is due not simply to competition, but also to compartmentalization in building layout. Career and geographic mobility contribute as well to social instability. For some, fellow workers and clients are little more than impersonal resources or obstacles to deal with. For others, the isolation is actually physical as well: "The venal customer, the gold-bricking workers, the lazy clerk, their sweaty and malevolent existence reaches him [the corporate manager] only in the palest reflections, in reports or printouts."[16] Work, neighborhood, family, friends: our ability to establish aesthetic relationships socially has eroded. The contemporary diagnosis of "alienation" refers not just to the fact of social separation, but also to the loss of *ability* and *opportunity* (power) to connect up with others.

Perhaps this is why so much current violence is done to strangers, while the loss of intergenerational continuity may explain why so much current violence is also done to the old. The ties that make us human keep us from violence by providing a counterpoise and conduit for once private desires. Without such ties in the present and with the past, society's members fragment; the society lacks what might be called an identity. Its "members," therefore, having little identification with or through it, are an aggregate of individuals rather than a community of participants. It may be a bit perverse to suggest that assertion violence is a social act, proclaiming the social significance of the individual, but the perversity would seem rather to lie in the unraveling social relations which give rise to it. Attacking someone shows more than apathy and in turn forces some kind of social response. This is true of one of the "no-future people" mentioned earlier:

> Cajo . . . a 22-year-old unemployed anarchist and squatter, has taken part in much of the street fighting. "The violence is attractive," he said. "If you hit a policeman on the head with a stone you are at least showing that you are not going to take it lying down."[17]

The revolution in mass communication revealingly illustrates the nature of social alienation, in that "mass communication" is another double misnomer. First of all, the individual is addressed apart, in the isolation of his home, rather than gathered with others in church or town hall. "Mass" refers to the quantity of those (perhaps simultaneously) affected, not *how* they are affected; they are not affected *en masse*. Secondly, there is not the give and take of real communication; television, radio, newspapers transmit in one direction. Mass communication renders us passive and alone. "Mass audience" has replaced an associating "public." Where the mass audience is fractured into so many electric "receivers," a real public is a politically active community in which members interact, make policy, reach decisions.[18] The difference between a mass audience and a public is the difference between a do-it-yourself home-study course (mass marketed) and the aesthetic classroom.

* * *

As indicated above, the anti-aesthetic environment (including the mass media) mutilates the imagination, sometimes in very subtle ways. I suggest that this imaginative impairment can extend to the way we see ourselves, or, rather, the ways in which we cannot see ourselves. More people cannot envisage themselves in the world as active, powerful people. And no wonder, since their impact on this world is minimal. The deprivation of the senses, therefore, combines with powerlessness to produce a second-level aesthetic erosion of power: the decreasing ability to *imagine* the self as acting on and in the world. The individual must struggle to see himself as a force in the society in which he feels lost. In assertion violence, the individual hurls himself into the social "picture" in a desperate attempt to portray himself as an agent; his imagination gives him few alternatives to violence. Because the opportunities for actually exerting power in the world are so few and so constricted, violence is needed to tear an imaginative space in which the self can be seen as acting the way real agents do. ". . . Power is the opposite of violence. The powerful man can respect the stranger, not fear him. The sense of being cut off makes men want to find reality through the ancient pride in blood-letting. Powerlessness corrupts; absolute powerlessness corrupts absolutely."[19]

The assertion of the individual as would-be agent is an *aesthetic* project: to insert the self into one's image of the world. The violent act forces the individual into the "public view," perhaps with the aid of the media. They "cover" the event and the individual can now see *himself* because the public sees him or his violence. (Television not only showed us President Kennedy being shot to death, but it covered his assassin's murder as well.) The act of assertion violence is, therefore, the process whereby the individual displays the *appearance* of agency. It is a parody of genuine power, since this public expression of self cannot go past a fleeting alteration in society. It does not, after all, effect real change in the social conditions that have stunted the individual's sense of self and imagination. This is to say that he is no more a real agent after the violence than before, evidenced by the fact that his force is spent, with no residue of himself left in the world except a media image. He has, at best, made a brief appearance on the public stage, to be replaced by the next bit of entertainment.

To say that there is an aesthetic basis to assertion violence is therefore to say several related things. The anti-aesthetic environment fails to educate our human strengths and capacities in humanizing ways. Instead, it degrades and cripples perception, imagination, and overall agency. We come to *feel* this lack of capacity and opportunity to effect our social world: our failure to envision ourselves as taking part in the world more felt than articulated or understood. Finally, the violent act is itself an image, transient and ersatz, of genuine agency. Aesthetic in origin, assertion violence is itself an aesthetic project aimed at providing the individual with the appearance of agency.

2. Ultraviolence

The aesthetic project of assertion violence culminates in ultraviolence. Like assertion violence, ultraviolence is concerned with the process of the act, except that in this case destruction is valued as an aesthetic process rather than as a self-affirming one. The self is experienced as producing the vivid sensations of violent destruction, but not as a social agent. At most, the individual asserts himself as originator of his own aesthetic experience, but this is not a social role. Of course, the same act can be violent in both ways and even serve practical ends as well, but ultraviolence marks a shift in emphasis. It "completes" assertion violence by calling attention to their shared social source: the disintegration of aesthetic relations in everyday life. Ultraviolence makes explicit the aesthetic ground of violence in society by explicitly seeking to force aesthetic enjoyment from society. Conscious of *its* aesthetic intent, ultraviolence illuminates the aesthetic root and project of assertion violence.

Ultraviolence goes "beyond" assertion violence by looking past the significance of the self to its aesthetic condition. Interest in self as socially powerful is replaced with self as aesthetic experiencer; interest in others as means to and testimony of social impact is replaced by the view of others as aesthetic "material" (in an aesthetically impoverished environment). As twisted and terrifying as assertion violence can be, it nevertheless bespeaks a recognition of the self as socially situated. It is a rebellion against one's disfranchisement and symbolically demands society's acknowledgement of the individual as a wielder of power. In ultraviolence, however, the individual is "lost," totally unmoored from the social fabric and values of power and participation. His is a totally private world, existing for his aesthetic delight. Society is important for his sake, whereas in assertion violence the individual wishes to be significant in and for his social world—to assert himself as a power within it. The ultraviolent individual is content to mean nothing to his society as long as it provides him with the material of aesthetic enjoyment. The social context in which assertion violence gives way to ultraviolence must be articulated, but first a characterization of ultraviolence itself is called for.

* * *

In ultraviolence, the violent action is valued for its aesthetic content—the sights and sounds of human destruction: the tearing of flesh, mashing of bone, letting of blood. Although it involves mangling or killing someone, death is but the climax of a sensuously rewarding attack. Dismemberment is pleasing not as a means to some ulterior motive (such as humiliation of the victim) but as a gory process in which a whole, living person is transformed into his or her sensuously striking components. The victim lacks significance save as something to be mangled. In *A Clockwork Orange*, we find a paradigm of the ultraviolent individual, Alex, who delights to the "...crack, crack, first left fistie then right, so that our dear old droog [friend] the red-red vino on tap and the same in all places, like it's put out by the same big firm—started to pour and spot the nice clean carpet..."[20] and "...then out comes the blood, my brothers, real beautiful."[21] The purpose of ultraviolence, then, lies within the activity itself—appreciation of its sensational content, its *aisthesis.*

As with beauty, ultraviolence must be experienced firsthand; it cannot be appreciated indirectly. Practical violence and to a lesser extent assertion violence do not require direct experience; we *need* not be on hand for the actual destruction we cause in order to rob a bank or see ourselves as a force in society. In these social sorts of violence, we are more concerned with the occurrence of the violence as a fact in the world rather than its availability to us. A newspaper report of his effectiveness *can* satisfy the individual who performs practical or assertion violence (even though he might prefer to experience the destruction); the violent act would have been performed even if it were known beforehand that there would be no direct perception, only indirect confirmation of its conclusion. When a terrorist or alienated individual blows up a building, he is not in it for the flames. To the extent that he *is*, his practical end or the goal of self-assertion is joined by an aesthetic interest. Just as we would not be satisfied with a report about a work of art, so is indirect appreciation of ultraviolence ruled out; without direct experience, there is nothing to take an interest in, in the case of ultraviolence. It is therefore "aesthetic" in nature on at least two related counts: the valuing of sensuous content and the necessity for directness. The ultraviolent act is valued for the sensuous qualities involved, and their appreciation requires direct first-hand experience.

The experience is viewed as an evening's entertainment, to be "taken in" like so much theatre. In ultraviolence the individual sees himself as a performer; he is self-conscious about what he does and why he does it, in a way not typical of other kinds of violence. Thus does Alex speak of getting ready for a "bit of the old ultra-violent." The "Ultra" suggests a fashionable novelty, part of the adolescents' jargon proclaiming proprietorship of what is so "super," so "far out," as to be beyond conventional description. It demands a style all its own.[22] At its most refined, ultraviolence is self-consciously undertaken, staged, and performed. Not only, then, does ultraviolence focus on the aesthetic qualities of the violent activity, but it includes an artful undertaking.

> With my britva [razor] I managed to slit right down the front of one of Billyboy's droog's [friend's] platties [clothes], very, very neat....[he] suddenly found himself all opened up like a peapod. ...It was stinking fat Billyboy I wanted now, and there I was dancing about with my britva like I might be a barber on board a ship on a very rough sea, ... to waltz—left two three, right two three—and carve left cheeky and right cheeky, so that like two curtains of blood seemed to pour out at the same time, one on either side of his fat filthy oily snout in the winter starlight. Down this blood poured in like red curtains....[23]

The doer of ultraviolence is removed from his society and his victim, at an "aesthetic distance" from both. Like a theatre-goer, he does not take them "seriously"; only he is real and his reality consists in little more than aesthetic appetite. Unlike those who engage in practical or assertion violence, the ultraviolent individual has no—perhaps miti-gating—personal end for which the violent behavior is a means. He has not been pushed by some jealousy or affront to his dignity. This very separation from pathos and personal involvement lends the ultraviolent a chilling antiseptic quality. It is "pure." In it there is no destruction for the sake of selfish ambition; neither venal nor honorable personal motivation infects the agent as the spur of his violence, nor is he swept away in a tide of feeling. As a connoisseur and performer of violence, the ultraviolent individual is in a way, therefore, *beyond* violent emotions.

Because he is not moved by violent emotions, he is not a "violent person" the way a frustrated, hateful, or vengeful individual is. In assertion violence, it will be recalled, the individual is likely to lash out from a sense of frustration or impotence; intense emotions govern his behavior. In ultraviolence, the individual is also psychologically disordered, but he is not emotionally driven; rather, his psyche is dominated by his *appetite*—his desire for sensation. His chief regard, then, is not with his self as such, but with the sensuous content of destruction. The ultraviolent individual is aware of his activity and its motivation to such a high degree precisely because he is so detached from himself and others.

But if the ultraviolent individual is not enslaved by his passions, neither is he humanly related to any of his victims. Emotions signify a relationship with others. Violent emotions involve negative relations, to be sure, in which energy is blocked and goals thwarted, but they nevertheless bespeak human connections. Even assertion violence is a human gesture made in and to society. But ultraviolence requires and reflects the culmination of the loss of the social connectedness in which human living (and much violence) consists. The ultraviolent person does not engage the other as human; his ultraviolence transforms a human being into sensible object(s). Writing of the Manson murders, Prosecutor Vincent Bugliosi notes: "They wanted to take out the eyes of the people, and squash them against the walls, and cut off their fingers."[24]

In objectifying the victim, however, the ultraviolent individual himself becomes objectified—in two respects. He becomes on the one hand a destructive force, on the other—a record of sensations. Neither involve the person as a truly human subject, whereas in assertion violence the individual tries to affirm himself as the subject of socially meaningful actions. The ultraviolent individual is at the same time a cold instrument of murder and a vibrating mass of sensations. Susan Atkins, a member of the "Manson family," said of stabbing actress Sharon Tate: "It felt so good the first time I stabbed her, and when she screamed at me it did something to me, sent a rush through me, and I stabbed her again."[25] It is as if in destroying what make the victim human, the ultraviolent person necessarily loses her own human self.

Therefore, ultraviolence exhibits an ironic sort of selfishness. It appears to be selfishness to an extreme, since its end is simply to enjoy the sensuous results of forcibly destroying another human being. But it is an ironic, deceptive appearance of selfishness because the self is immersed in the immediacy of both force and sensation. This cannot be real selfishness since the self disappears (as it does *not* in assertion violence). The emotions, interests, personal relations, and purposes which constitute the self are not called upon. They are neither engaged nor integrated with the forceful destruction or its resulting sensations.

Complete aesthetic experience differs importantly from ultraviolence. It makes subjective or human where the ultraviolent objectifies; it creates a whole where the ultraviolent atomizes. To begin with, the depths of the self are drawn upon, not obliterated, in complete aesthetic experience. They are brought to bear on external objective material—sounds, colors, shapes, word meanings. Manipulating such material in turn modifies the elements of the self: the individual's feelings, impulses, desires, and thoughts.

Both outer world and inner self are organized as they are brought into relation with one another. The inanimate objective materials are synthesized into a whole which seems to have a distinctive personality. Music, paintings, and poems, for example, seem to have moods, attitudes, and other human characteristics. The individual's desires, thoughts, and emotions, on the other hand, become ordered. Instead of being loosely connected, they receive the imprint of his personality. The individual's identity develops as the "inner" material of self is organized in relation to the "outer" material of the world. As a result, both the self and the external material are subjectified, made more fully human.

Complete aesthetic experience subjectifies by bestowing form on diverse constituents. And, as Marcuse observes, "Form is the negation, the mastery of disorder, violence. . . ."[26] The aesthetic experience ultraviolence affords is necessarily incomplete; it has only sensuous content or *aisthesis*[27] but no form or structure. When *aisthesis* captivates attention, as in ultraviolence, a selfless enjoyment results, because the forming activities which help define the self are missing. Form in aesthetic experience is not simply "given" to a passive recipient; it requires forming, integrative activity from the artist or appreciator. To do so, the individual must himself become "orderly."

The ultraviolent individual is not capable of the forming activity whereby the sensuous material is incorporated into a larger aesthetic whole. He *cannot order* diverse external material because he is *himself disordered.* Lacking the necessary self-mastery, he also lacks "mastery of the opposites 'without tension, so that violence is no longer needed.'"[28] He has not learned to limit and thereby give shape either to his self or to objective material.

* * *

In my view, this is not because most ultraviolent people are innately defective, neurologically fated to the attractions of lurid sensations and impervious to the value of form. Rather, their aesthetic desire fastens on the sensuous content of the aesthetic because the complete object of the desire—form as well as sense-content—is out of reach. Form is lacking in their lives in general and through little fault of their own. What is claimed here would seem true of human psychology in general: If an individual cannot attain complete love, then she "settles" or fixes on an aspect of it, such as sexuality or helpfulness. If someone cannot secure fulfilling work, then he occupies himself with an aspect or outward index of it, such as competition or wealth. The ultraviolent person pursues the sensuous through destruction because his environment has failed to educate his appetites and inform his senses. The forming capacities necessary for complete aesthetic experience are undeveloped in proportion to the individual's lack of self-control and psychic order. Ultraviolence is sympathetically understood as a radical response to an anti-aesthetic society, expressing the "radical social content of the aesthetic needs. . . ."

> For the aesthetic needs have their own social content: They are the claims of the human organism . . . for a dimension of fulfillment which can be created only in the struggle against the institutions which . . . deny and violate these claims.[29]

Everyday social life must provide the individual with opportunities to learn to limit and shape his desires by responding to what is independent of himself. Interaction with his culture, family, peers, at work and in political processes must modify the individual's senses and appetites. They then cease to be private and instead are penetrated by the nature of what intersects with them. Thus might our ambitions be restrained for the sake of friendship or redirected by family considerations, or our romantic attractions informed by religious or cultural ideals of love. As a result of such modification, the individual's relation to himself is qualified by these external relations; he is informed by friends and culture, work and politics. They "mediate"— come between and reconstruct—his relation to appetite and sense experience. These are the relations through which force can become power—whereby we are able to alter the environment to meet our needs. This should be understood to include the physical surroundings as well. J. B. Jackson sees with uncommon clarity the connection between individual growth and power over the built world:

> Not all of our development comes from contact with the environment; but much of it does, and when that contact is made difficult we are badly cheated. Each of us needs a chance to create or modify some part of our world—house or place of work or place of leisure; and an environment which is so mismanaged and disorganized that most of us are simply tenants or guests or spectators can be called impoverished. This is what has happened in many parts of America.[30]

Creating and maintaining such "mediating relations" also enables a person to shape sensuous material into an integral whole and enjoy complete aesthetic experience, form as well as sensuous content.

Through the modifying relations with objects and events in his environment, the individual's appetites and perceptions are sifted; they are refined and realigned in light of the nature of what he encounters outside himself. Thus does otherwise private sensuous material join with the everyday objects of work, friendship, politics, or art itself, and become redefined by intimate connections with external reality. Consider, for example, the ruddy rose of Robert Burns' "luv" or Stephen Crane's "red badge of courage." The vivid sensation of bloody red is given form by being socially situated, whether in a rose or the turmoil of war. Its appeal and meaning is subsequently delimited by the social objects with which it is integrated. Contrast this with the delight in the *isolated* sensation experienced by the performer of ultraviolence such as Alex: ". . . Then out comes the blood, my brothers, real beautiful." Just as the individual is isolated from society, so are his particular experiences cut off from one another and their social context. The ultraviolent individual is thereby untempered by any social consciousness. His force joins immediately with his desire for the sensuous. The two are not mediated by connections with other people, culture, or political processes. No mutual investment, no care, no cooperation, no shared decision-making relates his aesthetic desire to society.

Bereft of these everyday social relations that inform our appetites and sensations, the ultraviolent individual is absorbed in the sensuous. And the sensuous is itself limitless. Thus the circularity of the ultraviolent performer's psychology and experience. Psychologically unlimited within, he can produce only the sensible content of the aesthetic, without its formal limits. The enjoyment of the unbounded, sensuous content of the aesthetic, moreover, serves as fuel for his unlimited aesthetic desire. In this way the excessive individual is made more excessive by the consequences of his unrestrained behavior. Leslie Ann Houten, another member of the Manson family was at first reluctant to kill, but then "discovered the more you stabbed the more fun it was."[31] In separate episodes, Manson family members stabbed Rosemary Labianca forty-one times and Voytek Frykowski (friend of movie director Roman Polanski) fifty-one times. Killing alone could hardly have been the objective.

Aesthetic experience can be sought anywhere, in any thing: the arrangement of cracks in a sidewalk, water stains on a wall, or the patterns of people walking to work. This great scope is a great virtue; it means that we do not have to go to museums or art galleries to find aesthetic fulfillment—the textures and timbres of everyday life can be aesthetically satisfying. Yet this is also a danger of the aesthetic. As a way of appropriating the world the aesthetic can also appropriate us; we may seek it anywhere, at any expense, compulsively. This is what happens to the individual who pursues the aesthetic solely in its sensuous dimension, which is necessarily without limit because without form.

Aesthetc desire threatens destruction when it is realized only in the sensuous because the sensuous self is boundless, easily "carried away" as force gets "out of hand." Force is untempered by the personal purposes, which, found in both practical and assertion violence, limit behavior. Missing then is the commitment to others or self which can inhibit the temptation to aesthetic license. Nothing checks the temptation to do simply *anything* for aesthetic delight. The ultraviolent individual is unlimited in his striving and there are no inherent limits to the degrees or sources of sensation.[32] Perhaps this helps explain the association between violence and sex. Sexuality itself is intensely sensuous, which suggests why it is considered "sensual" and not simply sensible. It is therefore a likely or "natural" locus for ultraviolence, especially since isolating the "victim's" sexuality further objectifies and dehumanizes him. The influence of the sensuous, furthermore, grows in a self-generating way. We are easily seduced into viewing *everything* for its sensational value:"Had, having, and in quest to have, extreme," (Shakespeare, Sonnet 129). Like lust, the desire for *aesthesis* can expend the spirit, the individual consumed by his desire for ultraviolence.

Ultraviolence leaves its performer with nothing but the isolated content of agency—force. Thus, he perfectly mirrors his aesthetic experience: sensuous content without form. Both the individual and the aesthetic process are reduced to unformed content: sheer force on the one hand, sensations on the other. Given the failure of his society to provide the necessary environmental education, this is the best the lover of the aesthetic can do in such a situation. The world about him restricts the individual in search of aesthetic experience to the sensations of destruction by depriving him of the opportunity to engage in the aesthetic relations necessary for the development of genuine agency. This is, at bottom, a political problem, since politics is an alternative to force as a way for the individual to shape his environment in wholesale fashion. Because politics has a summary voice over our social relations, its failure signifies and symbolizes the failure of the individual to exercise his force as power.

3. Politics and Art

Assertion violence occurs within a context in which powerless individuals see others wielding power. Particular political figures or groups are perceived making decisions that affect the lives of many. The Organization of Petroleum-Exporting Countries controls oil prices; a community blocks construction of a nuclear power plant; a legislator promises and delivers on tax reform. The powerless, moreover, see the lives of those with power as rich in meaning; they have social, economic, political relations which are sustaining and over which they have control. Assertion violence is a distorted imitation of such lives. But for many people there is no such perception of anyone wielding much power. No one seems "in charge" of his own or another's destiny, or, what is practically the same, it does not matter much who is in charge because conditions will be the same regardless.

The prospect of self-assertion dims as power begins to seem not to exist in society at all; as plausible images of agency (needed in order to be imitated in assertion violence) fade or become hazy. To a growing extent this is true for a large segment of American society. The prospect of powerlessness pervades: cities go bankrupt; laws are unenforced; communities age and decay; and there seem to be no real differences among officials standing for election. An anti-aesthetic society becomes ultraviolent as its political integrity degenerates. There appear to be no *public* agents, no people with the power to reshape the social environment. If ". . . politics is the struggle to construct an optimum environment for the realizing and sanctioning of the aesthetic processes of living,"[33] then that struggle would appear to have been abandoned. So-called politicians appear helpless, their ersatz political activity merely a show—party platforms, speeches, legislative debates, and public appearances so much hoopla.

Whether more true today than in the past, more people *see* the political arena in these terms. Politicians are seen to be actors on a public stage, their miming of real political activity merely a way for self-aggrandizement—politics as cloaking influence-peddling in respectability. This parallels the aesthetics of ultraviolence. Just as the only available dimension of aesthetic experience is what is *apparent* to the senses, so the only thing political is its *appearance* in speeches, parties, ballots, and the media. Those with political authority seem to make little difference, at least too little difference, in how most of us live our lives.

This is to say that the agency so many individual members of society lack is missing from society collectively.[34] The lives of the people are increasingly beyond the deliberate, concerted reshaping that defines genuine political activity. To the extent that a society is beyond political remedy, it is an ultraviolent society;[35] only private ends such as security, force, or aesthetic delight have meaning. Ultraviolence blends force with the aesthetic for personal satisfaction. It grows as society's primary institutions of politics and art lose their viability. That their decline is concomitant, moreover, is no accident.

Artistic and political bankruptcy go hand in hand. Genuine art is always potentially an instrument for political awareness and change because it fosters self-consciousness in the widest sense. Art loses its reach into the public domain as political power dries up. When people see no chance to change their conditions through political means, including violence, art's call to action becomes a cry in the wilderness: spurring thought, stirring up new possibilities for experience that cannot be realized.

In a politically functioning society, on the other hand, it is not surprising to find what Marcuse calls an "ingression of the aesthetic into the political," political activity expressed aesthetically. Marcuse cites the example of the aesthetic protests of the 1960s in songs, sensuous long hair, and "flower power." More subtle and pervasive may be the way black culture takes a political stance aesthetically by appropriating and redefining white language: "soul" ("in its essence lily-white ever since Plato") for instance describes brothers, food, and music.[36] It follows, then, that loss of aesthetic creativity is a loss of political expression and power.

Perhaps, then, a society actually becomes depoliticized as it loses touch with its main aesthetic resource—its arts, its culture, for these provide an historical-ideological continuity that gives a society its identity, one it can self-consciously embrace. This identity is a basis for generating future options and political directions. A healthy society is one whose future is continuous with its past, mindful of what it has done and valued. Art is both part of that past and a fundamental way of reconstructing and keeping it before us.

As our art (and, more generally, our culture) dwindles in vitality, America is more liable to the identity loss that rots political life. Evidence of such dwindling can be found in the decreased attention paid to the liberal arts in colleges as they become more technically and vocationally oriented. Yet college study is one of the few ways for new generations to become acculturated into our artistic traditions. Like politics, art and culture occur within and in response to particular traditions out of which are developed novel formulations and revisions of human experience. Moreover, political life depends upon the effects of such traditions on society's thinking, feeling, and imagination. The "liberal" arts are thought to have a liberating effect on imaginaton and experience, much needed to meet the demands of political renewal.[37] The loss of care and respect for our cultural traditions as a society parallels the loss of connection between the younger and older generations. Each separation bespeaks a loss of self-identity, for the individual and for society as a whole; both become "hollow," without substance or a real nature. De-cultured people become de-natured.

4. A Social Aesthetic

How then *should* society limit the aesthetic desire which we have seen can be a motive for great destruction? Aesthetic quality seems to be an essential dimension of human well-being, but its attraction can have the monstrous consequences of ultraviolence. It is a painfully ironic form of violence because aesthetic desire, a distinctly human characteristic, motivates the person who is virtually without the social relations essential to becoming fully human. Without these relations, an intense human desire is transmogrified into a force for human destruction. It is apparent, therefore, that all societies, and perhaps ours more particularly, need to come to terms with the aesthetics of violence.

We could, as most commentators have, take Plato's provocative answer in *The Republic* literally: Society can blunt the danger of the aesthetic forcefully. It can police the streets more diligently, censor artistic expression or sponsor propagandistic art. The various forceful means of suppressing or rerouting aesthetic appetite available to society must, however, eventually fail to control our pursuit of the aesthetic. Forceful measures keep the aesthetic apart from society; they do not really domesticate it because they do not reshape aesthetic desire and sensibility. *The Republic* properly calls attention to the antisocial potential of the aesthetic; however, it also suggests how the danger lies not in art, but in the lack of the artful in everyday living.

Society properly governs aesthetic desire by itself becoming aesthetically educational. Quite simply, society must change the conditions which give rise to ultraviolence. Providing an aesthetic environment in which people wield power is also a remedy for assertion violence. Both contemporary forms of violence are overcome when everyday social living consists in opportunities for complete aesthetic experience, in the political, vocational, artistic, personal, and physical dimensions of daily life. In this way does the environment complete the aesthetic education begun in the classroom. There is no special place for art in *The Republic*,[38] for instance, because the society or *polis* as a whole is to be artfully formed. But what does this mean, specifically?

I can hardly here offer a blueprint for society, but if we think of social elaborations of classroom relationships, portions of an outline emerge: in particular, the place of *friendship* and *politics* in a social aesthetic. As paradigms of the personal and public, they are contexts for aesthetic give-and-take in which one's originally private energies and desires come to be modified by the agency of others.

The ultraviolent individual is disengaged from other people. Because he does not respond to the victim's person or purposes, they cannot modify who and what he is. This is the antithesis of what goes on in friendship, where each is involved with another through whom he comes to know and develop himself. Each friend mediates the other's relation to himself; the opinions, desires, and interests of each modify the other's as they are taken into account by him. Thus, under a friend's aegis might we alter our attitude toward someone else (finding virtues where before only faults were seen) or perhaps temper a tendency toward self-aggrandizement. Whatever the specific impact, friends necessarily make us step back from ourselves, and thereby foster if not require self-scrutiny and modification. The performer of ultraviolence, however, lacks this human mediation and so is immediately absorbed in the sensations of his destruction. So too is the individual in assertion violence closed off from response from others; he has a predetermined private goal and is not open to alteration from without. (More specific meaning is given to the aesthetic relations involved in friendship in the discussion of sexuality in Chapter IV.)

A more extended, political form of friendship involves harmony among the generations—sorely absent in the ultraviolent society. Every society is faced anew with the problem of socializing what sociologist Daniel Patrick Moynihan calls the "new barbarians"—its youth. But it must do so without enervating them. The extremes to be avoided, then, are alienation on the one hand and enervating conformity on the other. It is difficult to socialize without stifling, but society needs the challenge that disagreement with its youth offers. It needs the newness of the new generation. Without thoughtful response from the older generations, however, the youth will either give up their competitive challenge or strike out in pursuit of private satisfactions such as found in ultraviolence. Their creativity must be encouraged and accommodated by society.

Intergenerational cooperation requires that the new members of society criticize and build upon the work and thought and institutions of previous generations. It is against the history of their culture that the young must test their ideas, and the older generations more or less adequately personify that culture. The young, then, must question and interpret their culture's traditions: traditions of art, science, technology, politics, and education. Meeting within these traditions and even disagreeing about their value or direction, the lives of the different generations achieve continuity, and society neither alienates nor stifles its youth.

Harmony among the generations presupposes political interaction in general—each generation entering into public discussion with the others about that which is of concern to all. Political speech is aimed at reaching decisions about all sorts of practical activities and matters:

farming, building, defending, teaching, and the like. It is the means by which issues and activities of concern to all of society are coordinated, ideally, for the good of all the people in the community. This inclusive concern for all is the basis on which political decisions about specific issues such as farming or building are then reached.

Political activity is the way a collection of individuals becomes and remains a community. Community requires that people step out of their particular private perspectives and take the larger good of society as their horizon of deliberation. Political activity modifies one's private interest with concern for the whole (society), just as aesthetic interaction in the classroom modifies the individual's partial understanding. It thereby extends the concern for another which animates friendship. One's deliberations must take into account the opinions and welfare of the other, sometimes distant, members of society.

In the previous chapter we saw how the student can be brought to such a larger view through imaginative or hypothetical exercises, but here the issues concern the participants more immediately: family life, neighborhood, health, and livelihood are at stake. Without the sort of practice provided in the classroom, this larger social perspective is harder to attain. Each will tenaciously cling to "his own." As in the aesthetic classroom, however, the larger view should encompass rather than exclude the particular outlook. Private interest meshes with public good in the aesthetically unified society. It boasts a unity not purchased at the expense of the individuals who compose it; rather, the distinct talents and interests of each are furthered by his or her social relationships[39] (but more on this theme in the next chapter).

Only by taking part in those political processes through which the broad circumstances of his life are determined does an individual develop fully as an agent. Only in political activity does the individual's force systematically extend to others and into the socially shared environment. Even if he enjoys private exercise of power, when the individual is excluded from the basic framing of his circumstances he is without the power definitive of complete agency. Then he easily sinks back into the immediacy of his private interests and experience—as in assertion violence or ultraviolence. Society overcomes these contemporary forms of violence by building into its peoples' everyday lives the occasions for using power to structure aesthetic relationships. These include participating in the most overarching, collective use of the community's power—its politics.[40]

* * *

We have seen how aesthetic relations and qualities play a crucial role in the education of our human endowment, whether on the microlevel of the self-contained, controlled schoolroom, or the macrolevel of the hurly-burly social environment. The way we teach our young in the classroom is decisive for their ability to take part in the aesthetic processes which everyday social life should make available. Formal schooling is perhaps the most concentrated and self-conscious way a society has for preparing its members to make their daily social environment pedagogically effective. In turn, it is in his everyday social environment that the individual must cultivate the relations constitutive of complete aesthetic experience.

Complete aesthetic experience! Up until now we have elaborated upon the aesthetic character of human development and identity, human distortion and fragmentation. The aesthetic has emerged as the leading lady in a drama first about formal education, then about the violence attendant upon the deficiencies in the education social life must provide. It is time now to turn directly to this pivotal character, to examine more explicitly and fully the nature of complete aesthetic experience. The connection between the aesthetic and personal development, moreover, will not be abandoned, but will be pursued along especially moral lines.

Chapter Three
Aesthetic Experience
As Moral Education

RATHER THAN GLEAN the nature of the aesthetic from such areas of the everyday as classroom teaching and social violence, we need now to look at aesthetic experience "proper." Taking up aesthetic experience as an end in itself, we will elaborate the aesthetic relations found in the everyday, carrying forward the discussion of the preceding chapters and anticipating those that are to come. We shall be able to see more comprehensively and clearly, for example, what was briefly mentioned in connection with ultraviolence: that complete aesthetic experience requires that the individual actively organize and inform material presented to him. We will also explore the converse: the way the individual is liable to re-formation in the course of aesthetic experience. It not only prepares us for engaging in all sorts of pursuits aesthetically—simply by concentrating their potential aesthetic values—but disposes us toward morally relevant thought and action by nurturing far-reaching social habits. In discussing this instrumental moral benefit of aesthetic experience, I do not mean to slight its intrinsic worth, especially since part of its instrumentality depends upon valuing it intrinsically. Because we value aesthetic experience for its own sake, we have a motive for seeking its structure in everyday activities not usually thought of in aesthetic terms.[1]

Aesthetic experience can have profound if subtle impact on how we interact with others by its influence on our habits. This is not to say that aesthetic experience is either necessary or sufficient for moral education.[2] An individual's character might develop well without it and having such experience is certainly no guarantee of moral growth. However, its contribution may yet be considerable: Swimming at an early age prepares for expertise, although neither necessary nor sufficient for it, just as reading good authors is effective in honing writing talent.

Often our understanding of the good or ideal is sharpened through examination of the corrupt or deficient, as in the preceding discussion of contemporary violence. The moral value of aesthetic experience may be similarly thrown in relief by contrasting it with our delight in "cheap" art. Not all weak or disappointing art fails to contribute to aesthetic experience the way cheap art does, for it is actually antithetical to aesthetic experience and the constructive dispositions it can engender. The cheap does more than fail to call into play the powers and capacities crucial to human growth—it dulls the sensibility, inhibits imagination, and disposes toward intransigence. By inducing the very tendencies which blind us to its harmfulness, moreover, cheap art adds illusion to injury by being self-concealing.

1. Aesthetic Object

The center of attention in aesthetic experience is the "object" which emerges within it: the result of a creative response to something present to consciousness. It is what we designate within aesthetic experience when we speak of "Hamlet" or "Beethoven's Fifth Symphony." When the physical object, the work of art (words on a page, notes or sounds in air) enters into an aesthetic experience, it helps constitute an aesthetic object. What strikes us as singularly impressive about such objects is that they are complete in themselves. The sense of wholeness conveyed seems to suggest that we are in a self-contained realm in which every part has a necessary place. This sort of completeness answers the complementary and often competing demands of economy and adequacy. Each element seems essential to the character of the whole—none are extraneous, none are "idling." On the other hand, no further constituents are neded; all that are present are sufficient for the integrity of the others. Furthermore, the more complex the elements and relations brought into harmony, the more valuable the unity. The unity of an object which is low in dissonance or diversity is a unity too easily won, one in which there is little to take an interest. We miss the tensions responsible for the energetic cooperation necessary for the whole to have a distinctive presence or "personality."

Within the ideal aesthetic object, tensions and oppositions are synthesized. Resistances or obstacles to movement are converted into material for fresh episodes. Although the parts or moments are distinct and possess individual textures, the whole unfolds as if growing in a defined direction. Material in one section seems to open on to that of the next. Sometimes the affinity among the segments is grasped only retrospectively, sometimes what presently occupies us anticipates what is to come. The crucial thing is that the continuity includes time—we are never allowed to forget or file away what has occurred nor to ignore possible intimations of what awaits us. This does not mean that there are no rests or pauses, only that such moments punctuate, give meaning to what has gone before and what succeeds. Effective rests are different from dead spots; they are not holes in which nothing is "going on."

All aesthetic objects are temporal, on-going events; even plastic works of art which are present all at once as physical objects develop in time *qua* aesthetic objects (as taken up constructivley in a human consciousness). What is begun is carried forward, thematically and temporally, until its development reaches a culmination. The conclusion of the way in which each part grows out of another is aptly dubbed by Dewey "consummation." The parts and their relations are brought to fulfillment in a comprehensive way. They are "consumed," their meanings drawn out and penumbras filled in, by the time the end is reached. This is in contrast to the extremes either of petering out or of premature constriction.[3] In the former, there is simply no closure, no rounding out of what has transpired, but rather a loose, undirected expense of energies. In the latter, a blueprint or artificial pattern extraneous to the material seems imposed on it. This often happens in overly didactic works when the artist's "message" demands a specific ending even though his creation (plot or character, for example) does not. In the full or ideal aesthetic object, however, the moments are felt to mature to their conclusion in an unforced but forceful way. They are "consummated" in and through the whole even as human life and relationships were once thought capable of consummation.

This takes place because the thrust and meaning of each part is colored by its relation to others. The episodes are what they are because of their relation to one another as well as their situation in this particular whole. Each reciprocally modifies and depends upon the others. Consider the ideal work of fiction. The changing events help bring about the development of the characters even as these characters are partly responsible for making the plot move the way it does. Subjects or themes in the fiction are exposed by the characters developing within the context of plot, but the nature of the characters' change and plot movement are themselves made intelligible by the emerging thematic material. And so it goes for all the arts: The parts, moments, and events of each stand related reciprocally.

Reciprocity is central to human community, so we are not stretching meaning to say that an aesthetic object consists of a community of parts or members. This is to be distinguished, first, from a mere aggregate or collection of items, the case of a volume of water or a heap of sand. For there the members' natures are not altered by their relation to one another; in a different collection of some of these same a particular drop of water or grain of sand would not be changed. Conversely, changes in the arrangement of the parts would make no difference to the quality of the whole, the aggregate. Mere aggregates, then, lack the reciprocity that helps define community.

The aesthetic object must also be distinguished from useful or mechanical objects, even though the parts of such objects do stand reciprocally related to one another. In a useful object, determining whether or not the parts are reciprocally related in an adequate way depends upon whether, when so related, the whole fulfills a function external to it: whether the car transports, the gun shoots straight, or the typewriter prints accurately. The existence and appreciation of such useful or mechanical reciprocity, therefore, is determined extrinsically, by a purpose independent of the object. But an aesthetic object, including its parts and relations, exists only for its own sake, not to fulfill some extrinsic function. The success of the reciprocity of an aesthetic object, therefore, is determined from within, by the degree to which its parts form a community, complete and (consequently) valuable in itself. Since an aesthetic object is appreciated as an end-in-itself, its reciprocity is valued as a constituting relation rather than as simply a means to some extrinsic end.

2. Aesthetic Response

Aesthetic experience includes our *relation to* the aesthetic object. The integration and unity of the aesthetic object is not given passively in experience but is achieved through our discriminating and organizing response to something present to us. Although other things besides works of art or nature can be taken up aesthetically and provide the material for aesthetic objects, I shall speak of our response to art works for convenience and because they are obvious sources of aesthetic experience. Now clearly one feature of our relationship to aesthetic objects is our intrinsic valuing of them. Further, I think we value the relationship itself. Why? Because it is a relation characterized by a certain sort of freedom and an active receptivity I shall call "responsivity". Since this freedom and responsivity are enjoyed in connection with an aesthetic object, the communal structure of the aesthetic object informs and conditions them. Let us turn first to how the creation of an aesthetic object calls for a sort of freedom on our part.

Because the parts of the aesthetic object do not stand in any one determinate relationship, we are called upon to invent, to play freely at arranging parts and articulating a whole. There is no concept or rule to apply in this responding because we are not bound to come up with a definite object.[4] Think here of the difference between arranging colored shapes into a conceptually defined "thing" such as a house or car and arranging them simply into a "good" design. In the latter case, we are not inventing a something for some purpose external to our creation; consequently, we are freed from the restrictions of utility to explore imaginative possibilities. We are not limited to the specification of a definite concept: of a house, a car, or a means-of-sending-long-distance-messages. But this is a freedom *demanded* of us. We have the burden of entering into an open-ended, indeterminate creative process, denied the definite rules that practical ends establish for the fabrication of useful objects.

The making of useful objects, on the other hand, is circumscribed by the demand to satisfy this desire or meet that need. The practical end enters into the concept by which the object is determined and brought into existence. Depending on whether it succeeds or fails to fit the function at hand, a mechanical product is correct or incorrect, and there are techniques specifying ways to attain a correct result. But much more than techique is needed for bringing about an aesthetic object.

Furthermore, there are no correct or incorrect renditions of aesthetic objects and, because there are no extrinsically based measures to apply, something other than functional suitability provides criteria of worth. Rather, when there are works before us our *aesthetic* end—a notion of the complete aesthetic object—helps us judge the quality of our aesthetic creation. Thus, interpretations are more or less appropriate to works of art; more or less imaginative or original; more or less insightful or fecund in aesthetic qualities. Hence the virtuosity, and legitimacy of plurality, in interpretation whereby the critical audience is credited with contributing to the emergence of the aesthetic object.

In bringing about this integrated object, we are neither wholly active nor wholly passive, nor are we alternately exclusively one and then the other: We are actively receptive to what is before us. As indicated in Chapter I, we strike a balance between "doing" and "undergoing." What we do is conditioned by what we are taking in and what we receive is shaped by our active involvement. As we saw in considering classroom interaction, this is characteristic of genuine communication: active listening, receptive speaking. So too in aesthetic experience per se a kind of communication takes place. We must draw upon our personal histories, acquaintance with aesthetic and other cultural products, as well as associations the work evokes. This activity is described by Dewey as "funding"—bringing to the work of art our fund of experience, values, and cultural knowledge. This funding, of course, is in response to the ongoing perception of what the artist offers; what he offers determines whether and when our funding is appropriate.

Because we are actively engaging the work of art, the "present" moment in aesthetic experience is infused with past and future. The notion of funding already indicates the relevance of personal and cultural history, but active involvement also means that what has transpired during *this* aesthetic experience is kept in mind (how else appreciate the rhyme scheme of a poem or the variations on a musical theme?). Alert to various possibilities in what is undergone, moreover, "doing" includes anticipating what is yet to come: further tensions, complications, dissonances, resolutions. Past and future are united in the aesthetic present, with the result that, "Art celebrates with peculiar intensity the moments in which the past reenforces the present and in which the future is a quickening of what now is."[5]

As we take in, undergo, the artist's work, we must engage in the complementary activities of discrimination and integration. Each requires the other: "to evoke a clearer consciousness of constituent parts and to discover how consistently these parts are related to form a whole."[6] Dewey points out that analyzing and discriminating among the segments or moments of the experience should result in unification. We must "distinguish particulars and parts with respect to their weight and function in formation of an integral experience."[7] Without integration, all we have is "enumeration of details."

Our integrative efforts are facilitated by emotion or, more generally, affect. Emotion carries the experience forward, binding parts and moments to one another:

It selects what is congruous and dyes what is selected with its color, thereby giving qualitative unity to materials externally disparate and dissimilar. It thus provides unity in and through the varied parts of an experience.[8]

The ensuing pervasive affective quality strengthens the unity of the experience; moreover, the way emotion performs this task illustrates the mutuality between doing and undergoing. The emotion's active office of selection is performed after it is initially aroused—the effect of what is *undergone*. So, for example, does poetry or painting evoke a mood whose affective timbre determines how and what we select for attention.

From the delicate balance between doing and undergoing, a feeling of suspension arises. We are at once distanced from the aesthetic object while absorbed in it. We seem simultaneously to be aware of ourselves but taken out of ourselves: intensely involved but easily overlooked. This state of equipoise is "responsivity."

When responsive we take part in a process which begins and culminates in something distinct from us. This means that we neither fabricate from whole cloth nor have our activity totally determined from without. Responsivity requires that the creative upshot of our efforts, the aesthetic object, stand over against us, a publicly accessible object in whose composition we have participated. Were it merely a private child of imagination, there would be too much "doing" not amenable enough to what we should be attending to. To be responsive our doing must be shaped by contours not of our choosing. As a general character trait, responsivity is essential to taking moral responsibility for our conduct—that willingness to stand behind our actions as they intersect with the world in ways we could not have fully foreseen. (The importance of being open to the uncertain response of others will be brought home in the next chapter.)

3. Aesthetic Experience and Community

Our responsive freedom takes place in developing the aesthetic object. If the aesthetic object possesses some of the formal relations constitutive of human community, then those relations can instruct our responsive freedom. What we must now make out, therefore, is how the aesthetic object as described in the first section resembles (the ideal) human community. The impact of such resemblance on our aesthetically engaged freedom and responsivity would be to prepare us for living in community.

A social community is a whole, complete in itself. Since it consists in people in relation to one another, its existing for the sake of itself as an ongoing whole implies existing for the benefit of its members and their relations. The strength of the whole requires the integrity and autonomy of its constituents as well as their mutual support. Thus, in my understanding, there is a crucial difference between societies which function well as a whole at the expense of some of their members and those whose success is the result of the development and growth of all their people. Individuals who are neglected or exploited are not, in a real sense, *part* of the community since they neither participate nor partake as full-fledged members.

In true human community, the complementary aesthetic norms of adequacy and economy are satisifed in social and political relations. The contributions of the members are sufficient for the organization of the continuing community, and such organization squanders none of the talent, industry, or capacity of its members. As difficult as such ordering and husbanding of human ability may be, it nevertheless seems basic to both community and individual well-being. It includes the notion of mutual dependence and benefit. Each contributes completely, which results in each having a subsequent fuller contribution to make.

What we must notice here is that the interdependence of distinctively developing individuals mirrors the form of the aesthetic object. Themes in a musical composition, characters or dialogue in a play, or portions of a painting are distinct and often memorable in their own right. Each possesses a sort of individuality which nonetheless is *what* it is because of that part's relation to other parts within the whole. Individuality is not bought at the price of separation, so that when we recognize the climax of a symphonic movement, for example, we also recognize the motifs, variations, and inversions which it recalls and completes. It becomes impossible to grasp the qualities of one segment or moment without considering others and their relations. In the ideal human counterpart, it becomes impossible to pursue our ends privately or at the expense of others. Although distinct, our aims necessarily implicate each of us in the interests of others. Such interdependence also obtains between the individual and society as a whole. Since the individual and society are mutually constitutive, the health and development of the one presupposes the well-being of the other.

Others are not indifferent or irrelevant to our projects; therefore, more than a negative notion of freedom is implied in community. We must do more than merely avoid harming others by our actions. Rather, there is the "sharing in ends"; the activities and purposes of others enter positively into ours (as indicated in Section 3 of the preceding chapter). We commonly recognize the existence of a community by a common store of feelings, thought, and values. This comes about only because each incorporates others in his or her daily projects: "Similar ideas or meanings spring up because both persons are engaged as partners in an action where what each does depends upon and influences what the other does."[9] In this way the activity or object dealt with come to have social, community "meaning" for the individual.

A fair assumption about human development seems to be that the conditions under which we acquire new characteristics show up in their subsequent employment. This is to say that our newly acquired habits, tendencies, or attitudes are saturated by the context in which they are formed.[10] Consider the cluster of habits which go by the names of cooperation and discipline. If they are nurtured in the context of do-or-die competition, as is often the case in sports and business, these habits will more likely than not be impressed by competition's warp. What we attend *to* or work *on* generally does temper with its own character the way we attend or work: so, too, in aesthetic experience. The responsivity and freedom of aesthetic experience are cultivated in the process of organizing aesthetic elements into a community of design. It is reasonable to suppose, then, that the formal relations of community do condition this responsivity and freedom. What this means is that our responsive freedom is not "free" of the aesthetic object's communal character. Consequently, the freedom and responsivity we exhibit in interaction with other people are likely to bear the stamp of these formal relations. Let us consider responsivity first.

In aesthetic experience we respond in an attempt to compose independent parts so that they mutually modify and thereby enhance one another. Our aesthetic responsivity is invested with the reciprocity which holds among the parts of the aesthetic object. The fact that we respond in an effort to compose a whole, all of whose parts are so to speak respected, the contribution of each deepening that of another, can thus lead us more generally to be responsive toward other people. The reciprocity of the aesthetic object cuts against our seeing our responsive activity as isolated or opposed to that of others. The delicate balance between doing and undergoing *we* experience in relation to the aesthetic object is liable to be extended in our regard for others.

Aesthetic experience offers preparation for responding to others in the ongoing business of daily life. In human community we are neither the rulers nor the ruled, neither making the social world exclusively according to our own design nor merely implementing another's. We participate in the decisions and resolution of problems common to all the members. This requires that we respond to the institutions in whose midsts we find ourselves similarly to the way we bring to completion material selected and fashioned by another's sensibility in the aesthetic sphere. In the aesthetic we respond to a process begun by another; in human community we must respond to the responses of the other participants.

Whether in human community or aesthetic experience, responding presupposes perceiving either the moral or the aesthetic product of another's activity. Aesthetic experience itself further anticipates moral perception by demanding an exercise of detachment, separation from our everyday "selfish" concerns, without which we cannot really see (or hear, touch, or kinesthetically feel) what is present to us. Iris Murdoch claims that aesthetic experience thereby provides a "completely adequate entry into the good life, since it *is* the checking of selfishness in the interest of seeing the real."[11] According to Murdoch, aesthetic experience gives us practice in the sort of "realism" essential to moral goodness: a kind of mental ability to perceive what is real. Since we "grow by looking,"[12] "aesthetic situations are not so much analogies of morals as cases of morals, . . . selfless attention."[13] The attention to what is distinct from ourselves demanded by aesthetic experience would seem, then, conducive to the moral detachment required for participating in community.

Just as responding to the response-laden aesthetic material intimates the responsive role of other people in community, so our freedom to propose ways of organizing the material into an aesthetic whole implicates us in the freedom of others. Again, our aesthetic experience of freedom is conditioned by the result of that freedom: an aesthetic whole composed of parts whose development is distinctive but harmonious. Again I suggest that our experience of autonomy is infused by a sensitivity to a harmony which completes the development of individual elements. We are thereby inhibited from treating freedom as mere lack of restraint upon self, as freedom *from* interference by others. Freedom is, rather, experienced as integral to establishing cooperative relations. It includes positive alignment of others since the free play of *our* imaginations helps create a whole whose distinctive parts develop through their interdependence and mutual modification. This is how the aesthetic exercise of our freedom can inform its everyday social employment in ways which further a community of autonomous yet cooperative individuals.

The freedom of aesthetic apprehension has additional importance for moral thinking. The open-endedness and indeterminacy inherent in the enterprise of bringing about human community also define the aesthetic task. We lack definite rules and certain methods in the formation of both moral and aesthetic unities: each requires judgment, sensibility, and insight into the particularities of its respective situation.

Ordinary technical tasks set out determinate goals; we can conceive and state what we are trying to accomplish when making a useful object. Not so in the aesthetic. There, as Kant puts it, the play of our imaginations is free because it does not issue in a determinate, concepted thing. Therefore no rules or decision procedures can supplant the incisiveness of judgment or the sensitivity of taste. Each work confronts us with its particular demands, requiring renewed creative response even when falling within familiar styles or genres. This requirement might be considered our aesthetic responsibility: to incorporate independent elements into a whole without a determinate conception such as we have of useful objects. Among the alternative ways of organizing the aesthetic constitutents, we try to choose the one yielding an object richest in the formal relations characteristic of community.

The moral situation demands of us that we envision *people* as integrally related. Unlike the aesthetic, the moral demand involves real changes in the way people lead their lives, but the moral nevertheless resembles the aesthetic in several crucial ways. As in the aesthetic, we must contemplate the indeterminate organization of mutually modifying constitutents. We have neither a definite concept of moral community nor a set of rules for implementing or maintaining a moral order among people. The upshot of this parallel is that our aesthetic activity can be practice for the moral exercise of our imaginations, since in both the reconciliation of tensions and dovetailing of the diverse call for freshness in invention and vision.

When we consider the efficacy of rules or precepts in setting forth the conditions of moral community, we see that no moral system or set of rules can be adequate to the task without the help of our practical wisdom. Attempts at casuistry (rule specification of what course of conduct is demanded in various types of situation) snag upon the regressive difficulty of knowing how to apply the rules: How do we know this rule applies to this situation or takes precedence over another rule? Moral judgment is necessary because without it we would need ever higher-order rules to direct our employment of those more particular rules we wish to employ. In the attainment of a moral course of conduct there comes a time where precedent and maxims are inadequate and we must respond to the morally relevant aspects of particular situations with judgment, insight, and "sensitivity".

Aesthetic activity, however, can help delineate the moral *structure* which should govern our response to other people. The aesthetic freedom and responsivity we ought to extend to others fills in the form of community which should be guiding our decisions in concrete social situations. The parts of the real social whole—people—are to be viewed as free and responsive, themselves participants in the process by which community is achieved. Thus, the form of the aesthetic object and our relation to it readies us to outline a social organization in which we can respond freely with similarly participating individuals.

Of course, our practical judgment will be guided by the ideal of community *only if we hold it as an ideal*, only if we regard human community as an end in itself. This our aesthetic experience promotes because of *its* intrinsic value. Many things can be of instrumental value without themselves being intrinsically good, and most, in fact, are instrumentally good in just this way; cars, hammers, money, even intelligence, are useful without being ends in themselves. But part of the instrumental value of aesthetic experience derives precisely from its intrinsic worth. Because the aesthetic object is both the focus and outcome of this intrinsically good experience, we are encouraged to prize its form for its own sake. We then have a basis, perhaps an incentive, for valuing its communal structure in other areas of life. Because the form of community demarcates the horizon of our aesthetically enjoyed freedom and responsivity, moreover, aesthetic experience can enliven us to community as an ideal which regulates our freedom and responsivity in their social employment.

4. Critical Communication

Aesthetic activity is further wed to the moral in that art criticism resembles moral dialogue. The search for agreement in aesthetic matters is important not only for the judgment sought but also for what transpires in the search. Directing, discriminating, redescribing, and highlighting are common to both aesthetic and moral communication. The parallels between aesthetic and moral discourse are hit off nicely by Marcia Cavell.

And we don't so much justify our [moral] judgments as explain them in much the same way as the critic explains why a character is badly drawn, or how a musical passage is more or less banal than it seemed on a careless listening, or why a poem is false and sentimental. In all these cases explanation takes the form of pointing out details we have missed, giving a new kind of emphasis, showing us patterns and relationships that put things in a new light.[14]

Critical aesthetic exchange affords practice in moral interaction because of this resemblance. Aesthetic responsibility and communication can provide preparation in facing new situations which demand the harmonizing of diverse opinions or opposed courses of action. This preparation is necessary for moral deliberation and intercourse in which we are denied the clear prospect of a determinate integrated whole. As with the aesthetic, moral judgment has only the form of ideal community to guide it.

Art criticism also contributes to moral education simply by directing us toward aesthetic experiences. If my earlier contention that aesthetic experience is morally educational is correct, then the criticism which is instrumental to it derives instrumental moral value. Which is just to say that moral worth attaches to the means.

While this might seem here a fairly obvious approach toward art criticism, it runs counter to any number of theories which see criticism as an enterprise concerned with judging and ranking. For them it becomes a question of analyzing the logic of applying standards to works and mustering evidence for one's evaluations. On such views, judging works of art rather than the instructing of another's judgment is the critic's calling.

In opposition to such theories of criticism, I offer that the critic should be viewed as a teacher[15] aiming to help another develop those synthesizing and discriminating powers essential for aesthetic experience. The critic's task is to assist another to the best aesthetic experience possible given the particular work of art before him. This is what it means to "do the best one can for the work." We should strive to maximize aesthetic value in this way just because aesthetic appreciation is the immediate reason for taking up works of art in the first place. By doing the best we can for the work, we do the best we can for the other person in a wider sense, since helping the other to the richest possible aesthetic experience also puts him in the way of moral instruction.

Aesthetic criticism/communication consists in directing another's attention and thought in such a way as to help him form a complete aesthetic object. This direction takes two clear shapes: performance and commentary. For some modes of art the concept of performance applies straightforwardly, for others, a bit more subtly. Poetic and musical renditions, for example, direct attention to pivotal qualities of the composition. The critic may himself perform the text or score in different ways or simply call attention to different existing renditions. As the medium tends toward the plastic, such as in sculpture or painting, the performative dimension of criticism persists, although in a less direct or obvious way. How we *behave in relation* to the plastic work is a matter requiring decision. What we do with or in relation to the work "performs" it in a particular way, which determines its particular aesthetic features. How high is the painting hung? In what light? In what size room? From what distance is it viewed? Is it scrutinized closely or surveyed panoramically? The same painting qua physical object offers itself as a different aesthetic object to differing modes of inspection. The viewer must decide in what ways to appropriate the work. This involves him in a performative venture which is accompanied typically by commentary or prescription.

The critic's commentary calls attention to features of the work, offers his performance of it, or indicates the proper performance. Such commentary may take in the work as a whole. "Listen to the piece as an instance of jazz rather than as a classical work," we encourage. "Forget its allegorical implications and read the story as a character study." In discussing what he calls "aspecting," Paul Ziff[16] remarks that it is appropriate for us to "wander" through medieval tapestries and their poetic counterparts such as the *Faerie Queene*. This differs from scanning the meter, researching the literary allusions, and fathoming character motivation or metaphysical supposition in, say, *Paradise Lost*. This will also be shown, in Chapter V, to be evidenced in something as commonplace as sports. The various internal structures of the different sports require a variety of aesthetic approaches to them. Perhaps we must leisurely "stroll" through a baseball game, but assiduously tune in to how the guards block in a game of American football.

This last remark points to the fact that, in art criticism, focus on segments complements directions for taking in the work as a whole. The way the figures in a Giotto painting are grouped into triangular threes or a poem's recurrent morbid images grate against its jovial meter and rhyme are important in building toward the aesthetic whole. Emphasizing minor elements can reorient our perspective on the whole, just as taking a different standpoint in the large view shifts the meaning and play of the segments or moments. It should also be remarked that what is helpful direction or exemplary performance for one interlocutor may not be for another. The appropriate activity is determined both by the demands of the particular work and by the particular audience.

Clearly, then, aesthetic communication seems to include a combination of performance and commentary. Since it is an ongoing affair, I have doubtless omitted much that does or will count as communicating. But if my main claim is cogent, then the instruction provided by aesthetic communication, whatever its precise parameters, is derivatively of moral value insofar as the aesthetic experience it helps generate can inform our dispositions in morally valuable ways.

5. Cheap Art

If we take aesthetic experience to be our primary category, we can conceive of art, or good art, as the most reliable source of rich aesthetic experience. Yet art can be bad in a variety of ways. Some art strives for something genuinely worthwhile but comes up short, inadequate to aesthetic experience. Vulgar or cheap art, however, does not even aim for the full end; it is geared to facile amusement. The way it fails runs counter to the habits of community that aesthetic experience can help foster. Cheap aesthetic appreciation is more than mere privation of the genuine or complete article; rather, it has a distinctive composition of its own whose form is miseducational in impetus.

In the first place, the vulgar offers us types and formulas. As E. M. Forster remarked about thin characters in fiction, if turned sidewise they would virtually disappear like a phonograph record. In cheap art the "character" of what is presented lacks depth; its situation or complication does all the work and the work it does is to reinforce the familiar. The familiar is housed in a formula, a schema which arranges events for maximal excitement, "as though a newspaper consisted entirely of headlines."[17]

Someone might protest that the first time the formula is used or seen, it is not yet a "pat" device. But this is to miss the point, for its formularity stems from its relation to the realities of our lives, not to other art works. The simple linear progression, with its rising and falling directions of energies, is easily appreciated because typical of the movement in life we most easily, thoughtlessly master. The vulgar can trade upon what is easily understood or felt by us in real life;

consequently, we are at ease with it since to enjoy it we are all but passive. What we receive are new situations, settings, or convolutions to embellish banal relationships. In this way, cheap art piles on melodramatic incidence but does not structure the incidents dramatically.

Rather than show or embody the dramatic, it tells us what to think and feel. The event is a signal to feel a way we have felt before and are comfortable with. So we see earthquakes, open heart surgery, or lynchings, but there is no transformation in the underpinnings of the human situation. The cheap offers variations in magnitude but not in form.

We react by identifying the subject matter before us: "Aesthetic *perception* is replaced by mere *recognition*."[18] And this too is comforting. Once the artistic depiction has been categorized, we can settle back into the usual pattern of tensions and, if not resolutions, at least releases of energy. The often incredibly elaborate array of material— plot complication, colors, or instrumentation for example—falls into simplified forms. The complexity of invention does not realize itself in a complexity of formal relation or emotional transformation. If "cheap" takes its original meaning from the economic value of a specific level of craft, then its aptness as applied to art is most conspicuous in the quality of its emotional purchase.

The emotions enjoyed in the experience of cheap art are superficial and shallow, therefore lightly triggered. Since no effort is needed to feel them, their arousal is unconnected with the deeper-lying dimensions of our lives. The emotions excited bring no others in their train because their meaning is immediate. Thus, when the kind old man who never had any children is given a birthday party by the children in the village who do not suspect the truth that he is dying, we feel a sorrowful gladness, even though the old man possesses a nonexemplary species of kindness. More important, the situation presented draws upon—and only upon—easily aroused emotions, those which demand nothing of us save immediate identification of subject matter. It does not pull on deeper layers of our experience; it goes and takes us "nowhere." So, no thought or imaginative play works up and brings together less accessible emotions.

Emotions have conceptual content: food for thought is also food for feeling. As we connect new ideas or objects, new emotional patterns can emerge. Art can be the occasion for discovery of new relations in the world as well as emotional resources in ourselves. This cannot occur in cheap art, where everything conspires against emotional labor. Instead, ignited emotions dissipate or discharge immediately. Their impetus is unchecked by the novel or the complexity of structure which give emotions meaning. In Dewey's idiom, we "undergo" at the expense of "doing."

This is to say that the vulgar traffics in sentiment rather than sensibility. Sensibility is "a ready responsiveness to demands on our feelings."[19] Sensibility requires being controlled by and in sustained involvement with the object of emotion; sentiment requires but a cause, after which the object can be passed over. Cheap art excites intense feelings but with no direction, no entrance into what lies beneath the surface of things. These feelings are not deepened because not anchored in a sphere wider than ourselves. The vulgar has value only as stimulus, so that we actually appreciate nothing more than our own patently excited state. The broader cultural consequence of this is that liking replaces critical appreciation. The work either stimulates you here, now, and invites appropriate emotional release, or it does not. More appropriate to the cheap than discussions of beauty or aesthetic structure is, "Does it work for you?", as my druggist asked me about some cold medication. Does this particular play or song turn you on, get you off, or connect with you? The emphasis is on the patient, not the aesthetic object. I do not deny that real or good art can be of personal instrumental value, relaxing or invigorating, but I do deny that the vulgar can be anything more.

In an aesthetic experience we return to the business of forming an aesthetic object with our emotionally charged thoughts. Good art actually compels this return to the creative task by controlling our feelings via its own inherent movement. But vulgar art serves solely as a springboard for bathing in these associations. Epithets such as "corny," "sentimental," and "schmaltzy" (fatty) indicate awareness that we are revelling or are being invited to revel in aroused memories and emotions rather than in an aesthetically formed object. In aesthetic experience, emotions and memories are returned to the work. We actively join our store of experience with the work of art at hand, as "doing" balances the "undergoing." Our recollections of parents and children, our feelings and attitudes toward them, merge with the material presented by the artist to give us a fuller relationship of, say, Hamlet to his father or stepfather. Similarly, our own thwarted ambitions fuse with the narrator's in "Do Not Go Gentle into That Good Night," by Dylan Thomas, to flesh out the frustration he feels at his father's resignation in the face of death.

In the cheap, however, the incited memories and emotions terminate with us, never getting back to the work. Sorrow, for example, is immediately felt, and so we wind up feeling sad. In good art, the emotion is taken up into the larger whole of aesthetic composing. This is why no matter how depressing the subject matter or theme, we, if appropriately responsive, are not left depressed or sad. The sorrow is incorporated in a form whose integrity carries us beyond the emotion. In cheap art, the emotion sticks out and therefore sticks to us, separate from an aesthetic whole. This explains why vulgar art leaves us separate from the work. It is why neither we nor the work nor our apprehension of the real world is transformed. The audience and the work are causally connected, but not united.

It is by such union that we are drawn out of ourselves to a higher viewpoint. The vulgar cultivates no effort at feeling and seeing ourselves situated in new relations. It does not work so as to move us from where we are, to "broaden" our range of responses. Where good art challenges us, forcing us out of the comfortable patterns of thought and affect, the forms of the vulgar "are the recognizable and familiar rat-runs of selfish day-dreams."[20] Such art deepens our self-involvement or preoccupation, resulting in a larger loss to ourselves. The vulgar cannot "Invigorate our best faculties" because lacking "a perfection of form which invites unpossessive contemplation and resists absorption into the selfish dream life . . . ."[21] The cheap speaks to us as vicarious life; all but precluding the necessary detachment, it simulates the satisfaction of personal desires.

Cheap art further cuts against the liberating of our powers by shortcircuiting our perceptual processes. Cute puppies, breathtaking vistas, old Indians, sturdy peasants, tearful reunions, and the like, ask only for our habitual ways of pipe-dreaming or dealing with reality for enjoyment to occur. The appeal is immediate. No disruption of self occurs, since the vulgar conforms to our lives (as lived or fantasized) or presents a simplified, sensationalized version of it. Recognizing typical patterns of association, our present state is confirmed and we become educated away from the pleasures of reformulation, venture, and challenge.

It is not simply that what is presented is ordinary or commonplace, for challenging art can be fashioned from the most common items of experience. Rather, our ordinary emotional, perceptual, and intellectual capacities are not strained or enlarged in the enjoyment of the cheap. Well-worn grooves of reaction are simply deepened and overlaid with complacency. No new formal combinations are brought forth as familiar relations within us, in the world, and between us and the world become entrenched. This is why cheap art is ultimately conservative in the worst sense and it shows how we can be cheapened by it.

Challenging art, including weak art which is not cheap but whose ambitions outrun its strength, leaves us changed. It is a change of which we are aware, however uncertain as to quality or direction. The change occurs because what we bring to the work of art, our fund of experience, is reordered by our interaction with it. New relations emerge, new priorities are entertained, new facets brought together, as the ordinary is shown to be pregnant with the momentous. Something new is born within us yet independent of us. The aesthetic object stands distinct from us even as we are ourselves reformed in the progress of its composition. The concrete fleshing out of universal features of experience changes their meaning, whereas cheap art merely pastes detail on them. This helps account for why we feel revitalized by a work of art—as if seeing the world anew. By drawing together for us previously unconnected emotional objects, a work of art can generate new emotions. When we pause to digest this emotional or imaginative reforming, our understanding of the world is heightened.

Unlike challenging art, cheap art calls for a minimal amount of superficial funding. What we have brought to the work remains as it was. Without cooperation or conflict with the work there is no chance for our perceptual meanings to be reformed; consequently, we are not informed by the experience. This helps explain why we feel empty or cheated afterward. Often it shows up as a kind of lethargy, whereas after a genuine aesthetic experience we may be tired but not dulled.

In considering amusement in general, R. G. Collingwood argues that we become drained by titillation. A debit of emotional energy is incurred, leaving us shortchanged for everyday life.

> Amusement becomes a danger to practical life when the debt it imposes on these stores of energy is too great to be paid off in the ordinary course of living. When this reaches a point of crisis, practical life, or "real" life, becomes emotionally bankrupt; a state of things which we describe by speaking of its intolerable dullness or calling it a drudgery.[22]

We crave cheap excitations and find the problems that real life sets tedious because they demand disciplined attention. Since cheap art does little directly to tax us, its pleasure seems free, but as anyone knows who drinks or smokes, the notes eventually come due. Not only does cheap art arouse emotions in a way not conducive to living fruitfully in the world, it actually disposes us to quick undertakings with immediate payoffs. We become cheapened by enjoyments which do not accrue from the mobilization of our creative capacities. Not exercising the endowment which makes us human, we contribute to a civilization which values cheaply.

* * *

It is time now to return to specific everyday phenomena. The next two chapters apply and develop our present discussion of aesthetic experience to two everyday activities in which the aesthetic bears directly on the fact that we are physically embodied beings. Where sexuality is concerned with the private life of the body, sport calls our attention to its public performance. As might be expected, then, the chapters dealing with sexuality and sport take our understanding of aesthetic experience in different directions.

The first continues the theme of personal habituation in tracing the "practical" significance of aesthetic experience. The moral, social habits articulated here as central to aesthetic experience will be shown at stake in our sexual practices. The relationship between such practices and the development of these pivotal habits, I argue, determines whether the sex is good, deficient, or perverse. Aesthetic experience, therefore, ultimately functions as the basis for a critique of sexuality. It provides the grounds for evaluating what many of us unreflectively see as "unnatural" or deviant on the one hand, and "natural" or normal on the other.

The subsequent chapter examines sport in a more narrowly aesthetic fashion, with little consideration of its larger social or moral impact. We will not be concerned with the way sport shapes us for future activity so much as simply with what it has to offer us aesthetically. When criticizing the "professionalization" of sport, to be sure, I criticize a prevalent nonaesthetic attitude and disposition toward sports. The point of this criticism, however, is not to ensure more constructive interpersonal functioning, but to reinstate the aesthetic potential of sports in our everyday lives. Consequently, I explore the different kinds and nuances of sports for what they have to offer aesthetic experience.

Chapter Four
Sexuality: Good, Deficient, and Perverse

T
HE WINTER OF 1981 found police cracking down on prostitution in a Midwestern city of the United States by arresting the customers or "johns." Heading the list were prominent lawyers, ministers, and the president of a small Christian college. During this time, members of Congress in Washington were also arrested for homosexual advances in the Congressional washroom. Were their sexual desires so strong that they were willing to jeopardize career and reputation to satisfy them? People who lead otherwise exemplary lives seem to deviate, at least from socially accepted norms, in their sexual activities. The spread of "massage parlors" and "adult" book stores is mirrored in a radical transformation of "Tupperware" parties held in middle class homes by middle-American women. They now are selling erotica—lacy or see-through undergarments, oils, inflatable dolls, and sexual accoutrements—instead of plastic kitchenware![1]

These recent developments might seem to indicate the "liberalization" of sexual mores. What was once the taste of a deviant sexual underground is entering the daylight of the middle class. Sociologists John Gagnon and William Simon claim that we are experiencing an ongoing "erotization of the environment."[2] This is not to say, of course, that such practices as homosexuality, suggestive costuming, or "bondage and domination" have received widespread acceptance. The man-on-the-street no doubt continues to think of these and other sexual practices as "abnormal," "unnatural," or perverse, and the people who engage in them as sick or degenerate. To many their increasing popularity may seem symptomatic of moral degeneracy.

Surely this is the most common "common-sense" basis for criticizing sexual preferences and conduct. But what exactly does the man-on-the-street have in mind when he condemns a sexual practice as perverse because unnatural or abnormal? It should be clear what "unnatural" and "abnormal" do not mean. They do not simply reflect a statistical finding about what most people in fact do or do not do. Departing from the statistical norm would not meet with such vituperation or fear. People hurl the words "unnatural" and "abnormal" with disgust. What most who speak or think this way seem to have on lips or in mind is a biological notion: natural sex is heterosexual genital activity, and anything else, such as homosexuality or oral-genital sex, is unnatural and therefore perverted.

Now such a view, and it does seem to be the most popular, bespeaks a narrow understanding of human nature, for it construes the sexual component of human nature on strictly biological grounds, probably because reproduction is seen as the primary end of sexual interaction. This might well be thought of as the "Biological Fallacy": fallaciously reasoning about human beings in their physical activities, such as sex, as if those activities could be understood solely in biological terms. This overlooks how the psychological and social dimensions of being human condition even the most instinctual physical activities and invest them with meaning. There is both more and less to good or "natural" sexuality than is found in the conditions which make reproduction possible. More, because our sexual lives encompass our emotions, nonsexual needs and desires, thoughts, and capacities to interact with others. Less, because even without the possibility of reproduction sex still does not seem obviously tainted. Consider sexual relations involving the sterile, post-menopausal, or handicapped.

If we think of the natural as what is good for human nature, enabling its full development, then perverse sex is indeed unnatural. Becoming fully human is an achievement to which various practices and patterns of behavior can be obstacles. The perverse is unnatural in that it works against the formation of those habits and dispositions necessary for people to develop their human natures fully. It does so by constricting the social interaction through which the individual comes into full possession of his or her human capacities and powers. The perverse prevents the development of those habits which facilitate the full employment of distinctively human faculties for distinctively human activity.

To answer the question as to whether a sexual practice is "unnatural" and hence perverse, we must inquire into the valuable habits that good sex promotes and that the perverse undermines. Before condemning the suburban selling of erotic garments, the proliferation of gay bars, and the popularity of triple-X movies as indications of waxing perversity, we must *first* get clear on what makes good sex good. Then we can explore the connection between the perverse and this good.

1. Aesthetic Relations and Habits

Good sexuality is causally connected to the good of the people who engage in it. It helps initiate and perpetuate habits and dispositions which are, in part, responsible for human well-being. This is true to some extent of all our undertakings and interests: the way we treat members of our family, how we play at sports, drive our car, or the kind of art we experience. All have some impact on the sort of people we become. But some areas of life are more important than others, and our sexual behavior has a serious effect on what kind of people we are and will become.

> . . . Sexuality enters into the whole of man's life and qualifies all human reactions. . . . Its energies, psychic qualities, disturbances, and affective tone may modify, alter, enrich, or debase everything in experience. . . . What we do know from clinical experience is that personal interrelationships with their sexual dynamics reflect the whole life history.[3]

But why should this be? Perhaps because sexual experience can be so inclusive: affect and thought, desire and concern—all *embodied.* We touch and are touched and feel ourselves "in touch" with our bodies— basic physical urges modifying and modified by regard for self and other. Consequently, sex is intense, with wide potential for human expression. In sexuality we are intimate, revealing our human strengths and weaknesses in physical behavior. Naked, deception and conceal- ment require considerable resourcefulness. We are not only literally exposed, but we expose ourselves by what we do and how we do it.

If it be granted that sexual behavior and the propensity for it are important to the quality of human habituation, then the next question concerns the kind of habituation at stake. Good sex, in my view, is a form of interaction characterized by at least three socially important aesthetic relations, two of which are by now familiar from preceding discussions—responsivity and reciprocity. The third is a special sort of risk-taking, one involving the open-endedness of an indeterminate outcome. Unlike technical risk, in which we risk failing to achieve a set goal or series of actions, this kind of risk-taking is aesthetic in its openness to innovation and experiment. As we saw in the last chapter, aesthetic experience involves an experiment in which we must harmonize diverse external material with our personal experience. We risk failing to organize a whole without a definite concept or plan. As we shall see when we discuss this sort of risk-taking in more detail, it is closely aligned with the playful.

I do not claim that these relations exhaust good sexuality, only that they are crucial to it and that the more sexual interaction is characterized by these relations, the better it is (the less, the worse). They not only make the sexual experience itself more complete, and so inherently satisfying, but they also dispose us to reciprocally respond and risk in general, making the rest of life more complete. This is because the way we behave sexually helps determine general habits and dispositions, and the habits which correspond to these three particular relations contribute to a good life. They enable the individual to develop his or her human capacities and powers by providing fullness and freedom in social interaction. As we examine particular sexual practices, the discussion of the value of these habits, begun in the last chapter, should become more concrete, acquiring the "weight" of direct experience.

So much for a sketch of what makes good sex good. It follows from this conception that deficient sexual behavior is simply *lacking* in these aesthetic relations: like deficient art in which the parts fail to enhance one another or reach consummation. Impoverished sexuality comes up short and therefore does not foster the habits of responsivity, risk-taking, and reciprocity. Like art which is merely deficient, it is an *attempt* at what is aesthetically good; it is an attempt at aesthetic interaction that falls short of the mark. Something interferes with the filling out of these aesthetic relations—lack of mutual knowledge, fear, inexperience in sexual matters, lack of desire. But the failure is *not* due to the *form* of the sexual interaction itself. The form is such as to permit or even promote good sexuality. The failure is due to something in the circumstances, or the participants, or both. Indeed, much of our sexual life is less than ideal; complete responsivity, risk-taking, and reciprocity are difficult to realize. But this does not make our incomplete sexuality perverse, only deficient.

Perverse practices, on the other hand, *oppose* aesthetic sexuality and, consequently, human good. They are forms of sexuality that work against reciprocal response and risking: eroding and then supplanting these far-reaching habits essential to both aesthetically complete sex and social living. The difference between deficient and perverse sex is akin to that between merely incomplete and cheap art elaborated in the last chapter. The cheap is like the perverse in its destructive tendencies. Each provides a setting in which genuine challenge and confrontation are avoided by means of the predictably closed-ended. The very *nature* of the perverse works against the growth of crucial social habits and sensitivities. By "working against" I mean that it has destructive tendencies.

Like cheap art, perverse sex is a "force" for harmful habituation; it *tends* to undermine good habits, *inclining* us in an alienating, asocial direction. Perverse sexuality does not *necessarily* destroy the individual or his healthy habits; neither, however, is it merely accidentally related to such destruction. It possesses destructive tendencies by virtue of its structure—the way it situates and orients the individual toward others and himself. Where good sex disposes us positively, the perverse literally puts us in the way and direction of habits that are detrimental to us. Throughout our discussion we should keep in mind that perversity admits of a continuum: practices may be *more* or *less* perverse, just as they may be more or less aesthetically complete. Questions to ask about a practice, as a sort of "acid test," are: To what extent does it tend to engender or thwart completeness in social relationships? If it is the sole or primary mode of sexuality, what are its likely effects?

One way of thinking of a sexual practice as a "force" disposing us in a particular direction is to think of it as a contributing cause, daily non-sexual examples of which are plentiful. Treating a child with suspicion, for instance, *tends* to generate in him furtive, sneaky behavior and attitudes. Giving reasons for our actions disposes others toward reasonableness in a way that arbitrary use of superior force does not. On the other hand, actions or practices are also the *product* of habits and attitudes; the reasonable person eschews force in favor of reason. As Aristotle points out, the same practice is at once both cause and effect, not only bringing about habituation but arising from it. (The exercise which strengthens a muscle is also one which the developed muscle performs well.)

Thus can perverse sexuality also manifest *prior* loss of the aesthetic habits we are considering. This is why someone whose habituation is already skewed away from social interaction feels comfortable with or gravitates toward the perverse; he is "at home" with it. Whether contributing to or manifesting habit malformation, the sexual practice is cause or effect for the same reason: the relations which define aesthetically complete sex are missing from its structure. These relations, then, are central to understanding the behavior as either cause or effect of personality, but in what follows I wish to emphasize the *causal* tendency of sexual practices. This is where criticism most appropriately falls and where lies its significance for how we make choices.

As the *symptom* of a disturbed personality the practice itself cannot be condemned—it is diagnostically important as a clue to the original, causal factors. But as a force for such disturbance, as something within our deliberative control, the perverse is practically significant; it tells us something about what the future is likely to be (rather than simply helping us understand how the past shaped the present). To emphasize this causal tendency, the way practices can influence what we become, I will sometimes speak of *perverting* sexual practices.

Perverting practices, then, are "unnatural" in the sense that they undermine habits that contribute to the realization of our full human natures. Notice that we are speaking of a practice, a mode of sexual conduct rather than an instance or event. Moreover, we are speaking of the tendency of such a practice to affect adversely human nature or human beings in general; its structure is such as to dispose us toward habits destructive of those which are constitutive of our social natures. The cluster of aesthetic relations—responsivity, risk-taking, and reciprocity—help define both good and perverting sexuality. Whether or not a particular practice, say bondage or voyeurism, is perverting depends upon whether and to what extent it *works against* the habits fostered in aesthetic interaction.

Because "perverting" refers to the tendency of a practice to affect human beings or human nature in general, it is possible that a perverting practice not damage this individual or even the majority of its practitioners. And, conversely, a nonperverse practice could have deleterious consequences. But how could this be? It can be because of the specifics of the situation—the individual's or society's. In calling a sexual mode "perverting" or "aesthetic," we are considering it abstractly, its structure separated from context. Once the context is supplied, its tendencies may or may not be realized.

The circumstances or needs or previous experiences of the individual well may dictate that a perverse practice be beneficial; however, its general tendencies, considered in and of themselves, are still negative. In such a situation, which we shall be considering shortly, we would expect to find features which explain the beneficial effects, features which offset or convert the perverting tendencies. Think here of chemotherapy for cancer patients; it has damaging tendencies even though in some cases it produces an overall long-term benefit. In both sorts of cases—chemical poisons and perverse practices—the destructive tendencies must be so situated as to be beneficial or at least not harmful.

Our three aesthetic relation-habits provide criteria for gauging the tendencies of various sexual practices. I propose taking up each of the relation-habits to examine it in reference to various sexual practices, practices that are popularly thought to be strange, unnatural, or perverse. This should enable us to arrive at a tentative evaluation of these practices and also help us concretize and deepen the general understanding of these aesthetic habits first offered in the preceding chapter.

2. Responsivity

By now we are familiar with the concept of responsivity from the discussion of classroom teaching and aesthetic experience. Responsivity occurs when what we do is conditioned by what we are taking in and what we take in is shaped by our activity. Although discussed at length earlier, our present inquiry discloses responsivity more concretely, in physical interaction, since sex physically *embeds* the balance between doing and undergoing. This balance is physically realized, the body a medium through which we act and are acted upon in embracing, caressing, kissing. Where the cognitive was emphasized in classroom responsivity, sexuality subordinates and incorporates thinking to and in our bodies' intermingling. As indicated in Chapter I, the interlocutor is one who listens actively and speaks receptively, totally absorbed in neither his own nor the other's speech. Good sexuality must extend the interlocutor's conceptual-verbal responsivity to the whole body— the field for communication of desires, feelings, sensations, as well as thoughts.

Sexual responsivity often begins with simple awareness of the other person and blossoms into awareness of the other's awareness of us. Further, each party to the sexual encounter may be aware that the other is aware of the self as sexual, the self as aware of the other as sexual, and finally, the self as aware of the other as similarly aware in these ways. Thomas Nagel calls this process "reflexive mutual recognition" and notes that "the proliferation of levels of mutual awareness [found in sexual encounters] is an example of a type of complexity that typifies human interactions."[4] In sexual interaction in particular, awareness of the other's perception of mutual awareness both induces and includes sexual arousal.

However, sexual responsivity goes beyond this psychological stage and includes the body as receptor and actor. We interact with and through our bodies which provide the varied language for a "total" dialogue. Our physical response is to a *physical* expression: sighing and stretching, stroking and fondling, moan answers caress as anatomies interrogate one another. This is why perverting sex is more than the "truncation" of the "reflexive mutual recognition" Nagel thinks it is. Because sexual responsivity is a physical response to another's physical expression, perverting sex involves more than psychological interference. It subverts our responsivity as *embodied* beings. Not only our awareness, but our physical balance between activity and receptivity is undermined by the structure of the sexual practice itself; the structure disposes us toward one of the two extremes—activity or receptivity.

What then of specific practices that often come under attack, such as voyeurism, sadism, or homosexuality? I shall consider voyeurism or "peeping" as the practice of observing others in sexually arousing activity or postures (whether or not accompanied by the voyeur's self-stimulation). Most of us are voyeurs to some extent or at some times: We enjoy looking at people, their visual depiction, or reading about sexual activities. We are onlookers deriving titillation or gratification from the sexual behavior of others or its simulation. Such casual voyeurism should be distinguished from the practice of a *confirmed* voyeur: someone for whom it provides a primary or exclusive source of sexual satisfaction.

The practice of sexual onlooking or spectating is, in itself, predominantly passive. We might fantasize, imagining various possibilities for the participants, but this is not physically embodied activity of our own. If the onlooking is accompanied by masturbation, then clearly there is physical activity on the part of the voyeur. But is it an embodied response to another's response to *us?*

The self-stimulation is obviously influenced by what is undergone— the sexual scene—but what is undergone is not in turn modified by the voyeur's physical behavior. What is seen is not affected by what the voyeur does, since he does not interact with what he sees. Consequently, the voyeur is not poised between activity and receptivity; instead there is a *gap* between his undergoing and doing which is filled with another person's response in aesthetically complete sex. It is like talking to a television set: We undergo the "show" and are active in talking back, but our action is isolated, cut off from what we see (See chapter II, Section 1). The other's sexual behavior is not a response to the voyeur's—it cannot be, since it occurs on a different plane, at a distance (either real or virtual) from him. Therefore, the voyeur cannot shape his sexual activity to another's sexual response to him. Moreover, autoerotic behavior during voyeurism provides a rather limited sexuality compared with the possibilities held out by human interaction.

It seems reasonable to think that the structure of voyeurism is such as to tend to undermine the *social* habit of responsivity. The sexual pleasure generated reinforces the individual as sexual spectator, isolated from the bodies of others. It is socially passive! Its structure, then, is perverting, replacing responsivity with passivity and isolation. Without interaction, it is difficult to maintain our responsivity in general, and without embodied interaction, in particular, it is difficult to maintain *sexual* responsivity.

If voyeurism is perverting, as I claim, then why are more of us not actually perverted as a result of looking at sexually explicit films and reading sexually provocative literature? Obvious answers are handy. The sexual scenes are often part of a richer fabric: the humor of movies like "Tom Jones" or "10"; the sociopsychological observations in books like *Fear of Flying* or *Portnoy's Complaint.* So we are not receiving unalloyed sexual stimulation, for the sexual depictions acquire wider meaning because of their human/aesthetic situation. Paralleling this is the fact that most of us are not confirmed voyeurs, sexual onlooking making up but a small part of our sexual life, not substituting for it. If enough of our sexual life is aesthetically complete, the antisocial tendency of voyeurism should be minimal, counterbalanced by the healthy sexual diet. Although refined sugars and alcohol tend to affect the body adversely, if our nutritional diet is complete, their effects should be offset or blunted.[5]

Whether or not an individual, or the majority of a society's individuals for that matter, is actually perverted as a result of voyeurism or any other perverting practice, therefore, depends upon the nature of the individual's (and society's) overall sexual activity. Let us take the dietary-medical analogy one step further. Given an extreme or "unhealthy" situation, the deleterious tendencies of foods or chemicals (e.g., alcohol or snake venom) can be downright beneficial. Similarly it is possible for certain voyeuristic experiences to be beneficial to an individual—both sexually and in general. Thus Isadore Rubin quotes the view of psychiatrists and psychologists surveyed by the New Jersey Committee for the Right to Read in 1966 that "sexually stimulating materials" might help some people develop a normal sex drive.[6] And G.

L. Simons notes that a paper issued by the Danish Forensic Medicine Council indicates that "neurotic and sexually shy people may, by reading pornographic descriptions of normal sexual activity, be freed from some of their apprehension regarding sex and may thereby attain a freer and less frustrated attitude to the sexual side of life. . . ."[7]

In certain circumstances, therefore, a perverting practice can have salutary results. But if alone, as the sole ingredient in one's sexual diet, then these will either be undone or significantly offset by the perverting tendencies. Thus might the pleasure of pornography be dulled and its benefits countered by the lack of responsivity in pornographic voyeurism. Applying our "acid test," we would have to say that as the sole or primary mode of sexuality, voyeurism's perverting tendencies would be realized. Perhaps we can cautiously conclude then that if a practice is perverting in its structure, it should be regarded as an *indulgence,* dangerous without countervailing experiences.

* * *

Sadism presents the other side of the coin: overactivity at the expense of undergoing. Nagel nicely points out this lack of receptivity: "The infliction of pain is no doubt the most efficient way to accomplish this [evocation of *involuntary* response], but this requires a certain abrogation of one's own exposed spontaneity."[8] The sadist must be in control all the way, not permitting himself to "abandon the role of agent at any stage of the sexual act." Yet it is only by abandoning the role of agent to some degree (rather than simply *at* some stage) that we are poised between activity and passivity. "Exposed spontaneity" marks a juncture in doing and undergoing, indicating an openness to another's independent reaction and a readiness to be shaped, in turn, by it.

The sadist cannot be responsive since that would require not trying to determine totally the other's reaction, and that is precisely the goal—to circumscribe and thereby master the other. For this, the sadist must remain totally active. Clearly, sadism tends to foster the extreme of doing, thereby undercutting habitual responsivity.

Moreover, it is difficult to see how sadism could work benefits in an "unhealthy" situation or individual because of the psychological state it implies. Where many sexual practices can be characterized (and thus "individuated") on the basis of overt behavior—peeping, beating, heterosexual intercourse—we must also consider the *interior* dimension of intention and motivation. Sadism implies more than merely self-affirmation or forcefulness; it implies the intention to dominate and subdue the other.

Where voyeurism is isolated, sadism seems aggressive and violent. Our earlier analysis of assertion violence is probably apt in many cases of sadism: an exaggerated attempt by the individual to assert himself as a reaction to powerlessness (or its perception by the individual). As with assertion violence, however, sadism does not seem to promise a viable path to real self-assertion. Genuine self-assertion requires that the individual respond to and deal with the ever-changing input from others, input over which he has no determinate control. But in sadism, the other is forced to conform to a preestablished pattern. At best, the sadist may have the satisfaction of the *illusion* of a successful negotiation with a truly independent, unfettered agent. By definition, the sadist *intends* to dominate another so as to promote a sense of self-worth. This necessarily casts him in an exploitive role, which Daniel Day Williams claims "stupefies the spirit," resulting finally in insensitivity. In *this* regard sadism seems akin to ultraviolence: transforming a human into an object, a plaything. Just as in ultraviolence, the "objectifier," (in this case the sadist) is also objectified; without the other's genuine agency, the sadist cannot be fully responsive, and so goes through a mechanical routine.

Once we acknowledge this interior dimension of intention (*what* is pursued) and motive (*why* it is pursued), we see how a good deal of heterosexual, seemingly "normal" sex could indeed be perverse. The "Don Juan" syndrome of conquest is perhaps the most obvious example of *using* sexuality to satisfy unrealistic ambitions or shore up ego weaknesses. The Don Juan is not responding to the other's feelings and desires so much as scoring another sexual seduction. The case is nonetheless similar even when mutual and mutually acknowledged. Imagine two people whose sexual intimacy is predicated on the fact that each reminds the other of a former lover. Although not one-sided, as in the case of the Don Juan, responsiveness is still lacking since each is using the other as an occasion for remembering a past person or set of experiences. Response to the *actual* person is incidental to attention to the remembered *image* as each uses the other as a vehicle for fantasy embodiment. Treating the other as an object, therefore, can be more a matter of mental state than overt behavior.

When we consider the question of responsivity in homosexual relationships, there appears no reason to think that the practice works against it. The balance between activity and receptivity in no way seems foreclosed or undermined by the physical requirements of homosexual activity.

> Homosexuality . . . involves no oppression, no victimization. *Nearly all of the virtues* of heterosexual relationships can be embodied in homosexual relationships, in addition to virtues unique to same-sex behavior.[9]

It should be clear that homosexuality is popularly thought perverse because it is "unnatural" from the biological standpoint of precluding reproduction. But, as argued in the introduction to this chapter, that is too narrow a perspective to do justice to the "natural." If, instead, "unnatural" is construed as dehumanizing, then the structure of homosexuality is hardly unnatural. The extent to which practicing homosexuals (and perhaps even inhibited or latent homosexuals) are dehumanized is due more to social opprobrium than to the constitution of the practice itself. This should become more apparent in the next section when we consider homosexuality in light of risk-taking.

3. Risk-Taking

The second in our cluster of good habits that is undermined by perverse sex is a special, play-imbued kind of risk-taking. I speak of this risking as an aesthetic relation-habit because it is an interpersonal extension of the open-ended aesthetic venture discussed in the previous chapter. The undetermined, because under-determined, out-come essential to aesthetic experience requires a certain free play—of the imagination, the sensibilities, and in our appropriation of a medium. In sexual interaction, this free play includes the bodily expression of our thoughts, emotions, and desires. Unfortunately, with the increased professional attention human sexuality has received in this century, there has also come a "ludicrous and portentous solemnization of sex."[10] Our sexual interactions, notes C. S. Lewis, have "seldom a hint of gaiety," as psychologists all but suggest keeping Krafft-Ebbing, Freud, and Havelock Ellis on the bed-table. Overconcern with reaching orgasm (or achieving conception) has also trampled the playful under the heel of goal achievement. Lewis thinks that "sensible lovers laugh," not just because sex is best when fun but because the human body tends "to play the part of the buffoon,"[11] a fact which we ignore or deny at our own peril when we body forth in sexual embrace.

In distortions and perversions of sexuality, play and laughter *are* conspicuously missing, conspicuous because they are ideally as much a part of sexuality as of aesthetic experience per se. The open-endedness and indeterminacy which pervade the task of creating an aesthetic object also characterize aesthetically complete sex. It requires that we be open to uncertain outcomes and not prewrite a script which shields us from failure. To do so is necessarily to short-circuit our own or another's freedom to play, to experiment sexually with one another through our bodies.

And this is what happens in perverting sex: We flee risk. As might have already been guessed, this is a direct concomitant of the break-down in the delicate balance between doing and undergoing. In the assumption of either an exclusively active (doing) role such as the sadist's or an exclusively passive (undergoing) role such as the voyeur's, there is a loss of genuine risk. Odd as it may seem in light of the terrific nonsexual risk to self actually run, the perverse nevertheless affords a sexual and interpersonal safety. Risk is avoided because either our own agency is forfeited, as in voyeurism, or the other's is abridged, as in sadism. One of the two parties ceases to exercise choice or express desire, the other becoming the sole determinant of behavior and reaction. As a result, there is little risk of failing in *interaction*, in responding physically to the physical response of another.

If we are overly active, then we impose a definite outcome on the situation; if overly passive, then we install a safe pattern of nonpartici-pation. But the result is the same in either case: A structure is put in place which protects the individual from failing to deal with the originality that comes with the genuine interaction of free agents. The individual does not have to invent, to respond creatively to the unfore-seen or truly individual expression of the other. Either his own or the other's agency is circumscribed. This is why practices which are per-verting are also perverted—the recourse of one who feels inadequate to the demands of open-ended, demanding situations.

It may sound strange, but the playful exposes us to risk-taking. It signifies a willingness to try out new possibilities and to fail in the process. We *designate* certain activities "play" precisely to insulate such failure (and risk) from the "real world" and our investment in it. But as an attitude and orientation (to be developed at greater length in the next chapter) the playful takes its place in the midsts of our real, everyday lives. Perverting sex is decidedly unplayful, almost grim in its constricting behavior to narrow avenues, loss of the playful a price we pay for safety from risk.

Perverting sex routinizes us, inhibiting change in our behavior and ultimately our selves. Because of the risk involved in such change, we naturally resist it. Perhaps our natural resistance to change in self is exaggerated in sexuality because it includes so much self-exposure, the opportunity for physical intimacy an opportunity for many levels of disappointment. Perhaps the very invitation to exploration, experimentation, and playfulness that sex extends accounts for our wariness of it. Perverting sex represents the hardening of this wariness into a practice which essentially refuses risk. Failure becomes impossible because the risk of genuine agency is ruled out by the *structure* of the practice itself. In effect, it mobilizes a "pre-choice" which defines the terms of the situation so that it ceases to involve further choices and unforeseen possibilities.

* * *

Perverting sex disposes us (or expresses the existing disposition) to limit risk by limiting options in the sexual situation. Risk is avoided by the pre-choice which structures the situation so as to define roles which eliminate the demands of responsivity. Like cheap art, perverting sex follows a preestablished pattern whose familiarity breeds security. Without the social challenge of harmonizing our desires and feelings with another's we can rest easy in our assigned role. The voyeur perhaps risks being discovered or caught, but this is not a *sexual* risk. He cannot fail to respond adequately to another since he merely observes and does not enter into sexual partnership. When generalized, it means that the individual cannot fail to meet the demands of human interaction; he has achieved a pseudo-safety.

This holds equally well for the active complement of peeping—exhibitionism. I have in mind here the practice of exposing oneself with the intention of shocking or frightening the audience rather than the strutting and posing found at the beach or burlesque house. Such everyday or theatrical self-exhibition may well be part of normal flirtation (as found throughout the animal kingdom), a dimension of "the normal biological function of display which is [also] a part of courtship."[12] The exhibitionism which seems perverting, on the other hand, is calculated to elicit a reaction which will *terminate* the self-exposure and interaction, not further them.

I did it in laundromats, by schools, on open streets with the traffic going by. On [sic] laundromats I had the impulse before I went in, but on the street I'd see a woman and then have the

impulse. . . . When I do something like that the woman would be
shocked. . . . The more shocked they seemed to be, the better the
so-called enjoyment was for me.[13]

Once the reaction of fear, shock, or anger is registered, the exhibitionist can put his wares away. One patient reported that after a feeling of
sexual excitement and dread began, "He would then expose to the
female. . . . When the girl registered shock, 'the spell would be broken'
and he would flee."[14] He has not risked failing to be responsive, for
responsivity means having one's activity *shaped* by the other's reaction, not terminated by it. By exhibiting himself sexually (very few
women exhibit themselves in these ways), the "exposeur" forestalls
any real chance of entering into sexual communication with another,
his bravado masking the avoidance of sexual responsibility.

Perverse or "pathological" exhibitionism supplants social interaction with the genital exposure. Normal self-display, a prelude to sexual
intimacy, "becomes a disorder when display or viewing [voyeurism]
becomes a *substitute* for love-play."[15] Substituting a shocking exhibi-
tion for social interaction, the exhibitionist isolates himself from
others, both symbolically and literally. The exhibitionist is ultimately
self-oriented and absorbed, and exhibitionism is best seen as "'. . . regression, as poignant lapses into old childhood patterns and stages of
self-infatuation.'"[16]

The sadist derives satisfaction from thwarting the enjoyment of
another, hence he cannot risk failing to satisfy another's needs. He
thereby transforms what would typically be considered failure or
inadequacy into triumph. The only risk the sadist runs is that of
failing to elicit the requisite suffering, but, again this is not a sexual
failure. More generally, it is not an interpersonal failure: no failure to
"connect," to communicate completely or deeply. This is because the
very aim of the sadist necessarily excludes an interpersonal, joint
venture. In sexual sadism, it excludes physical give-and-take. As with
the exhibitionist, the outward show of aggression or virility is just
that, a show designed to cover up the flight from sexual risk.

Homosexuality would not seem to preclude such risk-taking since
sexual interaction is not truncated. It might be objected, however, that
the individual is avoiding the particular responsibilities of responding
with someone of the *opposite* sex. Are not those demands different?
While the demands may be different, the structure of homosexuality
is not in itself an indication that the individual is fleeing the
particular risks of a heterosexual relationship. Goode and Troiden

(Sexual Deviance and Sexual Deviants) reject a commonly accepted view, that homosexuality is *always* related to fears and inhibitions associated with heterosexuality. Against the position that homosexuality is always a type of heterosexual inadequacy, they argue that there is neither evidence of a "heterosexual destiny" for human beings, nor that homosexual personalities are "disordered." For support, they cite studies in which psychiatrists and clinical psychologists were unable to pick out homosexuals on the basis of personality tests.[17] More of a case must be made before we discount homosexuals as responsive, reciprocating risk-takers whose sex lives contribute to socially rich relationships.

In some pathological cases of homosexuality, the flight from heterosexuality may well be a prominent motivation, but, as indicated earlier, the motivation and intention at work in *heterosexual* relationships may also be pathological and perverting. If the individual *uses* homosexuality as an escape from heterosexual responsibility, then that *use* is perverting, but the structure of homosexuality itself would not serve to undermine or protect against risk-taking.

* * *

Fear of failing and disappointing others as well as ourselves seems an inescapable part of being human. Sexual practices are perverse when they generally contribute to flights from risk *just* when such risk-taking is particularly *important*. Such practices enable us to avoid confrontation, most especially with ourselves. They are doubly insidious because they so conveniently *veil* the risk avoidance from the individual.

This veiling occurs because the individual can readily see himself as engaged in an enterprise where interpersonal sexual failure just does not figure. He can describe or think of his activity as this other game: as spying on others—failing at which occurs only because of loss of visual prospect; or, as inflicting pain on another; and so forth. In this way, the important aspect of his behavior is easily obscured because it is negative in nature: what he is *not* doing by engaging in the perverse behavior. He is not venturing forth with another in such ways as leave him vulnerable. He is not risking the particular failures of sexuality or the general failures of human interaction.

This "not risking," I must repeat, is not accidental to the perverse activity, not a matter of mere happenstance. It is rather the very essence of the practice and what helps define it as perverse. For flight from and curtailment of those relationships which involve sexual fears in particular and interpersonal fears in general is hardly the best way of meeting these fears. What is of greatest moment is that retreat from risk-taking in the sexual area of life echoes in other contexts. Over such subtle and well-moored patterns of reaction we have less control than we might wish. In the retreat from human interaction, furthermore, we relinquish the very possibility of reciprocity.

4. Reciprocity

Reciprocity is the central relation missing in perverse sexual practices. Such practices are perverting just because they foreclose on the possibility of the individual entering into the give-and-take of reciprocal exchange with another. One-way social behavior, therefore, undermines the place of habits of reciprocation, habits which are crucial to social development both in their own right and because they encompass responsivity and risk-taking. In aesthetically complete sexuality, the responsivity of each is geared to the other's; the balance between our own doing and undergoing is maintained through the other's. The active/passive tension is mirrored in the sexual partners. Actually, reciprocation implies a still stronger connection. The active/passive tension is furthered *because* the other is also responsive. My sexual reaching out incorporates and is shaped by the perception of the other's earlier response to me, and vice versa. This is most clearly evidenced in its absence, by the awkward, unsure groping of those who are not mutually attuned and so do not respond sympathetically with one another. In reciprocal sexuality, responsivity becomes a mutual doing and undergoing in which each partner achieves a balance only insofar as the other does.

Reciprocity also encompasses risk-taking. The preceding discussion of risk-taking was on the individual level, but in inherently social activities such as sex I risk failing to attain not just my ends but those of another as well. Reciprocity means sharing in each other's ends, each taking risks in respect to the same things and with regard to one another at the same time. I risk failing to satisfy your sexual needs or desires even as you take the same risks with regard to me. Sara Ruddick puts this nicely when she remarks that one gives the same thing as one receives *by receiving it*.[18]

The giving of sexual satisfaction, for example, is accomplished in the process of receiving it; the receiving is also a giving. To the extent that one of us is frustrated or satisfied, so is the other. This is partly because your satisfaction and overall good has become part of my end and my sexual and social good has become part of your concern. Each then is able to give because of what is being given. The risk in sexuality is therefore shared and mutually dependent.

This requires that each must be open to an unguaranteed outcome, an outcome which results from independent initiative, shaped by individual desire. Responsivity indicates that this independence is attuned to the other's needs and responses, needs and responses it must be remembered which are psychological as well as physical. While the satisfaction of sexual desire is a foreseen sexual goal, how and whether it will be achieved remains undetermined in the openness of reciprocal risking. It awaits the concrete behavior of the partners and their adjustment to one another as sensing, feeling, thinking, embodies beings.

As we have seen, perverse sexuality shields the individual from sexual risk. Now we see that it also eliminates the risk of failed reciprocity itself, of that full responding and sharing for which sexuality provides such a rich occasion. The reciprocation which is lost in perverse sex is not merely cognitive; awareness of another's desire, followed by awareness of another's awareness of our awareness, and so on.[19] It is this, of course, but a good deal more.

Sexual reciprocity is also responding to another's physical response: moving to the other's movement, stroking the caressing hand, embracing the embracer. It includes acting on the needs and desires which we perceive the other to have. At the same time, our partner is responding in like fashion to us. Furthermore, reciprocity includes responding both for our own sake and for the sake of the other, independent of our personal stake. The openness to an outcome in doubt, mentioned above, is an openness to a result from the interaction of mutually caring people. The openness is to an outcome of behavior that is mutually modified, the passion and physical movement of each altering that of the other.

What each feels and does, then, depends upon the unrehearsed, to-be-discovered behavior and feelings of the other, and this requires trust. Each places his or her satisfaction and personality, to some extent, in the care of the other. The risk of misplacing such trust is crucial to reciprocity. It is worth noting that in sexual interaction the trust pertains to more than simply sexual matters, for acceptance, communication, respect, and vulnerability go well beyond sexuality, even though embodied in it.

Recalling our discussion of classroom reciprocity in Chapter I, it may be helpful to think of ideal sexual interaction as a physical form of communication. It complements our more typical verbal communication because the body seems to be a better medium for expressing feelings and attitudes than spoken or written language. Furthermore, perhaps particular kinds of feelings or attitudes are best conveyed by the body in its particular sexual activities—perhaps intimate touching best expresses care and tenderness or disdain and arrogance because, both more subtle and immediate than verbal language, bodily communication may be more emotionally expressive. In this view, good sexuality is reciprocal expression of feelings, desires, attitudes, and thoughts. When communicating clearly and completely, we express ourselves so as to elicit a similarly expressive response from the other.

Perverting sexuality must, then, be inimical to good communication in either of two ways: either in content or in form of expression. First of all, to the extent that there *is* communication (missing, for instance, in voyeurism), perverse sex communicates a nonreciprocal feeling or attitude:

> ... Sadism is not so much a breakdown in communication ... as an excessive expression of a particular content, namely the attitude of domination.... Masochism is excessive expression of an attitude of victimization, shame or inferiority.[21]

But what is so wrong with expressing domination and expressing it excessively? Clearly, that one intends to establish a nonreciprocal relationship—in *deed* as well as expression. Which brings us to what is truly central—the *form* of the communication. In sadism and masochism, actual dominating and submitting are taking place! The communication which occurs is *in fact* nonreciprocal. The attitudes and intentions are *embodied* in the behavior they produce—excessive, and so destructive of reciprocation.

The emphasis upon pain in sadism points to the antagonism inherent in the assumption of extreme roles, in this case, the extremely active role of domination. These role extremes, as noted in the preceding discussions of responsiveness and risk-taking, always make complete interaction impossible. And without complete interaction reciprocity is ruled out as a possibility of the practice. In a genuinely reciprocal relation one's interest or desire is satisfied to the extent that the other's is facilitated, which is exactly reversed in sadism. To this it could be objected that in sadomasochistic relations there *is* reciprocation since the sadist inflicts pain and the masochist happily receives it. Even if this *is* all that the sadist wants—to inflict some pain—then it is still not reciprocation because the masochist's enjoyment is incidental, not central, to the sadist's purpose and action; he does not inflict pain *in order* to satisfy the masochist. Rather, he does it for his own sake, treating the other as an object for his sadistic delight, in the manner of ultraviolence.

In my view, however, even this limited sort of mutual pleasing is not consistent with what the sadist really wants; he wants to control, frustrate, and dominate the other. He is not really dominating someone who enjoys suffering (hence the truth underlying the old joke. When the masochist begs to be beaten, the sadist replies, "Maybe I will, maybe I won't"). At best, the sadist would have to deny the masochist's enjoyment, deluding himself about his own mastery. If I am correct, then, in the case of the sadist an "inverse" relation obtains. Antagonistic concern and satisfaction replace reciprocal caring. This is why perverse practices such as the sadist's (and the masochist's, who is too passive) are not simply one way among many of failing to achieve ideal sexuality, such as misperception of the other's response, fatigue, and the like. They are actively aligned *against* the habit of reciprocating, encouraging indifference if not antagonism toward others. While other perverse practices may not be so virulently opposed to reciprocity, they nevertheless undermine it by supplanting it with their own brands of non- or anti-social dispositions. The voyeur, for instance, never need interact with those he or she espies, so reciprocity is cleared ruled out. My position requires that we take seriously the fact that these are not simply cases in which reciprocity does not occur; rather, they are cases where it is *sorely and deliberately lacking*. It *should* be taking place. And where what should obtain does not, then alternate and often opposing habits arise—making all the more difficult later acquisition of the disposition to reciprocate.

One result of failing to enter into reciprocating relationships is an overconcern with self or other, but more predominantly the former. C. I. Lewis points up the case of the music critic who takes more delight in his own "articulate analysis of the music than from listening to it."[22] One is led from an enjoyment of the music for which the analysis is intended to the relish of one's own criticism. The analog in sex is the partner who delights in his own "performance" or technique to the exclusion of the other, the activity, and the shared involvement. The perversions go further. They *guarantee* overconcern with self or other. The voyeur loses himself in the activity of others; the exhibitionist focuses on his self-exposure and the reaction to him (ironically fostering concealment of the nonphysical self). The fantasizing person is also self-preoccupied since it is his *image*, his escape object, not the other real flesh and blood person to which he relates and funnels his attention. The far-reaching trait is that of self-absorption. The price we pay is loss of the strictly aesthetic in Lewis' case, and the interpersonal nature of aesthetic sexuality in the others.

5. A Relativistic Conclusion

Odd as it may sound, the perverse may in fact be numbered among those sexual variations which are creative and beneficial, depending on the individual's condition and his or her social context. We have already noted how the voyeuristic consumption of pornography can be more than just a frill to a healthy sex life, and actually inform, relax, or uninhibit someone in sexual straits. Such practices as masturbation, voyeurism, or costuming in leather or rubber, while not aesthetically complete in themselves, can serve as the means to or medium for complete sexual relations—depending on the individual's needs and the social constraints on his or her sexual expression. Someone who has been taught to view her sexuality as dirty and ugly, for example, needs to learn to enjoy her body; erstwhile perverse practices may well be of instrumental benefit, liberating the individual from harmful inhibitions and self-denigration. It seems that experimentation ideally prepares for or facilitates complete sexuality. This would seem to be borne out developmentally by the normal maturation of children in which sexual viewing, costuming, and exhibiting are a matter of course. For the fearful, suppressed, or disturbed adult, therefore, the experimentation natural to the young may be therapeutic, even when it includes the perverse.

A perverse sex practice, therefore, is not always either the avenue a disturbed personality takes or one which leads to such disorder. It can, on the contrary, represent an original (and originating) response to a limited environment or a repressive society.[23] In a society which not only restricts sexual expression but which affords its members little control over their lives (recall the anti-aesthetic society of Chapter Two), trying out sexual variations can proclaim self-control or celebration of the body in the face of a disembodying environment. Group sex, bondage, or festishism could be experimented with in an attempt to reinvigorate an appreciation for the body and to deepen the individual's sense of embodied agency.

Like movements in modern art, sexual experimentation in the perverse, or otherwise, can be an extreme reaction to a socially rigid world: "The extremes expressed in modern art occur in proportion to the lack of flexibility and imagination characteristic of the cultural attitudes under attack."[24] As if to verify this parallel between art and sex, the 1980's are witnessing another extreme movement away from "commonplace" and promiscuous heterosexuality: the "new celibacy."[25] The *Joy of Sex* is being countered by the "serenity of abstinence." The movement away from sexual interaction as a self-conscious decision is as much a form of sexual experimentation as the varieties of "kink." Each may well be a reaction against human loss: disembodiment or the cheapening of the body as a mere vehicle for quick pleasure.

What I am here saying is an elaboration of the aspect of playfulness discussed earlier, in section 3: Sexuality is a fundamental sphere of venture and exploration. The evidence is that most people continue to be fascinated, whether personally or anthropologically, with the variety of sexual invention—despite the discouragement effectd by the considerable social and psychological fortifications against anything strange or statistically abnormal. Our interest is not just because these practices are forbidden or foreign, but because we sense the playful wherever the body is center stage. We also sense how much is to be learned about our bodies and how they succeed or fail in being integrated with our emotions, needs, perceptions, and thoughts.

There is, however, a danger in the playful: It can lead to novelty for its own sake or to extremes from which return is difficult. We may pay a steep price for the liberating possibilities which new experiences hold out. Without moorings in our everyday lives, without preparation for the experimental, we may eventually find ourselves at sea because of our sexual experiments:

> . . . Unless we come to them. [the novel and experimental] overland, anticipated relation by relation, their very intensity can sear off our past, rendering us 'strung out.'[26]

The playfulness of sexual experimentation, therefore, must be tethered to *responsibility*; otherwise, we fall into an egocentric indulgence, unreceptive to the meaning of responses *to us*. As a result, we can easily find ourselves addicted to "transient pleasurable excitations,"[27] thirsting after different, ever "kinkier" adventures. In such craving for the new, while the specific practice may not be perverse, the *way* it is undertaken is; the perversity of trying something just for the kick of its newness. We become jaded.

There also lies the further danger of finding ourselves marooned on a "sexual island," "strung out" by or on a practice that has *become* perverse over time. Fetishism illustrates what I am talking about here. A fetish can act in at least two ways:

> It may be an exotic stimulus to sexual intercourse or it may be a substitute. When it acts as a stimulus we speak of partial fetishism. If the object itself is so exciting that it brings on orgasm without the need of a partner we have total fetishism.[28]

On my analysis, the former is not perverse, but the latter is because it substitutes an inanimate object for the human. It thereby represents a retreat from social interaction and the loss of those dispositions central to it. At this extreme, the individual has withdrawn into a "private world of fantasy," no longer needing a human partner. Self-involvement replaces social involvement:

> Just as Narcissus fell in love with his own reflection, so in the more extreme instances the fetishist no longer attempts contact with a real man or woman and turns inward on himself.[29]

What concerns us here is the *connection* between partial fetishism, which can be sexually liberating, and total fetishism, which is always alienating and restricting. "The total fetishist has *passed beyond the stage* where his capacity for a sexual relationship is limited to some exotic stimulus. He has *lost interest* in sexual *relationships*."[30] Linking the fetish as stimulus and the fetish as substitute is the fetish as necessary auxiliary to sexual activity. This runs the danger of being a stage toward total fetishism and might therefore be thought of as *partially* perverse. Thus, what begins as a *stimulus* may become a *necessity* and culminate as a *substitute* for sexual interaction. While fetishes often are the result of earlier forces over which the individual could exercise no control (such as indelibly pleasant childhood sexual experiences involving the incipient fetish object), fetishes can also be gradually acquired and deepened by the experimenting adult.

Playing mood-setting music, watching oneself in mirrors, or wearing leather outfits may enhance the sexual experience. This sort of behavior, moreover, often has a distinct ritualistic aspect whose structure can heighten the significance of the activity or the relationship.

> . . . Sexual arousal and behavior are not dictated by mere body
> plus hormones, plus another body, plus opposite-sex hormones.
> Sex is symbolic, and the richness of another person's symbolic
> life cannot be predicted with commonsense information.[31]

The strength of ritualizing sexual life lies in its ability to reinstate the celebratory in what threatens to become either a hedonistic anarchy at one extreme or a dulling routine at the other. But the danger is obvious—a growing dependence on the stimulating object or situation which displaces the centrality of the sexual interaction itself.

Voyeurism and masturbation, for example, would seem liable to the same danger: gradual isolation of sexuality from the social round of life. What may begin as liberating and invigorating can become restrictive and alienating. This is to reaffirm what was said earlier, that we must be wary of perverse practices because they are dangerous. This caution must be balanced by an appreciation for their potential contribution to the individual and to society. The main thrust of this conclusion is to keep open the problematic nature of all sexual experiences. It is important to locate their beneficial and perverting tendencies, but the tendencies of a sexual practice are never the whole story. That awaits filling in by the individual's particular history and condition as well as the specific social context in which the sex is situated.

General tendencies and the specifics of the individual in his society: I take it to be a virtue of the view presented here that it accounts for both. Aesthetically complete sex is understood in terms of a cluster of important social relation-habits—responsivity, risk-taking, and reciprocity. Perverse sexuality then derives its meaning from a practice's structural tendency to undermine these positive social habits. Yet the realization of that tendency depends upon the details of people's lives. This is why a perverse practice, a "perversion," may not be perverting in a particular case, and, in fact, can be instrumental to aesthetically complete sex and human interaction.

Chapter Five
Sport—The Body Electric

W ILLIE STARGELL is "Pops," elder statesman of Pittsburgh's baseball team, the Pirates. His powerful body and mind as much as his age qualify him to be the team's leader. "Stargell Stars" for outstanding play grace his teammates' caps and even opposing players seek him out for his company and advice. Yet despite his weighty presence at first base, he is lighthearted, perhaps to a fault. At least, the umpires during the 1979 Championship Series (prelude to the World Series) found fault with him for "horsing around" with the opposing team's base runners; he was reprimanded for chatting, teasing, and playing good natured tricks on them. When asked about this by a reporter, Stargell first noted that the base runners never complained but seemed to enjoy fraternizing with him at first base. He concluded the interview archly, observing that it was awfully funny how people forget that just before every ball game, the umpires shout "Play ball!"; they never yell "Work ball!" It is a game, even if played for pay.

The problem with contemporary sports, especially in America, is that they have become too serious, or we have become too serious about them. Our attitude toward sports has been infected by their "professionalization": league expansion, salary and prize money escalation, media and consumer gluttony. Sports is a major industry, big business. In fact, *analyzing* the professionalizing of sports, especially in its "non-professional" incarnations in our schools and Little Leagues, has itself become a business. By now we are too familiar with the "Little League Father Syndrome" and the machinations of athletic recruiting on all levels. Easy pickings for sports debunkers.

1. Professionalization and Play

What calls for greater scrutiny lies hidden in this sports boom. The professionalization of sports reaches deep into what we appreciate in it—regardless of level of play. The "professionalized" fan has become obsessed not only with the details of sport as a business (salary arbitration, lawsuits, cable TV "packages") but with the business*like* side of sports: such bottom-line items as scores, wins, rankings. These consequences, abstracted from the actual events of the game, loom larger than the play which produces them. Our eyes are so fixed on end results that we lose sight of the means by which they come about— the "play" is no longer the thing. This seems a natural concomitant of the professionalization of sports. Former athletic director of De Paul University, Father Gielow makes the following comment:

> If college athletics is just big business, that's no good, even though I realize it needs a lot of very shrewd moves to pull it off. But never, because of my background, my priesthood, would I agree with something at the expense of good solid values.
>
> A serious question has to be raised: Does a student deserve a better ticket than a trustee? I think the students come first, I think that got me in a little trouble. I hate to say that I'm a victim. I don't want to agree so fast, because that saddens me. But it may be true.[1]

Something has gone wrong in our colleges. Not only is it virtually impossible for a (nonscholarship) workaday student to go out for the team, but he may not even get to see play those who are paid to play.

In this process we are losing something profound on the side of aesthetic appreciation: direct aesthetic appreciation of sport and consquently what sport has to offer for the aesthetic enhancement of daily life. Too often, we look to sport to satisfy our most obvious, private needs, with the result that we attend more to ourselves than to the sporting event before us. Our egos obscure much of the game from our own perception.

The traditions and rituals of the different sports are a wonderful thing, but without appreciation of the aesthetic of the sporting event the traditions and rituals are easily corrupting. They breed shallow enjoyments and self-enclosure when we look to sports merely as outlets for our aggression or as symbols of our strength. Rather than entrench the provincialism of narrow identifications, sport's rituals can enlarge us by embodying universal aspects of human movement and drama. For many of us, the traditions and ceremonies of sport have supplanted those of religion, creating new forms of congregation as we gather in stadia, arenas, and parks to witness the familiar forms reenacted.

The idea was that the ballpark—any ballpark—was a sanctuary. Once inside it, people were safe. Time stood still. The rules didn't change, like they did on the outside. There were no surprises. There was no death. Fanning liked to think that if somebody who had lived and died, say, in the 1920s or 1930s or 1940s could return to earth and walk inside a major league baseball park, they would feel immediately at home, and have the comforting assurance that a continuity had been upheld since their passing.[2]

The rites and sacraments of sport provide a stable structure for our enjoyments and anguish. Change occurs within the confines of the rules and traditions and so is always brought within an orbit of manageability often missing from the disruptions in our everyday patterns of life. What sport *can* be, then, is an aesthetic ritual of the body. This occurs when we attend to the incredible range and grace of human movement that sports are capable of exhibiting. As aesthetic ritual of the body, sport can inform our everyday movement and awareness of movement. Whether or not we actually participate in sports ourselves, our daily rhythms can be informed by appreciating the aesthetic sport has to offer. Simply watching sports is not enough for this to happen, it all depends on how we watch and what we watch for.

. . . . I had gone each lonely Sunday to the Polo Grounds where Gifford, when I heard the city cheer him, came after a time to represent to me the *possible,* had sustained for me the illusion that I could escape the bleak anonymity of life.[3]

There is nothing wrong with sport as a vehicle for dreaming, but it easily nourishes unrealistic projections of our personal desires or needs. Self-indulgent, we live on the unreal succor of fantasy. It is important to realize that, although unreal, such projections do not signify a playful apprehension of sport. They are too practical in the sense of self-serving. Absorption in fantasy clouds how sport can portray the possible in nonillusory, creative ways when appreciated as play: when its rhythms and proportions inform us of an aesthetic movement latent in our daily lives. Rather than dwelling on idiosyncratic illusions of success or fame, we can accept sports' invitation to celebrate our bodies' exuberance in movement—for the sheer fun of it.

* * *

What I want to suggest is that in the loss of the playful we deprive ourselves of entrance into the aesthetic dimension of sport. Sport especially lends itself to aesthetic appreciation because it is so naturally playful. The imperatives of the decidedly practical make aesthetic appreciation difficult in our everyday experience. Forced by need or moral constraint, we rarely are free simply to act for the sake of enjoyment of the activity: its inherent qualities, tensions, and resolutions. But something as nonpractical as sport should unambiguously invite our aesthetic attention. The sport situation is in a very obvious sense outside the "real" world. It is set up for the purpose of enjoying bodily activity toward no further extrinsic end.

In sports, we set up procedures, sometimes as games, and "pretend" that the activity and outcome are important. As Haywood Hale Broun phrases it, we enter into a "shared delusion." Because we set the rules of the activity and its consequences emerge according to these rules, we most completely define our freedom in play. Perhaps this is why such activities "disport" us, carrying us away from the everyday. We are quite literally free in *structuring* the play as well as in deciding *whether* to play (since not compelled by necessity). Broun nicely sees what is wrong with cheating in this respect: It puts us back in the real world[4]—the game becomes *really* important, pretense is lost. The goals and purposes of sport are not real; they serve no practical need outside the sporting arena. What real use is served in putting golf balls into holes or swatting tennis balls back and forth across a net? In this respect, sport takes the pretense of theatre one step further. Where theatre presents real ends and activities in a pretend setting, the significance of even the ends and activities are pretended in sport.

2. Individual Sports

A. Quantitative/Linear

Some sports obviously bear the practical stamp of their useful origins. Where once man ran or threw or jumped or swam in order to secure food, fight enemies, or explore surroundings, sport isolates these bodily movements for their own sake. Man now plays at activities that were once part of a practical enterprise, but in order to be transformed into sport, their practical value must be severed and the body appreciated simply as moving against the natural limits of space and time. Space and time form the matrix of all bodily activity, but in sports such as those which involve running, throwing, jumping, and the like, they stand out as the means by which man's measure is to be taken. Such sports in a way replace useful ends by *measurement:* how far the shot is put, the javelin thrown; how quickly the course run or swum (perhaps this is appropriate since counting or numbering is itself a practical activity). This kind of sport, then, is linear or quantitative in nature; its performance naturally includes quantification of time and/or space.

The nonaesthetic significance of the quantitative nature of these sports is clear. For one thing, the measurability of feats enables fairly accurate comparisons of different performances—performances separated spatially or temporally. We can compare a mile run in America to a mile run in Australia, or a mile run today with one run forty years ago, because people or machines *record* rather than *judge* accomplishment. Consequently, records are compiled and sometimes take on a life of their own. We can enjoy reading the records of performers whom we have never seen; indeed, one of the delights of linear sports lies in noting the progress human beings have made during the history of the sport. Progress in the mile run since Roger Bannister first broke the four minute *"barrier,"* moreover, is human progress, since the obstacles —space and time—are common to the species. To run a mile in less than four minutes or to put a sixteen pound shot sixty-five feet is the same anywhere,[5] making the same demands on the performer. And while hitting .400 in baseball or throwing forty touchdown passes in a football season can be compared with past performances, the issue is always clouded. These measures cannot be as pure since they are determined by an effort made against, and often with, other people rather than the abstractable dimensions of space and time. But this delight in records and progress in speed or strength is not itself an aesthetic delight. As interesting and enjoyable as record-keeping can be, it can distract us from the performance itself and encourage in us the anti-aesthetic penchant for counting and numbering.[6] The fascination with magnitudes, great and small, threatens to obscure the beauty of sports.

In aesthetic appreciation of the linear sports we grasp the relation between the human movement and the numerical result. The movement itself tends to be repetitious: either continuously—as in the swimmer's stroke or runner's gait—or serially—as in throwing, jumping, or vaulting sports. What we look for is the smooth, fluid motion

that suggests effortlessness. No wasted energy, no superfluous movement—just as the compression of words makes a poem trim and lean.
"Rhetorical flourishes . . . fussily blur the ideal of a straight, direct line
to conclusion."[7] On one level, we appreciate the smooth fluid style
because it simply *appears* to require less effort for the same result that
a jerky one gains. Thus, a truly fast runner, for example, *could* still be
aesthetically deficient if he ran with extraneous rolls, jerks, or flailing.
But this is sports, after all, and not dance, so we have an eye for results.
Because appearance is connected with measurement, we implicitly
judge that the herky-jerky performer *would* have done even better
were he more fluid. Grace really is efficient; the aesthetic value of
continuous, rhythmic movement has a measurable payoff. Measurement palpably confirms what our eyes intuitively register. Bob
Beamon *seemed to fly* in his 1968 Olympic execution of the long-jump
and *in fact* broke the existing record by over two feet! But perhaps
there is a larger perspective also at work in our aesthetic appreciation
of linear, quantitative sports.

Perhaps part of our aesthetic delight lies in the unwinnable struggle
with nature. Progress in these sports is ultimately infinite. We can
forever shave microseconds off our times, add millimeters to our
distances. On the fringes of our awareness is the Sisyphean spectacle
of human beings exhausting their resources against the natural limits
of physical movement. If we turn away from the particular records
involved and look at the overall effort, then space and time are seen as
the boundaries of all of our *own* daily movements. And in our own
graceful, efficient moments, their limits seem to shrink. When we
sprint for the bus or leap over a puddle, we feel ourselves, however
transiently, masters of our physical world.

B. Qualitative/Formal

In sports such as diving and figure skating, we are further removed
from real world concerns of usefulness and measurement. The athlete
performs *in* rather than *against* nature. Not worried about amounts of
space covered or time elapsed, we attend exclusively to the *look* of the
body in motion. Everyone dives the same distance in roughly the same
time. These are qualitative or "formal" sports whose excellence is
equivalent to beauty of movement. Measurement does not provide an
added aesthetic relation or means of assessment (although degree of
difficulty does). In these formal sports, we admire the fluid execution
of varied, difficult movement: the spring and flip of the gymnast in her

floor exercise, the skater's transition from a leaping double axel to the helix-like spin. Because difficult, we can appreciate the skill needed to perform these sequences. They are *aesthetically* noteworthy, however, because they display the suppleness and graceful strength of the human body. It is not the difficulty in itself that is aesthetically valued; rather, it is a performance with "the grace that makes strength the agent of art."[8] The linear sports are more limited in what they can exhibit, more focused on the struggle against our natural limitations. They seem workmanlike, whereas the formal sports provide contexts for liberation of movement—flight and gliding, air and ice. Here the human seems almost transformed into a creation of liquid motion.

The requirements of staging formal, qualitative sports as competitions reveal their fundamentally aesthetic nature. These competitions require judges, not recording officials who function as auxiliaries or substitutes for machines. Human beings must *evaluate* the performance of the athlete; *aesthetic judgment* is required. It must then undergo strained translation into numerical grading. The counting must be derived from the aesthetic judgment, indicating that the aesthetic, not the scoring or number, is fundamental in such sports. In the linear sports, on the other hand, keeping track of numbers is part of watching the performance itself and not a separate effort to be added on.

This is simply to say that counting is not integral to our appreciation of these formal sports the way it is to our enjoyment of the linear sort. Their central thrust is formal; their contribution to our everyday life is to be found in the grace with which human beings can accomplish varied, difficult movements. Aesthetic appreciation of these sports (and there is hardly any other kind of appreciation insofar as we are actually watching the performance) inevitably enlivens us to the body in motion—whether our own or another's. Thus does a skater's spin accentuate and complete our pivot to close the garage door or pirouette in slipping into an overcoat. Perhaps we even recapitulate the slalom skier's subtle weight shift when we veer out of someone's way in a grocery aisle. Appreciating the quality of movement of the most magnificent members of our species imprints, ever so delicately, images that are patterns for our own motion. Scale and degree are the only differences. If appreciating painting can enhance our everyday perception of light and color, why should we not expect appreciation of a gymnast like Olga Korbut to enhance our appreciation of physical movement, including our own?

The corollary of this is an aesthetic sensitivity to our environment as opportunity for movement and perception. Is it in fact conducive to aesthetic perception, movement, and perception-in-movement? Do our buildings, for instance, invite rhythmic movement of body or eye? Instigating aesthetic awareness of ourselves as moving in space and time, formal sports make us critics of environments that thwart fluidity and grace in movement. Aesthetic appreciation of sport, then, can combat the increasing *disembodiment* of modern life. Working at desks, encased in buildings and autos, pushing the buttons of appliances—*we lose touch.*[9] Perhaps more than any other single activity, qualitative sports reveal our bodies as more than useful machines, as an aesthetic medium with which we ought to be in intimate touch.

3. Competitive Sports

Competitive sports are the most popular, and for good reason. Only they require human opposition, offense and defense, for their play. Only they are *essentially social.* As we shall see in the next section, this added element of human confrontation (and cooperation) multiplies the aesthetic possibilities of competitive sports. While linear and formal sports *can* be engaged in competitively (and competition can enhance their performance), human opposition is not essential for their performance. We can run, pole vault, or dive quite well all by ourselves. But hitting a tennis ball against a wall or shooting a basketball is practice—it is not playing the game of tennis or basketball. To do that, opponents are needed.

Competitive sports transform the central features of both linear and formal sports by incorporating them within the structure of a game. As in linear sports, counting is a natural part of the play of competitive sports. Because brought about by overcoming human opposition, it is "scoring." And of course there are aspects of the game which can be isolated and measured, such as how fast a player can run or throw a ball. But such feats are subordinated to and transformed in the play of the game. We run to get to the football, jump to snare a basketball rebound, throw to get a base runner out. Achieving great magnitude without playing well ironically underlines the primacy of playing the game: With his 100-miles-per-hour fastball, Nolan Ryan is nevertheless much less effective than slower, more crafty pitchers (his lifetime won-loss record hovers about the mediocre .500 level). We appreciate "linear" accomplishments in competitive sports as *constitutive of the* play. Competitive sports, in fact, make the linear more playful, less feat-like by embedding it in a game.

Form as well as number is integrated into a larger fabric. Just as competitive sports transform the stark exertion of linear performances, so do they subordinate the "pure" grace of movement characteristic of the formal sports. We appreciate the athlete's balletic movements not in isolation, simply for their own sake, but within the framework of competitive play. A graceful jump and throw is marred by going off-target; it is supposed to serve a purpose internal to the game. The game thereby discloses the function inherent in grace. The best plays are graceful and while many who play well lack in grace, their good performance is not achieved *because* of their awkwardness. It is rather because they have compensated for the lack of grace and manage to "get the job done."

It is just because competitive sports have internal purposes whose final result is scoring or the thwarting of a score that we come to think of them as purposeful—aimed at winning by outscoring the opponent(s). The late football coach, Vince Lombardi, is reported to have said: "Winning isn't the most important thing; it's the only thing." Winning at games seems somehow more important than winning in a linear or formal peformance. Perhaps the term "performance" is a clue as to why. In linear and formal sports the athlete really *performs*, alone.[10] She may perform better than another but does not really "win" *at* something. Competitive sports, however, are *contests* between or among people, more like a human drama. Perhaps this is why Lombardi could sound plausible when he warned his football players that their "manhood was on the line" when they took the field. We seem to forget that winning the game is a goal *imaginatively* set up and accepted expressly for the purpose of playing the game, "as if" it were important.[11]

The reply, of course, is that for the professional athlete it *is* important. Granted. But why must professionalization infect all levels and appreciations of the game? Why have we spectators and amateur players forgotten that it is "as if" winning were important?

The irony is that while scoring/winning has been overemphasized, it has also been unwittingly underplayed. Overemphasized *apart* from the play of the game, it has been underexposed as an aesthetic constituent of the game. In examining the stress on winning apart from the play of the game, we need to see how it results from a mistaken understanding of scoring/winning as the *purpose of* playing. Because of this misunderstanding, playing the game is viewed as merely the means to the distinct, dominant end of winning. But we are mistaken if we think that winning is "an identifiable aim or purpose which is of far greater importance than the way it is accomplished."[12] The mistake will become apparent as we take a brief detour and recall the place of purposes in everyday activities.

The first thing to note is that the purpose of an everyday activity is the reason or basis for engaging in it. The activity *exists* for the sake of its purpose. We shingle our roofs in order to keep the inside of our homes dry; we take medicine in order to restore health. Were it not for the purposes of keeping our homes dry or restoring health we would not engage in these respective activities. But scoring is not the *raison d'etre* of competitive sport. It was not that in virtue of which the sport came to exist or is engaged in. "The play's the thing" and it *includes* scoring and winning. Since neither scoring nor winning is the reason or basis for competitive sport, it cannot be its purpose.

Scoring/winning is not, therefore, an end which could be accomplished by some other means; consequently, it is not distinguishable from or "external" to the game itself. Practical purposes in the everyday, however, are independent of their means and are rightly said to be the purposes *of* their activities since they are attainable by some other means. The practical activity is itself subordinated to the goal as its instrument. There are other ways besides shingling of keeping homes dry, other ways of restoring health besides taking medicine. These just seem the best, given our circumstances, resources, and know-how. But it would be ridiculous to suggest that we might try to score or win by some other means than playing the game of basketball or baseball. Another way of putting this idea is to say that we do not independently value scoring or winning and only subsequently alight upon the playing of this game simply as a means to the score or the win. Scoring is not an end which could be accomplished by some other avenue because what it *means* "to score" depends upon the particular kind of game being played. Obviously, scoring in tennis is defined by the structure of the game of tennis, and so on for the other sports.

Why then have so many people thought that scoring/winning is the purpose of sports? I believe that this sort of thinking rests on a confusion. People confuse two ways in which purposes relate to activities: as the goal *of* and as a goal *within* an activity. An activity may serve some purpose or function external to it—as in the cases of shingling and taking medicine. A purpose or end may, on the other hand, be included within an activity, regardless of whether the activity as a whole serves any further (external) purpose. This is the case with "taking tricks" in bridge; singing a harmonic in a barbershop quartet; or achieving validity in an argument. These are purposes *within* their respective activities. Scoring is not a purpose *of* sport but is an end *within* the play of the game, in fact, created as part of the game. By confounding these two sorts (and loci) of purpose, people falsely conclude that the play in competitive sport is purposeful in the sense of serving an end external to it.[13]

When a purpose is the purpose *of* an activity, it defines the activity. But when a purpose is a purpose *within* an activity, as part of it, the activity defines it! The subordination or dependency relation is reversed. The purpose *of* an activity helps distinguish it from others. The purpose of keeping one's home dry gives meaning to shingling; the purpose of restoring health distinguishes taking medicine from taking hallucinogenic drugs. But the mere fact that a goal is scored or a game won cannot define or differentiate one sport from another. On the contrary, the differentiation proceeds the other way 'round. The scoring (internal purpose) is distinguished by the manner of play of this or that particular kind of game. Sports are differentiated internally, by what is *required* to score, by the manner of play whose issue is scoring. The form or structure of the particular sport is the basis for our choosing to watch or play *it* rather than another. And it is this particular structure, then, which defines its internal purpose of scoring or winning.

What is crucial, especially from the aesthetic point of view, is *how* the score/win is made, not *that* it is made. To score or win as the result of accident or shabby play can by no stretch of the imagination be thought as achieving the "purpose" of competitive sport. Yet this would be of no matter if winning or scoring were in fact its purpose.[14] Even a professional athlete can transcend the practical concern for victory because of aesthetic interest. Speaking of those rare, magical moments when playing basketball was more like dancing than working, Bill Russell notes that those "spells" were fragile:

> An injury would break them, and so would a couple of bad plays or a bad call by a referee. Once a referee broke a run by making a bad call in my favor, which so irritated me that I protested it as I stood at the foul line to take my free throws. . . . He looked at me as if I was crazy, and then got so angry that I never again protested a call unless it went against me. . . . Sometimes the feeling would last all the way to the end of the game, and when that happened I never cared who won. . . . I don't mean that I was a good sport about

it—that I'd played my best and had nothing to be ashamed of.... When the game ended at that special level, I *literally* did not care who had won.[15]

Ideally, scoring or winning is valued as a sign of excellence in play because it is characteristic of excellence. Scoring or winning is part of our understanding of good play; the team that plays well *deserves* to win, the way a virtuous person deserves happiness. If by some strange change in nature good play went consistently unrewarded with scoring/winning, then we would modify the game so that it was—or just stop playing. Our very concept of playing the game would change.

Overemphasis on scoring and outcome in general focuses attention on ends at the expense of their connection with means—*how* the outcomes are achieved. This invites an attitude of expedience and inattention to the very conditions which produce the consequences we value so inordinately. It also disconnects the particular outcome—such as a thwarted scoring attempt—from subsequent events. The outcome, then, is sundered from its prior context and future effects. Too often ". . . so-called means remain external and servile and so-called ends are enjoyed objects whose further causative status is unperceived."[16] Sport ought not reinforce such discontinuities in experience. Rather, it should occasion the transformation of cause-effect relationships into those of means-consequence. This is epito-mized in play, in which the connections between means and ends is the chief source of delight, as it constitutes the situation's *meaning*. When we concentrate on ends, such as scoring or winning, at the expense of their means, therefore, the activity loses meaning for us. We then miss the fact that ". . . fulfillment is as relative to means as means are to realization."[17]

Rather than feed our growing obsession with results irrespective of how obtained, sports should give us an opportunity to see how events grow out of one another, how means enter into ends and ends further shape the future. When viewed playfully and as play, sports crystallize the way the purposes of scoring/winning are defined by the activities which produce them (and in turn determine subsequent events). It matters for all the world whether the 5-4 score was the result of a seesawing contest or the termination of a last-minute, furious rally (by *either* team). Perhaps we are too worried, in life as in sport, about the "score" and not enough about the quality of play.

The score itself is but an abstraction from the play. It tells us important information at a glance, like a newspaper headline, but is misleading even as a summary of play. This is because the score alone cannot tell us how and when the scoring did and *did not* occur; it is necessarily mute about nonscoring play, play which is sometimes the best in the game. "The score," therefore, indifferently represents widely different means and manner of play, abstracting from the way in which opposition is surmounted or frustrated. Put this way, it is odd to think that scoring/winning is more important than what it took to score the goal, defend the goal, or win the game. When this happens, games become uninteresting producers of statistics (not even justified in linear sports, where it is more natural). We revel in total football yardage, yearly and lifetime home runs, average rebounds per game of basketball—not noticing whether the yardage was piled up against weak opponents or the home runs hit when the game was out of reach. We make a fetish of quantity, number, accumulation. Infatuation with sheer magnitude is far more crippling and insidious than any fetish of sexual accoutrement. It keeps our attention on an ever-receding horizon, never on the moment. In sport it not only distracts us from the game's beauty but it even muddies the aesthetic role of scoring/winning. But what exactly is that role?

Scoring serves to define and articulate *overcoming opposition*. It helps determine the completeness of play and thereby the overall form of the game. It gives a closure to our experience of sport often lacking in everyday life. Unlike everyday life, sport gives us conclusive conclusion: to a game, a series, a season, a career. To appreciate the conclusion, though, we must see it as the fulfillment of what has preceded: whether it be a surprise 15th-round knockout by the apparent "loser" (as when Mike Weaver floored John Tate for a share of the heavyweight boxing championship in 1980) or the seemingly inevitable culmination of a football team's consistently superior play.

It is only when the play of the game is subordinated to external ends such as money or ego that scoring or winning is valued irrespective of the quality of play. In origin and ideal, games have no purpose other than the delight taken in their play. To play a game for monetary or personal gain, while not necessarily disastrous to its aesthetic appreciation, is always to introduce a purpose or basis foreign to the game itself. Scoring or winning, then, become independent purposes of the game only when extrinsic purposes become motivations to perform or watch. Our aesthetic expectations are satisfied when scoring and victory complete excellent play. Sport, then, provides clear-cut occasions for the joining of the useful (purpose-achieving) and the aesthetic (aesthetic execution of the play). When this happens our aesthetic appreciation seems to be of a second order, a "meta-appreciation" of the harmonizing of the practical with the aesthetic. Perhaps this harmony instantiates, as Kant would put it, the union of necessity (*needed* for a practical purpose) and freedom (the *free play* of the imagination which characterizes aesthetic experience). At any rate, we delight in victory which results from luck or shabby play only when we have some ulterior stake in the outcome. The more important these ulterior purposes are to us, the more we respond as if the umpire were indeed shouting "Work ball!", whether or not we are aware of it.

4. Social Drama

The complications introduced by human opposition multiply the aesthetic possibilities in competitive sports—dramatic possibilities due to social interaction. Nature provides a fairly constant standard or domain for linear and formal sports, but people must react and adjust to one another in competition. It is always a game of mutual readaptation and combination. A boxer must adjust to the weaving reaction of his opponent to his own initial, feinted jab; a defensive lineman must slip an attempted block in order to set up the tackle his linebacker will try to make. And this gives rise to a stunning variety of movements, rhythms, and situations. The social nature of games adds dramatic complexity just as the society of others complicates our daily lives.

In the individual sports, we focus on the human body: its motion and rhythms. In social sports the individual's movement is necessarily related to another's as well as to the movement of what ties them together—puck, shuttlecock, ball. Embedded in a contest, the athlete's movements and rhythms are taken up into the larger movements and rhythms of the game, creating a correlative mood or atmosphere.

Some games[18] are tense, stingy encounters in which defense dominates and scores are hard earned, as if squeezed from a resistant world. Our attention is tight in such contests, screwed to each moment since any play can be decisive. Ideally, their conclusion is a clean, incisive play, snapping the taut mood with its clarity. At the other extreme are sprawling, brawly affairs, scoring barrages threatening to last forever. There is a sense of luxury, opulence—always in danger of lapsing into the slackness that inflated wealth brings. These encounters "feel" lighter; we become almost giddy with the quantity of results and length of play. These two extremes mirror the poles of our everyday experience: now a seeming superabundance of riches, then a meager portion of sustenance.

At the beginning of a game, of course, we cannot know what is in store. What begins as a wide open slugfest can abruptly turn tense with firm defense. We look back on squandered chances and at our own false sense of luxury in scoring as we gather the two phases into an aesthetic whole. The shift of mood is itself an aesthetic transition gently felt as it happens, fully savored in retrospect.

On rare occasions, contests provide us with several shifts: in tempo, rhythm, or "dominance." The latter yields a sense of tug-of-war as one reversal succeeds another. Writing of the prizefight in which Rocky Marciano relieved Jersey Joe Walcott of the heavyweight championship, A. J. Liebling notes that in the first nine rounds the lead changed hands three times: "Walcott to Marciano in the third round, Marciano to Walcott in the seventh, Walcott to Marciano in the ninth."[19] Walcott then came back briskly to capture the eleventh and twelfth rounds, "the fourth switch in plot." This seesawing ended with Marciano's short, lethal left hook in the thirteenth round.

As with many *potentially* aesthetic experiences, games often fail to fill out into discernible wholes possessed of strong aesthetic qualities. Some never find a rhythm and in others tension is all but dissipated in early lopsidedness or lackadaisical play. The latter mars the drama of a game by destroying that particular dimension of rhythm which depends upon crispness of execution. An aesthetically complete game, moreover, requires balance between the opponents, otherwise the emotional tone will flatten. "Torpid" and "loose" do not so much characterize an emotional mood as indicate a lack of one. Without approximate equality, at least in a given encounter, the game as a whole goes slack; there is little anticipatory quickening as events do not seem to harbor interesting future possibilities. Aesthetic attention is then rewarded only episodically in the close or spectacular play. Such games gradually degenerate into their linear and formal components; we thrill to a long pass in football or an acrobatic shot in tennis, but that is all.

Balance, however, does not mean "sameness." Contrasting styles within balanced, even performances provide aesthetic richness. In *Levels of the Game*, John McFee reflects upon the difference between Arthur Ashe's flamboyant, "all-out" play and Clark Graebner's conservative, steady game of tennis. The contrast between Ashe's "shot-making" and Graebner's "play-making" was accentuated by the further contrast *within* each of the opponents. Ashe's flamboyant play was accompanied by a cool, calm demeanor, while Graebner's steady game was played demonstratively, heatedly. The dramatic tension between style and temperament *in* each of the players magnified the pair of differences *between* them. The sharp differences between each man's technical style and character leads the spectator to such dramatic speculations as: Can Ashe afford to play with abandon *because* he is so controlled, so cool? Aesthetic expectations were fulfilled in this particular match when Ashe triumphed with a series of low-percentage, high-voltage shots. Perhaps Ashe would not have had the opportunity or been moved to such dazzling display against a less steady opponent. And this is something we should be alive to, for it enlivens the drama of the contest.

Just *this* opponent makes the sort of demand on the individual (or team) which presses him to his utmost effort. There is a cooperative basis to all competition, at the very least on the level of fair play and agreeing to compete. But more, it is a "contest" in which each *tests* the other and *testifies* to his effort and ability. Each depends upon the other to bring the best out of him, as in a friendship or educational exchange. In this way the opponents are united, forming a whole whose opposition is also a cooperation.

> Every so often a Celtic game would heat up so that it became more than a physical or even mental game, and would be magical. ... *Both* teams had to be playing at their peaks, and they had to be competitive. . . . It never started with a hot streak by a single player, or with a breakdown of one team's defense. It usually began when three or four of the ten guys on the floor would heat up. . . . The feeling would spread to the other guys, and we'd all levitate.[20]

The dynamics of such interaction are as important an aesthetic dimension of sport as the graceful flick of the tennis backhand or the daring streak of the base stealer. In such situations are we likely to see "peak performances," tensions reaching toward crescendo after crescendo. Continuing his description of those games when everyone "heated up," Russell notes his need for both teams to keep the rhythm moving:

> Then the game would just take off, and there'd be a natural ebb and flow that reminded you of how rhythmic and musical basketball is supposed to be ... and I'd actually be rooting for the

other team. When their players made spectacular moves, I wanted their shots to go into the bucket. . . .[21]

In such tensions, give and take, and finally resolutions, competitive sports exhibit something of real-life struggle and resolve. Now obviously the drama of sport is considerably less than that of either real life or the theatre, but in its way it offers what they cannot. The dramatic development in sport is a distilled, circumscribed version of reality's. The unravelling of events is confined by the form of the game, its rules "shrinking" conflict to manageable proportions. The confrontations of the game are simple and starker because physically enacted. Because more obvious, almost a caricature of everyday life, the drama of sport indirectly suggests the greater subtleties found in the everyday. Sport can give clear and definite conclusion to dramatic confrontation in a way not possible within the ambiguities of either real or theatrically portrayed life, as if the rules and physical movement of the game supplant the complexities of plot and character. Yet precisely because of this, it can point to the bases for ambiguity and indefinite resolution in our daily dramas.

When aesthetically rich in dramatic qualities, the game builds to a consummation. The delicate balance between offenses and defenses establishes a rhythm which is fulfilled in its conclusion. The strengths and weaknesses of the opponents exhibited throughout reach their final reckoning in the outcome which is in doubt until the last possible moment[22] and the closing of the uncertain story can then be experienced as a climax, not simply a terminus of motion. Such a conclusion seems to put all the scoring and smaller duels and tensions in their "proper" dramatic place. Thus do we retrospectively hold the entire game before us, looking for omens, portents of what seems at the climax to have been inevitable.

Of course not all games fill out so nicely; they can fail to develop aesthetically for many reasons: ". . . But if the play of the Minneapolis Miniatures depresses us by its sloppiness, so, curiously, the precise rigidities of the Soviet Army Six depress us by their mechanical evenness."[23] Broun nicely points out the two extremes that the genuinely aesthetic avoids—loose aimlessness and mechanical rigidity. These are the extremes our daily activities tend toward: the meandering, pointless browse through the shopping mall; the overly circumscribed routine of a student's classroom schedule. The aesthetic mean combines the structure which is exaggerated in the mechanical with the freedom which is dissipated in the directionless. At its best, sport demonstrates the place of improvisation in the competition; jazz-like, the competitors respond in the moment to the opponent's own modification in play.

We must improvise in the face of human opposition in a way less called for in the linear or formal sports. The greater constancy and predictability of nature demand less alteration in strategy or immediate performance. But when Julius Erving finds his path to the basket blocked by a surprise move by the opposition, he suddenly veers at a tangent, shifts the ball to his left hand and with a swoop flicks the ball off the backboard as he has never done before. Invention by the other begets answering, unrehearsed creativity. Sometimes the result is a spontaneous variation in bodily motion that can alter the flow and rhythm of the whole game. The beauty of improvisation is magnified, moreover, when the social dimension is elevated, when *teams* play the game.

* * *

In team sports, each individual must adapt to the play of his mates as well as to his opponents'. This increased range of human interaction enlarges the game's aesthetic. As in art proper, we have the chance to see the parts integrated into an organic whole when players' movement and ability are complementary. In memorable teams, noted for their teamwork, the whole really is more than the sum of its parts. The Bill Russell-led Boston Celtics come quickly to mind; each player realized his excellence because of his relationships with the rest of the team's members. Each developed fully through his fellows' play: on the fast break, switching defense, or simply moving without the ball.

The play of the Celtics contrasted sharply with that of the contemporaneous Los Angeles Lakers who were led by three exceptional individuals (Jerry West, Elgin Baylor, and Wilt Chamberlain). They excelled *as* individuals; when one had the ball he put on a show—a solo performance. While their individual virtuosity was aesthetically breathtaking, they did not conspire to create an aesthetically integrated team.

Balance is needed within a team (as well as between teams) in order to achieve the cohesiveness of aesthetic unity. When the team members seem to be functioning as parts of one organism, the individuals' movements are felt to be determined by and attuned to the rhythm of the whole team. The action of each member of the Celtics' "fast break," for instance, seemed essentially suited to those of the others: Heinsohn's defense freed Nelson to help Russell rebound and then pass to Jones, who assisted Havlicek on his lay-up. It is practically impossible to give "credit" to one without including the contributions of the rest; they so jell that we can hardly tell where one's play begins and another's leaves off.

The excellent play of team members is a direct function of their interaction, as they flourish under one another's influence. The relationship among the players resembles that found among parts of a work of art: words in a poem enhancing one another's meaning; harmony complementing a musical composition's melody. On the experiential level, we perceive the cohesiveness of team play as the gracefulness of a "larger" organism; we experience something that may be thought of as interactive grace. This is what I was getting at above in describing a Celtic "fast break," when individual grace of movement is absorbed into the fluidity of the team's flow. We see it in the continuity of a smooth relay in baseball when the infielder takes the outfielder's throw and, pirouetting, relays the ball to home plate. The path of the ball is a straight line from the outfielder to home plate, the infielder a seemingly magical conduit.

Where the linear sports call our attention to time or distance, competitive sports emphasize *timing* and *place.* The timing and location of a pass in football or hockey is usually more important than its speed or distance: *Where* a ball is hit and *when* a pass is made is crucial. By incorporating them into its structure, games transform sheer speed and distance into timing and location. The old baseball exhortation to "hit 'em where they ain't" signifies placing the ball deftly, not merely whacking it hard or far.

"Timing" refers not only to the play among the teammates, but also to the occasion within the course of the game itself. Does the spectacular catch stave off a rally? Does the brilliant lob win the tennis match? The building and sustaining of dramatic tension obviously depend upon *when* the play is (or is not) made. We appreciate what does *not* happen as much as what does, just as a pause or inaction in the theatre punctuates speech or behavior. We savor chances missed, imaginatively rearranging events. Our mouths fill with "if only's": if only he had hit the home run in the eighth inning when two men were on base instead of in the fifth when no one was; if only he had not fumbled on fourth down with one yard to go for a touchdown. Without a sense of timing there is no appreciation of a game's decisive play:"... Every game's got its own special moment . . . that defines all that's happened before it and all that's gonna happen after it."[24] To feel, to perceive such decisive moments immediately, without cognitive analysis, is what aesthetic sensibility is all about. Surely there can and should be a carry-over to a sense of timing in our everyday lives, an immediate perception of opportunities lost, friendships ignited, deceptions uncovered. The turning points in games publicly dramatize the defining moments in our lives that we are so apt to miss for what they really are, so blind are we to the drama of our own living.

* * *

The batter swings and lofts a long fly down the foul line. At the last second the ball veers foul by a foot. What luck! Good luck for one team, bad for the other. Perhaps. It depends on why the ball sliced foul. The pitcher may have succeeded in fooling the batter ever so slightly and that slight advantage is spatially translated into one foot, foul (or one foul foot, for the team at bat). As in daily life, what seems to be luck often is the result of talent or effort well-timed. This is the sense of Branch Rickey's aphorism, "Luck is the residue of design." Careful attention discovers the little displays of intelligence that make up the design. But if the ball is blown foul by a sudden gust of wind? Surely that is not the residue of design. And surely when a player gets a favorable outcome from what is plainly a blunder, he is "lucky" in the ordinary sense of the word. The drama of competitive sports includes the hand of chance, just as does the drama of everyday life. Another's illness becomes our opportunity; a wind-blown hat occasions intimacy; or a power failure dims our business plans. Sport does not distort the aesthetic role of luck, it merely unclutters our perception of it.

* * *

The Green Bay Packers are one yard from a touchdown and victory with seconds to play on the frozen tundra of Wisconsin. The ball is snapped for the last play of the championship game; Jerry Kramer, lineman, gets a tentative toehold, pushes the defensive tackle slightly off balance, and Bart Starr, the quarterback, squirms into the end zone. The audience erupts. They have not only witnessed but have taken part in a "Great Moment in Sports!"

The dramatic qualities of sport are pinpointed in "great moments," those performances which stand out in the collective memory of its fans. Like classics in the art world, these moments become almost but not quite hackneyed, trotted out in film clips and reminiscing banter. For all their repetition, however, Beethoven's Fifth Symphony, Orson Welles' "Citizen Kane," and Hamlet's Soliloquy are nonetheless great moments in art. We may rely on them too much, asking them to provide more enrichment than they are capable of, but that is our failure, not theirs.

As with a work of art, a great moment in sport may well take more than a moment. Don Larsen's "perfect" pitching performance in the 1956 World Series took a couple of hours, as did Wilt Chamberlain's 100-point basketball outing. But the paradigm of the great moment is probably just that—a split-second catch, shot, or pass—a moment frozen in time. Only the moment freezes time and takes our breath away. The moment of excellent performance consummates all that has come before, rounding out our expectations, resolving the game's conflicts.

As its name indicates, great moments are a matter of timing; they come at crucial moments, usually in important games. Not only is the play dramatically timed, but it is a dramatic response to demanding play by the opposition. Unless Vic Wertz blasts a baseball nearly 400 feet, Willie Mays cannot make his spectacular back-to-homeplate catch during the 1954 World Series; unless Joe Frazier is boxing like a juggernaut, Muhammad Ali is not forced to display all his ring virtuosity (perhaps lack of worthy opposition deprived Marciano of his greatest moments). After a wonderful hockey play-off game between the North Stars and the Islanders, columnist Dave Anderson wrote:

> Hockey, or any game, is seldom played at that [Great Moment] level because the exquisite elements which create that level seldom fall together. Such a game requires two quality teams at peak performance competing for high stakes in a cauldron of emotion. And at that level, the outcome is almost incidental.[25]

The Great Moment is epitomized in a moment because in a moment our attention is riveted. Time seems frozen for our breathless appreciation as we attend fully and are filled. The possibility of a great or even a *good* moment should quicken our attention, keeping us more alert than usual and perhaps altering our usual level of discrimination. The technical innovations of television (such as "instant replays," slow-motions, and stop-actions), even television itself, lessen the premium of careful observation. We need not be "on our toes" when we know that videotape replays will show us the outstanding play from several angles, at varying speeds, over and over. Whereas, "being there" means being on the lookout. And, of course, when we are on the lookout for the great play, we see so much more: the shifting of the boxer's feet; the football player's subtle change of speed; the deceptive dip of the tennis racquet. Being ready for the great moment quickens us to the movement in each moment upon which the great performance ultimately rests. And this is really what aesthetic attention is all about: noticing the features and qualities of whatever is present to us.

Dramatic tension screws our senses to the present, and this is good, but aesthetic attention in the first place discovers the minute dramas within each moment—whatever the significance of the situation. Aesthetic attention in sports can and does affect our everyday perceptions of physical movement. Watchful for a great moment, we are awakened to the flows and interruptions within each, however mundane. At a jazz concert recently, a stagehand climbed down a ladder after adjusting some lights. On the last rung something went wrong, he stumbled backwards, and smashed into the bass violin—irreparably damaging it. Most of us saw only the thunderous climax of his movement and gasped our concern. But a friend just quietly nodded, seeing this "awful moment" prefigured in each of the stagehand's earlier, little, awkward steps. While careful attention may mean fewer surprises, it will be because we see how movements unfold out of one another.

5. Micro-Rhythms, Meta-Rhythms

The "great moment" shines at one end of the temporal continuum for aesthetic appreciation of sport. But, we can appreciate such long-range projects as the mazy turns of a team's history or an athlete's blossoming career as well as the quick and bright. This continuum also has a spatial counterpart, ranging from the flashing glint of a skater's blade to the panoramic surges of soccer teams. As in everyday life, we manage to appreciate a fair share of the micro-rhythms, accents on the "small" end of the continua: the left-right, jab-hook tattoo of a boxer's "combination"; the promise of the poised racquet, stick, or bat. Sometimes we perceive a pause and anticipate the accented beat that is to follow. When the baseball pitcher chooses ". . . not to throw on a man [to trap the base runner off base]. Whole thing about *base* stealing. It's like a dance."[26]

The turns and twists, leaps and lunges comprise episode events within the larger contexts of games, competitions, seasons. Appreciating each moment need not preclude seeing how the moments build upon one another until, finally, a season or career has come to a close. Does the star performer go out blazing like a meteor, the way Ted

Williams and Rocky Marciano did? Or does he "hang on," a sorry reminder of what he once was? Even serious injury can add a dramatic dimension when seen in the context of a player's whole career and place in the game. Thus, Chuck Bednarik's crippling tackle of Frank Gifford "...was the rather brutal homage the league was paying him for catching one too many passes, for winning one too many times...."[27] Yet the drama of Gifford's football career was not over; defiantly, it reversed field, as he was wont to do, for he returned to play, sometimes spectacularly, yet another day. It takes an effort of memory and imagination to grasp with aesthetic firmness the events which make up team or individual biographies, but it can be done. Such breadth of apprehension is needed lest the meta-rhythms of the sport escape.

Within the meta-rhythms of sport, time and place are redefined. Their meaning is modified by the seasons and locales of the different sports. Each has its time and its place—in the sun, on the urban concrete, or under the creaking rafters.

> Perhaps if sports have their inner rhythms, ... there is a larger rhythm, like Ecclesiastes' list of the times for this and the times for that. Perhaps if baseball is the game that runs its leisured way through the whole of hopeful spring and lazy summer, football should be the game of brief intensity, a search for a great day.[28]

But with the professionalization of sports their seasons have become blurry. They no longer unambiguously claim their own time, so that the relationships among them have lost their clarity, their meta-rhythm gone slack. Basketball and hockey stretch deep into May when the balmy weather makes rink and court the wrong place to play or watch. Conversely, baseball's slow flow threatens to freeze in October winds. Why lay this loss at the doorstep of professionalization? Because longer schedules are largely responsible for loss of seasonal hegemony, and longer schedules are the result of league expansion and televison commitments. Of course, league expansion and television contracts add up to more revenue—professionalization includes commercialization. Abetting the cause of "more" is the gradual loss of the outdoors as setting for such sports as soccer, football, and baseball. "Indoor" (American) soccer and domed stadia have brought these sports "in from the cold," out of their natural seasonal niches. When any sport can be played any place we are in danger of forgetting their distinctive aesthetic personalities and the way their differences harmonize in the yearly round of play.

6. Aesthetic Attitude

The notion of the "aesthetic attitude" helps distinguish aesthetic orientation and valuation from a variety of other possibilities. The aesthetic attitude is different, for example, from the economic, social, or historical. Each kind of attitude is characterized by its respective value and therefore determines the sort of appreciation likely to be had. For example, we can view a piece of land as an investment, site for low-rent housing, or the scene of a Civil War battle. But when we attend to the piece of land simply for its appearance, its contours and colors, texture and rhythms, then we take the aesthetic attitude toward it. We turn away from a host of everyday interests and look for aesthetic relations and qualities.

We may say of all these nonaesthetic interests, and of "practical" perception generally, that the object is apprehended with an eye to its origins and consequences, its interrelations with other things. By contrast, the aesthetic attitude "isolates" the object and focuses upon it—the "look" of the rocks, the sound of the ocean, the colors in the painting. . . . Its whole nature and character are dwelt upon.[29]

The same applies in sports. The aesthetic aspects and values are distinct from whatever practical interests we may bring to the performance or contest. To appreciate a sport aesthetically is likely, moreover, to conflict with viewing it from a practical standpoint; the interests of the "professional" athlete or spectator incline him least toward aesthetic appreciation. It is difficult, for example, to appreciate the grace of a boxer who is demolishing the home town boy. And when we are playing another team for a prize or money it is practically impossible to value their teamwork. The aesthetic attitude requires that we "distance" ourselves a bit from such realistic, everyday concerns.

So far so good, but we must further distinguish different expectations and orientations *within* the aesthetic attitude itself. It is not appropriate to expect the same aesthetic riches from different art forms or styles. We should not expect to find the same sort of aesthetic values in a sonata as we anticipate finding in a symphony.

So Spenser's great *Faerie Queene* is ignored because fools try to read it as though it were a sonnet of Donne, for the *Queene* is a medieval tapestry, and one wanders about in it. An epic is not an epigram.[30]

Even within the same medium, then, our general aesthetic attitude should be specifically determined by the form and style of the particular object or performance at hand.

And so it goes for appreciating the aesthetic qualities of sports. There are inherent structural differences among sports: A sprint is over in a flash while a marathon takes hours, and hockey is virtually continuous movement while baseball and football have pauses after each play. It should be no surprise, therefore, that aesthetic potentials vary from sport to sport, some variations greater than others. This is why it is foolish to expect or demand similar aesthetic rewards from structurally different sports.

And yet this is exactly at the heart of much popular (misplaced) criticism of particular sports or particular performances of them. We hear people faulting baseball, for example, for slowness of pace or deliberateness of action. Spectators more than likely are looking to baseball to supply the aesthetic qualities more easily found in such sports as football or basketball; only the season changes for such spectators. But this is like faulting a war movie for showing violence or a surrealistic painting by Dali for being "weird." Part of the general description of the aesthetic attitude is that it includes a "sympathetic" openness to the object or event before us. For sport, this means giving the structure of the particular game or activity a chance to show what it has to offer.

Because it has come in for much harsh criticism by today's fast-paced generation, baseball is a good candidate for close examination (and if I dwell too long on its "innings and outs," forgive an enthusiast). To appreciate baseball, we must first cultivate a sense of its setting—a park, a field, or "grounds." Its context is that of a leisurely outing during which we bask in the sun, enjoying friends and food.[31] There is no rush. We are to savor the moments of player and manager decision, the slow building of tension as the batter repeatedly steps out of the box, trying to guess the pitcher's mind while at the same time upset his rhythm.[32] Contributing to its patient pace is baseball's atemporal nature. Structured by outs and innings, baseball does not move to a game-clock, so there is no rush, no frantic play against time. Relaxing in the abundance of time, we are suddenly brought up sharp by the explosive home run or the flashing double play. The quick steal or rapid pick-off stand out within the game's overall easy pace.

The regular tempo and even, staid pace of baseball are determined by its structure. Former baseball player, Ken Harrelson, once pointed out that baseball is the only sport in which the defense controls the ball by putting it in play. Conversely, once the defense commences the action, only the offense can score. There is no immediate, sudden transition from offense to defense or defense to offense. Each team waits to "take its turn" and we must wait for this regular alternation to occur. In football, basketball, hockey, or tennis, however, a sudden shift in advantage can occur; either side can mount an attack at any time regardless of who happens to "possess" or put in play the object of "interest" (literally, that which connects and engages the two sides). But in baseball, scoring opportunity (and number of outs) is fixed. And because the defense controls the ball, the sense of order and fixity is increased; the offense must wait, it cannot take matters into its own hands by initiating play.

It may be stretching a point, but I think that the fixity and orderliness of baseball are reinforced by its circularity. Scores occur when players go *around* the bases, returning home, and the game progresses by going "through" each team's *recurring* batting order. Goal-sports (football, lacrosse, basketball, hockey, soccer, and the like) are linear: Play moves back and forth, surging and ebbing. In most, space is consumed and finally invaded by the ball or puck at the goal. The players on each team do not "wait" around, but are in the thick of the linear flow all the time. It is not just that the action is continuous, but each player is in or near the action continually.

The aesthetic appreciation, and therefore the criticism, of a particular sport must, then, be appropriate to the possibilities of that sport's particular aesthetic. Bill Russell notes, for example, that basketball is played essentially in the air, and football is a game of territory. We can, of course, still find aesthetic fault with a baseball game, but not because it lacks those aesthetic qualities displayed by other sports. We should fault a game for lacking such aesthetic qualities it is capable of.[33] While baseball's aesthetic may not appeal to everyone, just as a waltz tempo may not suit polka lovers, its pace and rhythms should be felt in relation to its general structure. Its aesthetic possibilities are determined by its style and structure. The aesthetic moral of this extends all the way into our daily activities: We should not expect a lecture to offer the same rewards as party chitchat, or a walk in the woods to provide what a plunge in the surf can. Our minds and bodies move within determining contexts which, like those in sport, structure time and space.

7. Participation

"What attracted me was the sound of the swish, the sound of the dribble, the feel of going up in the air."[34]

What is *distinctive* about each sport, and what should shape our aesthetic expectations as spectators, should also contribute to the aesthetic enjoyment of participating. So Bradley might have included the sound of a shot being blocked, the feel of the ball flicking off the fingertips, or the look of a spinning, weaving lay-up. Basketball: Its textures and rhythms are so different from those of tennis or football, running or swimming; we simply "feel" different playing in each one.

More Americans are participating in more sports but we do not seem playful about it. We compete to win tournament and trophy, or work on shape and health. Eyes fixed on glory, waistline, and heartbeat, we do not pay much attention to the aesthetic qualities inherent in participating in the sport itself. We do not play. When we play our senses are alive. Not only is the body the receiver of sensory news from the environment, but it is itself an *object* of sensory awareness. This is especially true in individual sports in which no response to others is called for.

Isolated with and within his body in its environment, the performer is free to appreciate the rhythms he makes with it. The runner, for instance, can appreciate from the "inside" the pattern his arm, leg, and breath movement creates. For him, shifting, breathing, and muscular exertion are viscerally felt and heard, whereas spectators can only infer this experience from what they see. Even the weariness of muscles and, finally, pain can be appreciated by the performer as the accompaniment of motion.

The grace that the spectator only sees the performer feels. Moreover, he feels it as instigated by himself since he is "in charge." He controls the angle of the dive, the thrust of the pole before the vault, the rhythms of the run. The kinesthetic experience that results, therefore, is *felt as the result* of the athlete's own will or choice. Slicing into the water, soaring up to the bar, or loping across a meadow are experienced as the completion of mental as well as physical concentration. When the body does the mind's bidding, the aesthetic of performance includes mental-physical continuity. We experience ourselves as one. Attending to our body's movement is also attending to our control. This requires harmony between our active and passive capacities: responding to our present performance, readied by current feedback for subsequent movement. This "self-communication" is experienced immediately as "listening" to our body, which shapes the messages we then send it. Continuity in movement results from moving in *response* to antecedent motion; we are, in effect, responding to ourselves.

In individual sports we can attend to the coordination of the whole body's movement. The hand-eye coordination so crucial in social sports and everyday tasks is virtually nonexistent. Especially rhythmic are such "repetitive" sports as swimming and running, in which the same motion is repeated; arms and legs, trunk and head, are synchronized in a pattern of beats and rests, thrusts and recoveries. Consider the coordination involved in the rhythms of swimming the crawl: head turns, inhaling; right arm pulls down, left arm reaching; kick-kick; face down, exhaling; left arm pulls, right arm lifting from side; kick-kick. No wonder we can be so attuned to our bodies' rhythms that we experience a meditative refreshment.

We also tune in to our interaction with the environment. Consider swimming again, where environment plays such a significant aesthetic role, so palpably does it depart from our ordinary surroundings. Not only are we moving through a "foreign" medium when we swim, but we are horizontal rather than upright, buoyed up. Supported from below, feeling lighter than normal, the water envelopes and caresses us. Its softening effect includes opacity of sight and diffuseness of light: a striking sensuous context for the rhythms established by breathing and by head, trunk, and limb movement. We beat out these rhythms as we slide through a medium that resists and then fluidly yields to the pull of our arms and the push of our legs.

Our participation in social sports, on the other hand, is informed more by other people than environment; rather, other people comprise our environment. Here we must react and adjust to what others, opposition or teammates, are doing, as well as anticipate what they *will* do. As we run to the ball in tennis, we must anticipate where our opponent will be on the other side of the net. The response to ourselves paramount in individual sports is now situated within the larger context of social response. The "aesthetic" field of perception and initiation of movement is widened. It is further deepened when teammates are added and we must adapt cooperatively to their response to us—all of which aims at overcoming the opposition!

Spectators, as we have noted, appreciate continuously recoordinated and readjusted play, but their perceptions do not issue in any immediate physical response on their part (unless standing, shouting in appreciation). It is the continuity between perception and physical response that adds an aesthetic dimension to participation. Similarly, the participant not only feels the dramatic tension, as does the audience, but must play *in* it. "Grace under pressure" is an exquisite aesthetic experience with which the audience can perhaps sympathize. But when we ourselves are playing, our running, throwing, leaping, or shooting are crystallized by the pressure of competition.

As much as our enthusiasm for victory has warped our appreciation of sports, keeping score does dramatically structure our participation. The score informs our perception of the situation and our anticipation of action. It adds directionality, a sense of "building" to the play. Whether we play in a seesaw contest, a game in which one team doggedly claws back from repeated setbacks, or one in which a comfortable margin suddenly, inexplicably melts away, keeping score with winning and losing in mind certainly provides a felt horizon to our play.[35]

This directionality, however, is typical of a conventional Western aesthetic. If and when we forego keeping score in our play, we tend to tune in to the rhythms and other nonlinear components of the game. When we appreciate playing a game in this way, our orientation is more akin to an African or Eastern aesthetic perspective. Such a nonlinear, nonincremental aesthetic has clearly influenced twentieth-century Western art: threads of meaning, swatches of color, patches of sound laid side by side or end to end but with no "escalating" or "progressing." Describing John Coltrane's play on the tenor saxophone in the early '60s, Leroi Jones writes:

> The seeming masses of sixteenth notes, the *new* and finally articulated concept of using whole groups or clusters of rapidly fired notes as chordal insistence rather than a strict melodic progression . . . to try to play almost every note of the chord separately, as well as the related or vibrating tones that chord produced. The result, of course, is what someone termed 'Sheets of Sound. . . .'[36]

Can we sometimes, forgetting the score, not worrying about winning, give ourselves up to the rhythms, grace, and body-tempo of the game so that we experience "sheets of movement"? In such moments we would feel how the rhythms change and modify one another. We might sense our energies and actions as part of a flowing repetition rather than building toward a climax or progressing along a linear route.

But perhaps the ideal of aesthetic playing should involve both the progressive aspect of competition *and* appreciation for directionless "layers" of play. Maybe neither has to be sacrificed and we can savor our roles in the dramatic build-up without forfeiting a "non-Western," nonincremental enjoyment in the horizontal dimensions of play. Every now and then Bill Russell seemed to have both; his peak moments were realized through intense competition but the competition sent him "over" its edge, into the horizontal textures of play.

At that special level all sorts of odd things happened. The game would be in a white heat of competition, and yet somehow I wouldn't feel competitive—which is a miracle in itself. . . . The game would move so quickly that every fake, cut and pass would be surprising, and yet nothing could surprise me. It was almost as if we were playing in slow motion. During those spells I could almost sense how the next play would develop and where the next shot would be taken.[37]

Chapter Six
The Drama of Decision-Making

W E HAVE JUST CONCLUDED looking at two areas of life—sexuality and sport—in which aesthetic experience should play a significant part. Yet they are but two interests among many; we must also make decisions about whether and whom to marry, how to raise our children, what sort of work to undertake, where to live, and so on. The great number and variety of decisions we face raise the following question *about* deliberation: How should we choose; What method of deciding what to do will conduct us most happily into the future? The thrust of this chapter is to argue for a mode of decision-making which is essentially aesthetic in nature. Thus, to the claim that specific areas of life such as sexuality and sport should be aesthetically informed, I add that decision-making *about* such interests ought to be aesthetic in nature.

The method for making decisions most relied upon, unwittingly relied upon, is the procedure of counting up the benefits and drawbacks, reckoning the pleasures against the pains in each of the alternative courses of action. This calculative way of making decisions evidences the force of the particular conception of self which it presupposes: that the self is a collection of states, an aggregate of desirable and undesirable experiences. Calculation is challenged by an (aesthetic) alternative for making decisions and the theory of self which supports it.

This rival method is what John Dewey has called "dramatic rehearsal."[1] It situates the agent in a sequence of events imagined in anticipation of real action. This imaginative play enables the individual to foresee not merely moments of pleasure and pain, but relations among far-reaching habits and interests. This treats the self as the more or less successful organization of habits and interests which ultimately determines a way of living (including our positive and negative experiences).

Rehearsing our options in the imagination provides a procedure for *discovering* and not simply rehashing sources of value. It is not irrevocably tied to the delights and disappointments of the past as a calculus must be. In this respect, calculative decision-making is an extension of the vulgarizing process analyzed in Chapter III. As with cheap art, it entrenches us in what we are used to liking and does not help cultivate our powers of dealing with the new or of effecting continuity between the new and the old. This is true largely because the calculative model offers no real *standard* for making decisions, just the injunction to accumulate more of what has seemed enjoyable before.

In dramatic rehearsal, on the other hand, the form of aesthetic experience itself is a standard by which to judge our deliberations. We judge whether our imaginative projection of alternative futures proceeds in an *aesthetically complete way*. In a sense, even to question how we deliberate already signifies a break with a quantitative, calculative way of dealing with the world. It indicates that we have made the "meta-decision" to examine our usual mode of practical thinking. This kind of self-reflection is encouraged by the open, imaginative, improvisational nature of the response characteristic of aesthetic experience. The aesthetic structure of dramatic rehearsal impels us to reexamine how we make decisions in a way that the quantitative format of calculation actually discourages.

1. Methods of Decision-Making

A. Calculation

When trying to figure out what to do, we often go through a counting procedure: adding up the good and bad points of the different options open to us. We perform a sort of cost/benefit analysis of the alternatives. Going to an evening party, for example, will require traveling some distance and making "small talk," but the gathering could be spirited, include good food and drink and the prospect of meeting new people. On the other hand, the museum is close by and has a new exhibit, but that will be interesting for a shorter period of time than the party and will be more somber. And so it goes. We try to tally up the pluses and minuses of each option and pick the one with the greater net gain of "plus."

We do this in small decisions like the preceding, as well as those concerning more momentous choices such as what career to enter into, where to live, or whom to marry. This procedure sounds feasible enough, but let us look into the details of calculation.

When we do, we notice that "plus" usually translates into pleasure or some other positive mental state, "minus" as pain or some other negative mental state. Our goal, then, is to choose a path of action which will produce a fairly large collection of pleasant or positive states and a small collection of painful or negative states. This is, after all the final *meaning* of listing the good and bad features of the dinner party and the museum outing. We make our decisions on the basis of anticipated collections of sensations or states, as if accumulating grains of sand or money in the bank.

The first thing to note about this method of making decisions is that we are necessarily tied to our past. What has pleased and pained us in the past is all we have to go on. While this is not disastrous for immediately realized decisions, such as what to do this evening, it is certainly dangerous for long-term decisions such as those concerning career or spouse. There is little assurance that what has been pleasant and painful will continue to be so for the next twenty, thirty, or forty years. If this be granted by the calculator, then what is he to base his estimate on? Calculating pluses and minuses, pleasures and pains, does not project us into the future. Even if all indications point to our prospective mate retaining her beauty and charm, how do we know beauty and charm will continue to captivate us or that our taste in them will remain the same?

This shows that the calculative model of decision-making ties our ends or interests to the past and cannot take account of change—whether in us or the world. The contemplated actions or action plans can appear only as means to *prior* ends: what has been positive to date. This stems, in part, from the fact that in calculation we regard ourselves as so many collections of separate states and sensations. We are not invited to view ourselves in an interconnected way, as a "self." Rather, we see ourselves as repositories of benefits or burdens. Although this criticism will be enlarged upon shortly, it is important to note here that this lack of a picture of an integrated self explains why calculation is so deficient for long-term decisions. There is no framework (of self) within which to project the consequences of our contemplated choices.

In addition to these difficulties, calculation faces added problems posed by the nature of pleasure and pain.[2] These problems revolve about the comparison of quantities. Even if quantification (however exact or inexact) were possible (say, some notion of *units* of pleasure versus units of pain), it would still have to deal with two independent dimensions: extensivity (how long-lasting) and intensity (how much per unit of time). Since these two vary independently of one another, an individual must sometimes decide whether to opt for either short but very intense periods of pleasure or long but mild periods of pleasure. The same difficulty holds for pains, but is compounded when we try to *combine* the pleasures and pains of each option. Yet this is clearly what calculation requires us to attempt.

There is a still further difficulty in comparing pleasure/pain pairings: whether to opt for greatest *net gain* of pleasure or greatest amount of pleasure *proportional* to the amount of pain. Generalized, we might call this the dilemma of choosing between the method of simple subtraction and that of proportional advantage as our procedure for realizing "more" pleasure versus pain. Suppose, in our previous example, that the dinner-party option looks to yield 100 units of pleasure and 50 units of pain: net gain, 50 units of pleasure (remember that we are overlooking the gross implausibility of estimating such units). The museum option looks to yield 60 units of pleasure at a cost of 11 units of pain: net gain, 49 units of pleasure. While the museum option comes out slightly behind in (anticipated) net pleasure, it has the advantage of producing *much* less pain. In *proportion* to the pain calculated, therefore, its pleasure is greater: roughly 6:1 instead of a mere 2:1. There seems to be no reasonable way for someone to decide between the "net gain" approach and the "proportional advantage" approach, indicating once again the basic irrationality of the calculative method.[3] Whether we think of pleasures/pains, pluses/minuses, or costs/benefits, the problems remain. Assuming that some form of gross quantification *were* possible, comparing those quantities poses insurmountable difficulties. I suggest that this is because what is at stake—human happiness or well-being—has a *qualitative* cast that must be taken into account in an adequate model of decision-making. And this is precisely what calculation cannot encompass; because different pleasures and pains themselves are qualitatively different, they are fundamentally incommensurable. Describing their "polymorphous character," Alisdair MacIntyre writes:

And pleasure or happiness are not states of mind for the production of which these activities and modes are merely alternative means. The pleasure-of-drinking-Guinness is not the pleasure-of-swimming-at-Crane's-beach, and the swimming and the drinking are not two different means for providing the same end-state .... The happiness which belongs peculiarly to the way of life of the cloister is not the same happiness as that which belongs peculiarly to the military life. For different pleasures and different happinesses are to a large degree incommensurable: there are no scales of quality or quantity on which to weigh them.[4]

B. Dramatic Rehearsal

" ... Deliberation is a dramatic rehearsal (in imagination) of various competing possible lines of action .... [It] is an experiment in finding out what the various lines of possible action are really like."[5] For Dewey, decision-making should be an imitation of life. We imagine ourselves taking a particular course of action, embarking on a path that will involve a series of well- or ill-related activities. By engaging in dramatic rehearsal we do not simply abstract the pleasures or pains expected to be gained, but rather imagine ourselves acting in concrete situations. By trying out different scenarios we hope to anticipate what they will "feel" like when we actually put one into play.

In our imaginations we think through the consequences of possible action plans; we see and feel them as wearing or stimulating, repetitive or novel, demanding or relaxing. Not only do we get a feel for the action and its consequences in isolation, but we anticipate relations among activities. One of the important consequences of any action is its effect on us for further conduct. Will we be ready for the important meeting tomorrow if we go out on the town tonight? Or, in decisions with a larger scope—Will taking this new job leave me time enough for my family and avocations? Thus we should look to see whether this action will prepare or hinder us for other lines of conduct we may wish to try out in future.

In contrast to calculation, dramatic rehearsal focuses attention on the nature of the activities and their impact on the individual who engages in them. Dramatic rehearsal gives us an imaginary taste of the kinds of demands actions will make on us, how well they satisfy our interests, and the sort of habits they encourage or frustrate. By seeing ourselves performing the contemplated actions in specific situations, with other people, we derive some idea of the concrete meaning of the alternatives for ourselves. By seeing ourselves going through the actions we can more specifically foresee difficulties and the solutions to them.

Suppose we are planning a vacation. Two alternatives seem attractive, but for rather different reasons. By rehearsing each, these reasons emerge and with them a third, better alternative. A trip to Paris should satisfy our interests in art, meeting new people, sight-seeing, and adventure. It will, of course, entail struggling with a foreign culture and language as well as planning a day-to-day agenda. These latter demands oppose our desire to relax and our habits of passivity. The alternative of a leisurely stay at an ocean resort is more attractive on these grounds. But, alas, an ocean stay is less adventuresome, fewer acquaintances would be met, and our cultural interests would not be satisfied. Each alternative suits us in some ways, grates in others.

Rehearsing each option, we imaginatively see ourselves moving through days at Paris, days at the shore. A sense of the rhythms, pace, and tone of each emerges. We project the satisfaction or frustration of our interests. We picture habits and propensities acted upon or curbed. This enables us to uncover difficulties in each option. By anticipating them, we give ourselves the opportunity to avoid or overcome them with an imaginative revision. In our vacation case, we might hit upon the possibility of taking a *tour* in Paris. This would eliminate the stress of coming to grips all on our own with a foreign culture and tongue, and also relieve us of the responsibility of working up daily agendas. The restriction in our freedom would appear to be a small price to pay.

Dramatic rehearsal is therefore a way of *discovering* possibilities in action in a way that calculation is not. Calculation simply tallies up the benefits and drawbacks of each option, each vacation plan, but cannot of itself get to the basis of such benefits and drawbacks. Dramatic rehearsal uncovers this basis by showing how action sequences fit together or jar; by showing how different options satisfy or thwart our interests; and by showing us following through on these habits and those propensities. Dramatic rehearsal gives us something concrete with which to work and revise: story lines open to our imaginative retelling. Because it can uncover *why* a possible course of action is likely to be pleasant or painful, dramatic rehearsal can suggest new possibilities of action, beyond those entertained at the outset of the decision-making.

In considering careers, most of us perform calculations. We think of the benefits of status, income, opportunity for advancement, and *maybe* the kind of work involved. We perform a cost/benefit analysis to see if the long, hard climb will be worth it. Dramatic rehearsal, however, would have us imagine day-to-day life in the job. A career in law, for example, is made up of specific activities, not simply numbers of hours of study and then toil, amount of salary, or the kinds of cases. Dramatic rehearsal projects how the everyday reality of such work involves research; writing briefs; interviewing people; collaborating with other attorneys and assorted experts; developing arguments and plans of attack; dealing with clients.

The question we must ask ourselves is whether these sorts of activities, over a period of years, will be good for us. Will they broaden our interests? Will they contribute to our life outside of work? Will they promote habits of community and intelligence? And while dramatic rehearsal cannot answer such question definitively, it can give us a basis for making thoughtful evaluations.

C. Further Comparison

After a decision is made and a line of action chosen, we see whether the choice we made was a good one. Often it takes awhile before all the "returns" are in; the more momentous the decision, the more long-ranging its repercussions usually are. But in reexamining the dramatic rehearsal in light of the results of our actual choice, we are able to see *why* it was good or bad. The rehearsal *continues* to have value by helping us understand ourselves more fully.

Because it helps us understand ourselves, the dramatic rehearsal explains why this turned out to be pleasant and that painful. It shows us what sorts of activities are congenial to our nature, whether our interests are furthered or frustrated by a choice, and so on. We can pursue "feeling" distaste for an option in our imaginative projection to uncover some trait of ours that explains why. Consequently, appraising dramatic rehearsals in light of the actual consequences of our choice can improve our future decision-making. Dramatic rehearsal gives us a method for learning from our mistakes.

This is what is lacking in calculation. Failure in choosing means simply that we guessed poorly with regard to pleasant and painful future experiences. True, we learn that such and such was painful and this is a fact about us. But we do not learn *why* it was painful because we are not led by the calculation to a deeper understanding of our motives, interests, and habits. The best we can do, therefore, is avoid particular unpleasant situations in the future. In making future calculations, we cannot generalize on the basis of our underlying trait.

Suppose we go to Paris, without a tour, and have a disappointing time. If we had originally calculated, then we would blame our cost/benefit analysis. We figure out aspects of the situation which we overlooked or how we erred in estimating the particular amounts of pleasure/pain involved. This can, of course, be worthwhile. We might, for instance discover our saturation point for sight-seeing or how easily language barriers discomfit us.

But had we originally engaged in dramatic rehearsal, our disappointment would have more impact on subsequent deliberations. By scrutinizing our vacation's shortcomings in light of our previous dramatic rehearsal we could discover more about who we really are. We could learn, for example, that our initial dramatic rehearsal completely overlooked the conflict between our need for adventure and our habits of passivity. The Paris trip was exciting, filled with discoveries, but took too much effort for a vacation. Calculation has no way in itself to reveal this as the *cause* of our disappointment. Appraising previous dramatic rehearsal enables insightful diagnosis of the choice, which subsequent decision-making can then make use of. The benefits to future imaginative rehearsals extend even farther because diagnosis of past decisions enabled *modification* of how we make those in the future. Not only what but *how* we imagine action is open to revamping. This will be pursued at greater length in Section 3 below (while the "what" will be discussed in Section 2).

Although there are striking differences between the methods of calculation and dramatic rehearsal, each to some extent enters into the other. When we calculate, we imagine particular outcomes: tasting Parisian cuisine, the exhibit at the Louvre, attempts at speaking French. And, certainly, in dramatic rehearsal, having to work out daily itineraries is imaginatively painful, the excitement of a foreign city and people enjoyable. But the differences are nonetheless striking and are more than merely a matter of emphasis.

What each method takes as its *content*, as the *basis* of choice is radically different. Consider briefly how a director determines whether a particular gesture should be included in a scene in a play. He must reflect on its meaning in that scene—how it connects with the scene's dialogue, pauses, movement, and thrust. He must also consider the scene's overall contribution to the play. The costs and benefits of including the contemplated gesture should thereby *emerge*. This is radically different from trying to make the decision on the basis of the gesture's (isolated) value, which is then added to or subtracted from the calculated values of the scene's other ingredients. A particular gesture may be brilliant, illuminating, but grate against the rest of the scene (perhaps be "out of character"). This sort of consideration typifies dramatic rehearsal and indicates its difference from calculation. In the latter, pluses and minuses are considered in isolation from one another. Like profit and loss entries in a ledger, they cannot be *related* to one another—only added or subtracted. This is because the conception of self which underlies calculation is inferior to that which grounds dramatic rehearsal.

2. Conceptions of Self

A. A Collection of States

The method of calculation treats human beings as repositories of disconnected states. Figuring out the psychical costs and benefits of each action deals with the individual as a place for credits and debits to be recorded. The self so conceived is without structure or form—a loose bag of positive and negative experiences. The meaning of actions is understood to be exhausted in their particular outcomes; they appear to leave no traces in the individual's personality or character. If there *is* an enduring structure to the individual which can explain why this experience pleases now but will not please two years hence, the calculative method cannot reflect it or take it into account.

Because it cannot take an enduring structure of the self into account, projecting future gains and losses is very chancy. It amounts almost to blind guesswork based on what has been pleasant or painful to date. As indicated earlier, change in self or world cannot be intelligently anticipated. Obviously, the more distant the future for which we calculate, the less accurate the calculation is likely to be. Moreover, certain features of calculation indicate that the conception of self upon which it rests is false or, at the very least, inadequate. The *nature* of calculation itself repudiates the theory of selfhood on which it depends.

This becomes apparent once we notice that calculation is itself a habit and is part of an interlocking system of habits. Built up over time, we acquire the habit of guessing at the pluses and minuses alternative courses of action appear to promise. Sometimes this way of dealing with the future grows out of one area of expertise, such as business. But for most of us, various aspects of our everyday experience conspire, directly and indirectly, to habituate us as calculators.

Directly, everyday life presents innumerable instances of calculation. Candidates for office have scored well or poorly in the past.

Products have *lists* of good features. We see people weigh the advantages and disadvantages of adopting children, filing joint income tax returns, and renting versus buying commodities. But *why* has adding and subtracting become the prevalent method of decision-making so that even God is thought of as a super-accountant?

Calculation is demanded as the means of coping with a fragmented life. It fits nicely into a life which is a "patchwork of independent interests."[6] Each interest in life has its own territory, institutions, and rewards. Business, recreation, education, art, social intercourse, family, religion, sports, and politics each possess "a separate and independent province with its own peculiar aims and ways of proceeding. Each contributes to the others only externally and accidentally."[7] Calculation is eminently "suited" to such compartmentalized living. Within each sphere a cost/benefit analysis can be conducted. More important, calculation appears as the most efficient way of connecting isolated spheres of activity and interest for purposes of action. The net gains of competing interests, such as raising a family versus embarking on an all-consuming career are tallied up and then compared. Quantitative comparison *appears* the best way to relate the different compartments of our lives. Quantity seems to provide the necessary common denominator.[8]

The connection among these diverse areas of interest, however, is only on the surface, only in terms of outcomes that appear comparable. It should be noticed that calculation facilitates this segmentation; by reducing all spheres of activity and interest to quantities, no continuities (or discontinuities) in the lived life can be discovered. Calculation thereby educates us away from a conception of life as a unified whole.

> So work is divided from leisure, private life from public, the corporate from the personal . . . . And all these separations have been achieved so that it is the distinctiveness of each and not the unity of the life of the individual who passes through those parts in terms of which we are taught to think and feel.[9]

The calculative method would have us think that paintings, houses, college educations, sports, and clothing could be truly and well connected by costs/benefits or price alone. By summing up the advantages and disadvantages of each segment separately, the calculative method, as indicated above, actually reinforces the segmentation of everyday life—which brings us to the other habits with which calculation is wed. Its connection with them is the other aspect of our everyday lives which conspires to habituate us as calculators. The fragmentation of interest and activity which calculation is so geared to deal with ironically does not hold in calculation's snug fit with several other pervasive habits.

Calculation is a *habit* and is reinforced by its place in a *network* of habits: to mention the more powerful ones—quantification, manipulation, and acquisition. Each contributes to the scope and strength of the others, coalescing into a consistent way people respond to their world. We quantify virtually everything, and anything that cannot be measured by number is discounted in significance.[10] Money, mileage, production, efficiency, houses, cargo, beauty ("1-10"), earthquakes, children, success: The disparity among the items in this list shows the range of quantification in which we engage. The professionalization of sport examined in the last chapter is yet another, more publicly visible instance. The fan's obsession with scoring, winning, and ranking simply reflects the owners' and schools' preoccupation with that most complete representation of quantity—money. The professionalization of the fan has clearly kept pace with the commercialization of the game, each an expression of the national pastime of quantifying everything possible. Calculation is but the servant of such quantification—awkward and inexact since concerned with qualitatively diverse mental states and moments of experience.

By *calculating* we hope to hit upon the best way to *manipulate* our environment so as to *acquire* the greatest *quantity* of net positive experience. All the habits tie neatly together. Nature, other people, even our selves are viewed as resources to be handled and exploited. The Bible's assertion that humans were given dominion over the earth has come to mean: Nature is ours to harness and wring profit from. Our goal is to *control* every aspect of nature, from seas to weather. But other people are also viewed as potential contributors to or detractors from our comfort. Even one's own talents and abilities must be "used" for profit. Manipulating for acquisition treats the human self as the ultimate storehouse for the benefits generated by all the commodities actually stored in one's house.

Calculation is thus part of a tightly woven fabric of reinforcing habits. The point in exhibiting its place in this larger pattern is to show that there is a basic contradiction between the conception of self presupposed by the method of calculation and the conception attested to by the habitual nature of calculation itself. Implied in calculating outcomes as described above is a conception of the self as a collection of unrelated states or moments. No enduring structure of the self enters into the calculative way of making decisions. However, calculation is itself a habit, entwined in a deep-rooted structure of habits. The "facts" about calculation, therefore, belie the conception of the self upon which it rests. As a method of making decisions, calculation pays no heed to the reality it exemplifies.

Treating the self as a collection of states is therefore inaccurate. The nature of calculation itself ironically reveals this. It follows, then, that calculation necessarily directs our attention *away* from a complete understanding of who we are. With its fellow habits, calculation takes hold of us unawares. Blinding us to *its* real nature we are also blinded to what *we* really are.

I would tentatively suggest that any method of decision-making (or education, love-making, competition, etc.) that is "false" to what human beings really are cannot be the best one for them. It cannot do the job well because it rests on an inaccurate conception of personhood. Calculation is not the best way to make decisions even in its own terms—of pleasures and pains. Thus, an additional irony of calculation is that dramatic rehearsal is a better means of achieving its very ends, better because more attuned to what a self really is.

B. Organized Habits and Purposes

Dramatic rehearsal treats the self as habits and purposes organized through action. Focusing simply on the content of experience, calculation neglects its form. Dramatic rehearsal, on the other hand, sees contemplated actions as developing or disrupting, re-forming or de-forming the self. The signficance of this view of the self is brought home when we return to how dramatic rehearsal considers actions.

Actions, after all, are the immediate object of thought when we make decisions: "What shall we *do!*" is the main order of business. When dramatizing possible courses of action in an imaginative rehearsal, the action's meaning extends well beyond its consequences for pleasure and pain, positive and negative states. Rather, the action is seen as bearing on the individual's present and future array of habits and purposes. Does the action realize or clash with habits and purposes already in place? Does it begin to cultivate new ones? Does it equip the individual for future action, for the pursuit of unforeseen goals? In dramatic rehearsal, the action's import is understood as penetrating into the makeup of the individual.

When we rehearse an action imaginatively, therefore, we envision ourselves as *continuing* to respond to its consequences. We imagine ourselves, modified by the presently contemplated action(s), performing in the more remote future. *Subsequent* habits, purposes, and experience, then, will be influenced by the way *this* action modifies us. Dramatic rehearsal thus conceives action as helping to make and define who we are. Choice of action is not merely choice of some positive or negative state(s) but of *what we will become.*

Instead of making primary the question, "What will this act make me feel?", dramatic rehearsal asks, "What will this act make of me in my everyday living?" Sometimes a particular choice even determines our whole way of life. For some time now the United States government has bought land from American Indians (for development, dams, minerals, etc.). A tribe is offered a great deal of money for land that is, at the time, their home. Indians can decide in either the calculative or dramatic rehearsal way. In the calculative, they figure what the government's money will enable them to buy. Will their standard of living go up if they sell? Quantifying, they estimate what they will be able to acquire and try to guess at the amounts of pleasure and pain accrued. When they engage in dramatic rehearsal, however, they imagine what their *way of life* will be if they sell. They project themselves into a new daily routine. Will they be able to continue customary hunting, ritual, family, and tribal interaction? What will become of their overall relation with nature? Habits and purposes are brought into perspective by imagining day-to-day life off the present tribal land.

The difference between these two approaches is radical precisely because in the latter a conception of self as an ongoing pattern is thought through. "What will become of me in my daily life?" places the self at the center of the contemplated actions. Actions are seen as instrumental to a way of life: how the individual(s), as a result of this action, will subsequently interact with his (their) culture, other people, and nature.

Since this depends on his habits of perception, thinking, and acting, let me offer a characterization of what a habit is. This I will do primarily in terms of what it *does*, how it functions in our lives. Habits organize other elements of the person such as impulses, desires, perceptions, thoughts, muscles, as well as other habits. This organization enables the individual to respond more or less effectively to his environment; fortunately, it is open to change. We can acquire new and shed or modify old habits because of our "plasticity," which, according to William James, "means the possession of a structure weak enough to yield to an influence, but strong enough not to yield all at once."[11] The latter obviously indicates that, as noted in earlier chapters, habits take time to develop—or diminish. This is why, for example, it takes more than one experience of a perverting sexual practice to entrench perverse habits of social interaction.

As suggested above, there are different sorts of habits: habits of thought as much as habits of physical behavior; habits of perception as well as habits of emotion. What James says about actions counts doubly for thought, perception, and affect: "The great thing, then, in all education, is to *make our nervous systems our ally instead of our enemy, . . . make automatic and habitual, . . . as many useful actions as we can,* and guard against the grooving into ways that are likely to be disadvantageous to us . . . ."[12] What we are mostly concerned with here are psychological rather than strictly physical habits, although all habits no doubt have a neurological base or correlate.[13] These habits coordinate perceptions, emotions, and thoughts so as to dispose us to particular ways of behaving and reacting. Kindness, for instance, involves the habits of perceiving need, sympathizing with it, and acting to meliorate it. It creates particular expectations, discriminates among elements in our environment, and prepares us to respond to particular situations in determinate ways. Habits are therefore a readiness or openness to respond to particular situations, and to respond to them in definite ways. They are not always actively engaged, but are "latent", awaiting an appropriate context to call them into overt action. Thus, if there is no context of need, the habit of kindness will not be manifest. And the same for habits of communication, competition, recreation, and so on. It follows from this that, at any given moment, most of our habits are not acted out but are waiting to be called into play.

Habits are also general in their influence. There is no one-to-one relationship between habit and action. Any number of particular actions may manifest one and the same habit. For example, kindness can be manifested in encouragement, silence, or criticism. Conversely, several different habits can be responsible for one and the same act. Thus, criticism can exhibit kindness, competitiveness, or cruelty. A particular sort of action is never always and completely determined by a particular habit. This is because of two things: variations in the situation in which the action is performed; and various combinations of habits.

Both habits and actions have objective, knowable properties. The mental states which calculation focuses upon, however, are subjective—states of the individual subject. Because so open to change, as noted above, these states are difficult to estimate in advance; calculating future pleasures and pains verges on the arbitrary. The picture that is produced in dramatic rehearsal is not nearly so subjective or arbitrary because the actions and habits in it have objective *tendencies*.

The tendency of an action is general; actions of "this" sort *generally* have "these" kinds of effects on us. As James puts it, "... It is not simply *particular* lines of discharge, but also *general forms* of discharge, that seem to be grooved out by habit in the brain. ... If we often flinch from making an effort, before we know it the effort-making capacity will be gone ..."[14] When we act this way rather than that, we tend to become one sort of person rather than another: quick to judge rather than deliberate; obdurate rather than reasonable.

Because we are social beings, our actions usually affect others as well as ourselves. Thus, a parent has to be concerned with his child as well as himself in considering an action's tendency. "Spoiling" a child is a set of actions which produce and reinforce complementary habits in both parent and child. The parent is subservient to the child's tyranny. Getting all she wants, the child becomes unappreciative, demanding, and overly dependent. The parent, lacking firmness, habitually feeds the child's unlimited appetites. The point is that these consequences *tend* to be produced by certain sorts of actions and we can learn or imagine beforehand what these tendencies are.

The habits our actions are likely to engender also have general tendencies. The habits of overdependency, unappreciativeness, and demandingness obviously issue in behavior which is rather different from that which typifies a self-reliant, cooperative, generous individual. Habits, then, tend to be realized in certain sorts of actions, depending on the circumstances which call them forth.[15] Charity, which usually means donating time or money, has in fact a wider scope. We are charitable when we impute positive motives to seemingly questionable behavior. It dovetails with generosity: the readiness to give the other person another chance, the benefit of the doubt, or our largesse. Charity and generosity combine to direct our attention away from ourselves, toward others.

A habit's tendencies, like an action's, are general and open-textured; they cover a range of circumstances, will vary with circumstances, and change over time. The full meaning of a habit changes with circumstances and by combining with other habits. "Always our old habits and dispositions carry us into new fields."[16] We must relearn this meaning by observing how well or poorly experience confirms our dramatic rehearsal.

Dramatic rehearsal thereby calls on us to project a scheme of action-habit-action. We imagine which habits are likely to be fostered by a course of action, the actions that a person so habituated is likely to perform, and so on. Ideally, an objective pattern emerges and we build a fuller understanding of how choice helps shape who we are.

We can and perhaps should now ask how the question, "What will this course of action make of me?", pertains to decision-making itself. Many of our actions have implications for what sort of a decision-maker we will be in the future. Some actions will foster habits that are conducive to good, comprehensive dramatic rehearsal; they will develop in us those habits of mind that enable us to project ourselves as an organization of habits and purposes. Action accomplishes this both directly and in roundabout ways.

Discussing our lives with a psychologist should give us practice in self-examination in a straightforward way. It is a direct way to develop the habits involved in noticing the objective tendencies of actions and habits. A less direct way might lie in one's choice of spouse. Suppose that Tom is equally fond of Jane and Sue. Jane is a giving person, has a fairly low self-image, adores Tom, and rarely criticizes him. Tom enjoys her adulation and easy-going nature. Sue, on the other hand, is tough-minded, lets Tom get away with no hypocrisy or self-contradiction; and, while she loves him, does not place his needs above her own.

In considering which woman to wed, Tom should take into account which one's typical ways of interacting with him are likely to encourage in him habits essential to intelligent decision-making. Dramatic rehearsal, therefore, can include considerations of habits which are germane to itself. In dramatic rehearsal we can imaginatively try out actions that will promote " . . . habits which experience has shown to make us sensitive, generous, imaginative, impartial in perceiving the tendency of our inchoate dawning activities."[17] Dramatic rehearsal, therefore, is not only the means by which to reach particular decisions, but is also the method by which we can decide how to become better decision-makers in general.

Marrying Sue rather than Jane would contribute more to Tom as a *future* decision-maker. Interacting with Sue would make Tom more self-reflective, more sensitive to the implications of what he is doing, and more aware of the interests and needs of others. He is more likely, living with Sue, to develop the discrimination and sensitivity needed to assess the success and failure of his dramatic rehearsals.

This reveals how dramatic rehearsal is the opposite of calculation. While the latter fosters all sorts of habits in us, it obscures them from us; our attention is fixed on states of pleasures and pains. And we are led away from thinking about the underlying structure of ourselves.

This is why calculation cannot help us become better at making decisions. Until we begin to examine our habitual ways of acting, we cannot learn the significance of our different choices. That significance often burrows down into our habits, surfacing much later to betray our calculations. Actions change who we are and what will subsequently please us, but the calculative procedure has no way of exposing this to us.

Dramatic rehearsal, on the other hand, has the advantage (in principle) of being self-improving. It can enable us to see how actions will have ramifications for our ability to make subsequent decisions. Living with someone who loves us but criticizes fairly, for instance, will encourage the habits of impartiality, self-scrutiny, and imagination needed to become better at rehearsing options in the imagination. By engaging in dramatic rehearsal, we can see ourselves hindered or helped, by the different options, in our future decision-making. The complete story of *how* dramatic rehearsal includes within itself consideration of how well we make decisions involves the *standard* whereby we judge the dramatic rehearsal.

3. Aesthetic Form As Ideal Standard

We have seen how the method of dramatic rehearsal affords a means for criticizing itself. Within its framework we can ask whether the alternatives under consideration will promote such habits as enable us to make future decisions intelligently. By looking forward to see whether a course of action will better equip us to deal flexibly and with imagination in future decisions, the ability to engage in dramatic rehearsal itself is a criterion for judging the rehearsal we presently perform. Dramatic rehearsal thereby provides a way of evaluating decisions without going "outside" itself. There is, however, a more complete way in which the nature of dramatic rehearsal itself provides a basis for evaluating choices.

Dramatic rehearsal is like a narrative art—a story, play, or film. A line of action imaginatively begins, runs its course, and ends. People react to the envisioned actions, situations are created, events occur. We imagine the people changing, for better or worse. The narrative property of these imaginative rehearsals of action suggests that they be held up against the aesthetic form by which the narrative arts are themselves judged. The form of aesthetic experience can then provide a basis for deciding among the various choices of action. Actions, interests, and habits are the content of our dramatic rehearsals, but aesthetic experience provides the form to test their organization.

This ideal serves as a standard, a way of deciding among various alternative choices. What is a standard? Consider standards for buildings or lectures, two rather different kinds of thing. A building should facilitate entrance and egress; the traffic pattern within should be suited to whatever occupies its occupants; it should be well ventilated and lighted; and durable as a shelter. What of a lecture? A lecture should state its main thoughts clearly; develop their exposition in an orderly way; include examples to concretize the conceptual connections; and perhaps draw to a dramatic conclusion with a bit of humor or anecdote along the way. In both cases, a standard is a set of good, related qualities—qualities in virtue of which we value the building or lecture.

While calculation offers a "measure," it has no standard in the sense just sketched. It has no place for qualitative differences and relationships in outcomes. Of the possible choices, the one which "weighs" most heavily in favor of pleasure and least heavily in pain is the best. It "measures" out to have the greatest net positive weight. Even here, the difficulties of comparison noted in Section 1 reveal the lack of a truly common measure or denominator among pleasures and between pleasures and pains. These difficulties notwithstanding, calculation lacks a standard in the sense of a conception which can be more or less completely satisfied. It lists and tabulates but cannot organize the items being tabulated into a coherent (or jarring) picture. Consequently, there is no structure in the calculation procedure itself; before the action is undertaken there is no way to evaluate the calculation itself as an activity with such qualitative criteria as we found apply to a lecture or building.

The form of dramatic rehearsal, on the other hand, does admit of evaluation. Qualitative criteria apply to it so that it can be well- or ill-formed. By discussing how aesthetic experience provides the ideal which serves as a standard for judging this form, what is meant by a standard should be further clarified.

Let us briefly recall and enlarge upon several central ideas from Chapter 3. In aesthetic experience, the diverse constitutents cooperate to form a whole. Each is enhanced by its relation to others and its location in the whole. This cooperation produces integration; it is, however, deeper and more worthwhile the more numerous and varied the elements. The integration of a few similar components is uninteresting or shallow (the weakness in most popular music). Thus, the ideal in aesthetic form is a high degree of integration but not at the cost of complexity.[18]

Complexity includes the relations among the different elements, as well as their number and variety. Not only, then, should the elements be numerous and varied, but they should connect up in many and varied ways. The meaning, assonance or consonance, rhyme, rhythm, and images of a poem, for example, ideally admit of varied and numerous connections. Since *relations* among components increase integration, the more numerous and varied they are, the more complexity *and* unity are achieved.

The introduction of new elements and their increasingly cooperative relations occurs over time. Over time, a whole tapestry develops from the contributions of the elements in combination with one another. The implications of the parts are drawn out in the growth of the whole as they are transformed and reformed. Thus, the varied elements grow together and out of one another; an integrated whole *develops* over time.

While not, strictly speaking, a formal element, freedom is germane as a quality of the form. The form just outlined arises from the free play of imagination and is experienced as such. Unconstrained by practical demands,[19] the individual feels the form to be, in part, his free invention. Aesthetic experience requires *him* to make imaginative connections, as the form is not handed over ready-made. His freedom is, however, limited by the qualities of the presented material and the aesthetic ideal (of a diversity of elements developing into a whole). The aesthetic ideal of how the material should be formed can be achieved in different ways—think of the multiplicity of interpretations "great" literature or music admits of. This freedom, the invitation to try out different possibilities in forming an aesthetic experience, is sometimes conspicuous by its absence. When a work of art *tells* us what to think or feel rather than evoking our active response, we are coerced. Our imaginative play is cut off as we are channelled into a rut of thought or emotion. When a work deals merely with situation- or character-types, for example, it presents us with plot formulas rather than the life material out of which plot develops. Gothic Romance and television "soap operas" are notorious for their pat situations and cardboard characters.[20]

By whatever means, such art makes us especially *unfree*: our imagination is not given the chance to make connections, draw out hidden possibilities, and enlarge upon the presented material. Achieving the formal qualities outlined above requires this free play of the imagination. This is why freedom is a quality of that form when it is achieved.

How does this ideal of aesthetic form apply to dramatic rehearsal? The ingredients of dramatic rehearsal are actions, habits, and interests (though I tend to emphasize habits because of their permanence and scope). Thus, according to the aesthetic ideal, these ingredients should be diverse and numerous, deeply and variously related to one another, and developed in an integrated way. Finally, we should look to see whether at the conclusion of the rehearsal we seem to be free to respond to whatever further variety and novelty our environment may offer. Let us look at these components of the aesthetic standard one at a time.

The notion of variety and number of elements—actions, interests, and habits—seems straightforward enough; what needs more explanation is the idea of variety and number of *relations* among them. Possible relations would seem to range from mutually antagonistic (the habit of sloppiness and an interest in stamp collecting) through the merely compatible (an interest in stamp collecting and the habit of optimism) to the mutually enhancing (an interest in stamps and an interest in history). The latter promotes integration. The more we are able to integrate diverse habits and interests in a coherent imaginative rehearsal, the more we realize the ideal of aesthetic form. The same holds for the connection among actions themselves.

A contemplated action is likely to be a good choice if we can envision it initiating a connected chain of subsequent actions needed to satisfy interests. Think here of how a block initiates a play in American football (enabling a subsequent chain of run-block-maneuver-run-block) or of how cleaning a wood surface on a house initiates later stages of painting (enabling more effective sanding, priming, painting). We should look for action which facilitates consequent action and further interests directly, but does more than that; the ideal of integration also requires that action help *prepare us* for future action by fostering the right habits.

The "right" habits are those which enable us to respond successfully to varied and numerous situations. The aesthetic ideal puts a premium on habits which equip us for change—in our environment and in our interests. An action that narrows our interests or tends to confine our attention necessarily works against this ideal. To be sure, there may be ways of offsetting or compensating for this, but it must be recognized as the objective tendency of the action. Thus, someone who is already compulsively orderly should see the rigorous neatness demanded by a contemplated field of study as further restricting her. Whereas, such an area of study would complement the habits of someone of great creativity but little discipline.[21]

We have next to consider the dimension of development or growth. On the immediate level, the ideal is approached when action paves the way for further action and pursuing present interest begets new purposes. Continuity and increment signal ongoing development in action and purpose. We look to see whether the contemplated action will issue in growth over the span of time imagined in deliberation. But we should also think of growth in the long run, which recalls the importance of habits for agency. For the criterion of growth also means that the present choice develop in us capacities for further growth in the more remote future. Do the habits bred by the action ramify into new areas, encouraging the development of other beneficial habits? Does the choice bode well for the future cultivation of talents as well as tastes?

An aspect of this was discussed in Section 2.B, when we considered the self-corrective nature of dramatic-rehearsal; it can and should include envisioning habits essential to future good decision-making. Since so much depends on our ability to make good decisions, growth in these particular habits would seem to be a prerequisite for growth in virtually all others.[22] This brings us to the subject of freedom, for without the sort of freedom about to be sketched, there really is no growth.

The freedom of aesthetic experience, it will be remembered, lies in the play of the imagination, unrestricted by practical needs such as food, shelter, or work. Obviously, decision-making is practical, if anything! But the play of imagination is essential to it. It carries over from the aesthetic ideal in two ways. The first is rather obvious, since dramatic rehearsal is itself an imaginative venture. It cannot succeed without a vigorous, pliable imagination, one which can range over possible combinations of action, interests, and habits. Although *ultimately* practical, issuing in action, a dramatic rehearsal must focus on what is not *immediately* pressing. Fantasy should, for example, enter in so as to remind us of what we really want, where our true interests lie. Then imagination can be set to the task of exploring the possibilities for approximating these interests in reality. Imagining unlikely events—such as the death of someone we depend upon—can reveal how vulnerable or reckless we have become. "What if . . . " projections make the apparently nonpractical, far-ranging play of imagination of immense practical value.

Freedom also figures in dramatic rehearsal with regard to choice and action. Freedom of choice and action results from the overall achievement of aesthetic form in dramatic rehearsal; the ongoing integration of numerous, varied interests and habits produces freedom. As freedom is a quality of the form of aesthetic experience, so is it the *condition* of the individual whose deliberations are aesthetically formed. At the conclusion of a well-formed dramatic rehearsal, we should feel free. Why should this be so and what is meant by this freedom?

Let us consider the second question first. The sort of freedom I here have in mind involves the openness and readiness to respond to new situations, an ability to adapt to change in circumstance. This freedom is a flexibility, a freedom *from* the rigidity which *routine,* "grooved" habits enforce.[23] It is the ability to continue to integrate diverse habits and interests. This sort of freedom is the embodiment or summary of those habits of observation and largeness of view discussed in Section 2 as defining good decision-making. But why should a well-formed dramatic rehearsal yield this sense of freedom?

The answer is to be found in how the integration of diverse habits and interests contributes to the form of dramatic rehearsal. Dewey contrasts the development of a chicken's abilities to that of a human's. The chick, which can peck accurately at food shortly after hatching, quickly develops its expertise in behavior because it stems from few original tendencies. Its immediate efficiency, however, is "like a railway ticket, . . . good for one route only." Whereas, "A being who, in order to use his eyes, ears, hands, and legs, has to experiment in making varied combinations of their reactions, achieves a control that is flexible and varied."[24] Coordinating habits and interests that tug in different directions actually gives the individual greater freedom in the future. What Dewey says holds for psychological as well as physical development.

> In learning [or rehearsing] an action, instead of having it given readymade [as the chick's is], one of necessity learns to vary its factors, to make varied combinations of them, according to change of circumstances. A possibility of continuing progress is opened up by the fact that in learning one act, methods are developed good for use in other situations.[25]

We can now see why a well-formed dramatic rehearsal should intimate the freedom to respond to new situations in appropriate, creative ways. Such freedom emerges from the integration of diverse habits and interests. Each of the integrated elements is "freed" to reenter into new relationships with other habits and interests. This appears paradoxical, since the freeing up for recombining is claimed to result from a fitting together. The air of paradox evaporates when the key notion of variety reenters our thinking; variety in habit or interest, *and their relationships,* keep each from becoming cemented into a narrow range of pattern. The habit of observing, for instance, is freed for further tie-ins as a result of combining with different habits and interests in microscope work, pheasant hunting, social gatherings, basketball playing, and aviation. Similarly, a person who must cooperate with radically different kinds of people develops a range of responses which embody many of the same habits in varied combination (like using the same muscles to play a variety of sports). At the same time, the individual is becoming adept at the very process of integrating habits, both in practice and beforehand, in dramatic rehearsal. The latter facilitates the former (the way envisioning the procedures involved in driving an automobile facilitates its successful execution). The habits that are responsible for this imaginative integration are those "master habits" of decision-making. They "engulf" and oversee the other habits, yielding the freedom that lies at the root of all other freedom. For this is the freedom involved in anticipating contingencies, planning for the untoward, and foreseeing opportunities of action.

Improvisation, perhaps more than anything else, combines the two senses of freedom operant in the ideal by which we evaluate dramatic rehearsals: scope of imagination and plasticity of response. Our ability to improvise in the face of the new stems from habits that are recombinable upon the promptings of an imagination that itself is flexible. Such an imagination is able to project lines of action involving subtle and far-reaching connections among interests and habits. It is able to glean their objective tendencies from experience. And by envisioning the choices that best integrate them, it prepares us for what is as yet unforeseen.[26] Our discussion of freedom can appropriately be seen as elaborating the imagination's role in the development and deployment of agency—a central issue in the book's first two chapters. What matters here is the way dramatic rehearsal prepares us for realizing the aesthetic dimensions of agency by aesthetically situating our freedom in an imaginative performance.

Having worked out the way the ideal of aesthetic form applies to dramatic rehearsal in general, we should now get down to some concrete cases. Consider someone who is deciding on a career. Here are the sorts of thing the aesthetic ideal calls into question in such deliberations.

The first option may be working in a business that requires

extensive traveling and meeting new people. This demands that the individual respond quickly to new situations and make efficient use of her time. She must develop habits of quick judgment, decision-making, and action. She must navigate in unfamiliar places and circumstances, interact effectively with new people, and deal with the unforeseen or accidental with equanimity. The travel and interaction would most likely satisfy a variety of interests and provide the opportunities to develop new ones. The habits that would be encouraged are also varied and have clear contributions to make to the individual's world outside of work. They would enhance her poise at social gatherings, make her less provincial, and enable her to acquire new interests or to respond to those of friends.

But a life of travel might be difficult to integrate with the demands of raising a family, belonging to a neighborhood association, or taking part in the political life of the community. Would the task-oriented, quick-paced business life cut against habits of nurturance central in relations with spouse, children, or friends? Would the business habits tend to foster superficial, shallow interaction rather than the development of deep emotional relationships? There is the danger that the enormous self-reliance demanded by the job would harden the individual to the needs and dependencies of others. Applying the ideal of aesthetic form, our dramatic rehearsal should pose these as difficulties or possible shortcomings of the envisaged career. They are not necessarily insurmountable, but dramatic rehearsal reveals them as potential obstacles to attaining the aesthetic ideal.

The individual must take these difficulties into account, therefore, in considering other aspects of her life. If other valuable habits, either present or possible, are negated by those which emerge in the course of the dramatic rehearsal, then compensatory means must be projected whereby the opposition can be overcome. Of course, this hypothetical case has said nothing about what sort of person the individual is now. If she already possesses deep, developing friendships and the habits that go with them, for example, then the picture changes radically. The same holds for the other difficulties posed above.

In the same way, someone considering a career that focuses attention on the self must consider where her self now is. The self-centeredness of such careers as politics, entertainment, and sports is not in and of itself bad, but must be seen in light of the individual's present habits and interests. Someone who has been working "behind the scenes" for many years, say as an advisor, speech writer, or campaign manager, might do well to take to the political stage.

Although the idea should be fairly clear by now, let us consider one more career—college teaching. The opportunity to develop a variety of habits and abilities is certainly there, given the great diversity in activities: reading, preparing lectures, lecturing and leading discussion, research and writing, administrative work, dealing informally with students and colleagues. There is, in addition, considerable flexibility in selection of course material and scheduling of work. There is usually the chance to grow in the area of specialization as well as to branch out into related areas. The demands of performing in the classroom, moreover, are nicely balanced by the solitary nature of scholarship and research.

The challenge is to *integrate* these varied activities and their corresponding habits. Research should contribute to teaching, habits of administration should improve interaction with students, and so on. The ideal of aesthetic form suggests that these habits and interests should also connect with those which grow up outside of work. The relative autonomy of teaching for example, has to be harmonized with the collaborative demands of family and friends. The main problem, however, is that the enormous variety in the work threatens disorder. The aesthetic ideal can guide our considerations so that we not only foresee difficulties but can envision ways of overcoming or avoiding them.

Applying the aesthetic ideal can lead to a *discovery* of possible courses of action by which greater integration, diversity, or growth are achievable. Thus, a teacher (or prospective teacher) might foresee how not knowing statistics, or Greek, or Medieval history could hinder her growth or versatility and take remedial steps *before* frustration occurs in her actual work. Thus, applying the ideal of aesthetic form to dramatic rehearsal not only enables evaluation of competing lines of action, but also suggests how they can be revised.

* * *

So far we have been examining the aesthetic ideal only as it pertains to the individual engaged in the decision-making. But, as dramatic rehearsal often includes the impact of contemplated action on others, so too can the ideal of aesthetic form include the decision-maker in his relationships with other people.[27] In some cases—a team in sports, a family, a business group—the aesthetic ideal would seem to apply rather obviously to the group as a *whole*: The group would seem to be the most natural unit of consideration. Yet, often the alternative actions are assessed solely for their impact on each member *taken separately*. This is especially misguided where the functioning of the members *as a group* is clearly important. Let us consider briefly the smallest possible group—two people. In this case, drawn from a television movie, a young man and an older woman are trying to decide whether to marry.

He *calculates* and argues that their pleasure together, married, will far outweigh the pains of isolation or occasional embarrassment. They love each other; they are kind to each other; each helps the other see the world differently; they enjoy doing things together such as jogging and dancing, listening to music and going to the theatre. His portrayal is convincing and we in the audience think, "Yes, of course, love should triumph over the slings and arrows of foolish conventions." The love they feel and we see appears more than a match for the pale, distant stupidities of society; there is even the added satisfaction of bucking convention and being true to one's passion.

But the (older, wiser) woman protests. Instead of countering with a different calculation of the costs and benefits, she offers a *rehearsal* of their lives together as a married couple. She asks who they will go out with; his friends seem childish to her, hers "dated" to him. Her friends' interests are not his, his not hers. Each would be out of place in a gathering of the other's peers. Aside from the obvious, direct loss of social life, their relationship will lack the freshness and stimulation social life brings. Their marriage will not be able to grow or their interests expand through the natural channels provided by intercourse with people outside of their immediate relationship.

The two are at different places in life, with different needs, at different stages of growth. "You're ready to pick up and move at a moment's notice," she observes, "but I don't share your wanderlust." What will her role be in his exploring and testing of himself? She has raised a family and does not wish another. What if he decides he wants children? In short, their social isolation as a couple echoes the difficulties they would face in trying to mesh their lives as a husband and wife. They do not have some overarching cause or vocation (a political or religious calling, for example) to unite their energies or give them a social subculture. Even if her rehearsal does not capture or allow for all the ways they could try to make a go of marriage, it does point to likely discontinuities and constrictions which must be faced. The ideal of aesthetic form reveals a likely lack of variety and number in their interests and habits as a couple. Integration of them in varied relations does not appear in the offing; growth seems stymied, freedom jeopardized. The tensions presented by marriage under the best of conditions would appear to be exacerbated, the couple hemmed in by circumstance.

* * *

Calculation misleads us because it is really considering possible choices in the abstract: abstracting the rewards and drawbacks of actions from the everyday patterns of action, interest, and habit. Dramatic rehearsal, on the other hand, situates the individual or individuals in a lived context. There, we can hold our deliberations up against the form of aesthetic experience and evaluate the imagined living as if it were a work of narrative art. Where it falls short of the ideal form we are naturally led to try out ways of restructuring it so as to approximate that form. Where our dramatic rehearsal does approach it, we have a conception of how and why our decision is a promising one. Upon subsequently acting on it, we can assess it and say why and where it was adequate or inadequate to the circumstances in which we acted.

To the extent that our lives are envisioned as works of narrative art, we imagine them taking shape, if not with beginnings, middles, and endings, then at least with temporal stages marking shifts of interest and manner of living. We see our decisions precipitating continuities and discontinuities in and between the phases of our lives. Such dramatic rehearsal of the whole of life, or rather life-as-a-whole, requires attention to the place of death in both actual life and the way we imaginatively rehearse it. To the place of death in the time of our lives, then, we now turn.

Chapter Seven
Death and the Time of Our Lives

J UST AS THE IDEAL of aesthetic completeness gives direction and form to our particular deliberations, so can death give contour to the perspective we take toward our entire lives. The prospect of finally coming to an end lends shape and meaning to our everyday pursuits, but it may be better instead to say *can* make these undertakings meaningful, for many of us see in death a black event and consequently dread it. The result is that we really avoid considering its positive significance and so miss the chance to grasp its aesthetic role in how we see and do our living. As mistaken and fruitless as this attitude toward death is, it is still understandable. Getting straight on what lies behind this plausible mistake will clear the way for us to examine what it means to accept death as "mine".

Confronting death as "mine" personalizes our lived time, making all that we experience truly our own. When we appreciate death in this subjective way, not just as something that befalls "anyone," the temporal nature of all experience is especially brought home. In particular, the meanings of local endings within life are vivified, with the result that the episodes they culminate are made definite and intense. Individual moments, such as this outing or that conversation are then more fully structured because located within the boundaries endings draw.

Accepting, perhaps even appreciating, death as "mine" plays two complementary aesthetic functions in how we view and consequently live life. By providing a temporal limit, death enables life as an entirety to have the form necessary for it to be articulated and lived as an aesthetic whole. Seeing our lives as a process developing toward closure, we can appreciate its directionality—it is not felt to be simply a collection of unconnected events. Viewing ourselves as developing over time, passing through stages of life, moreover, enables us to *act* so as to unify our lives aesthetically. In this way death enters into the overarching dramatic rehearsal of our life-as-a-whole so that we may live it as a whole.

Complementing this "big picture" of life is the way we notice each passing moment. Accepting death can help us live *in* the moment: paying attention to whatever happens to be going on in and about us: as Henry James once put it, being one of those people "on whom nothing is lost." The subjective acknowledgment of death can detach us from distractions which easily clog or interrupt attention to and in the *present*. We are living in the moment only when we pay close attention to the details of present experience, which can include the passing of time itself.

Here I argue (with the support of William James and Henri Bergson) that we experience the passing of time, the flow of consciousness, as an aesthetically unified process. This parallels the continuity for which dramatic rehearsal tests the consequences of action plans; events imagined as jibing or jarring, interests and habits envisioned as enhancing or frustrating one another. In this way, dramatic rehearsal takes its cue from the unity of time directly experienced. The immediate quality of the time of our lives, therefore, both empirically vindicates and is an essential ingredient for an aesthetic perspective on the whole of our lifetime.

1. Epicurus' Catch

There is nothing odd in the fact that we often account another's death our loss, and therefore a bad thing for us. But we also believe such a person's death to be a bad thing for him, as when we say things like "What a shame, he had so much to live for, poor Harry." The belief that death is a bad or an "evil" for the one who dies is revealed in our typical reactions to the thought of our own death: We are often frightened, anxious, saddened, or depressed by such considerations. To discover whether such reactions or attitudes towards our own death are "rational," we must first try to figure out in what way our own death is a bad thing for us. For it seems that, if death is not a bad thing, then we are irrational in dreading it.

In what follows I presuppose that "death" means the terminus of our existence, our identity: that there is no life after death. Aside from avoiding the insurmountable difficulties which arise in trying to decide whether there is life after death, if we presuppose that there is not this has the virtue of retaining the import of our ordinary use of the term, "death." If we wish to claim that there *is* a life after death, then we must be prepared to give an extended sense of "death" such that it is not a real "end" of life, but a modification of it.

Death is the termination of life, and life is a necessary condition for all sorts of good things. Without life, no other good is possible; therefore, death is the loss of the "ground" or condition for all that we value. It would seem, then, that death is bad for those of us who die. But, at the time of the "loss," "we" no longer exist. As Epicurus puts the matter: "Death, the most dreaded of evils, is therefore of no concern for us; for while we exist death is not present, and when death is present we no longer exist."[1] The problem may be put in this way: we ordinarily think that our death is a bad thing for us, but how can it be if we do not exist when we are dead? Since death is the ceasing of our identity, there does not seem to be a subject, a "who," for which the death is an evil.

I call this "Epicurus' Catch."[2] What we heedlessly take for granted as real is exposed as impossible because our lives are temporal. Everyday thinking and speaking foster the illusion that death is really an experiencable event. This illusion evaporates once the thrust of Epicurus' Catch is appreciated, since the individual and his death cannot coexist in time.

We ordinarily think that death is an event with dreadful possibilities —a potential danger for the one who dies. It *appears* as though our death "happens" to us in a sense analogous to the way in which an illness or accident happens to us. Epicurus' Catch reveals the falsity in such an appearance. The danger associated with death is illusory because by its very nature death cannot be cotemporaneous with our existence. One cannot be dead and continue *to be*. To clean up our language, it might be less misleading to say: "Harry has ceased to exist," or "Harry is no more," rather than "Harry is dead." The latter sounds as though Harry is going through something, as though the person called "Harry" is somehow still available to experience events in the world (of which his death is one).

Epicurus employs his Catch in an argument designed to show that no one ought to fear his own death:

        (1) One ought to fear only those things which can be evils for him.

        (2) Unless one exists, nothing can be an evil for him.

        (3) When dead, one does not exist.

Therefore (4) when dead, nothing is an evil for one.

Therefore (5) one ought not now fear that which [—death—] can never be an evil for him.[3]

Epicurus' Catch (premise 3 above) yields two related conclusions:

Death is not a bad thing for the one who dies; and; Therefore, we ought not fear our own death. The "ought" refers to "rationality," meaning that it is rational to fear only things which are in some way bad for us. There must be some grounds for believing that this or that will be bad for us, otherwise, fearing it is irrational—without rational basis. Epicurus' Catch reveals why there cannot logically be any such grounds with regard to one's own death.

It is frequently asserted that death is bad because we get upset thinking about it—thinking about our nonexistence and loss of life. But this is to miss the full force of the Catch. Once we understand that we do not exist cotemporaneously with "our" death, then we see that the death really involves no such loss and that our nonexistence cannot be a genuine concern for us. Thus, as Epicurus himself insists, unless the death itself be bad, the thought of it cannot be a rational ground for anxiety. "So, too, he is foolish who says that he fears death, not because it will be painful when it comes [more generally, "bad" or "evil"], but because the anticipation of it is painful; for that which is no burden when it is present give pain to no purpose [is not rational] when it is anticipated."[4] What seems to be a reason for being upset is really no reason at all: We are caught by the Catch.

It was said earlier that death marks the end of the condition necessary for all good things—life. Perhaps, then, death is bad for us by *depriving* us of this necessary condition for all good things. We are deprived of time and all that can take place in it when we "lose" our lives. But this clearly will not do either. To be deprived of or lose something, we must exist. We cannot be deprived of something unless we are "there" to be deprived.

But when the "loss" (death) occurs, we are not "there" to be the losers. The loss is the world's, not ours. We have dropped out of the world. When we are dead, we can be deprived of nothing; yet until dead, we are deprived of neither life nor time. Thinking that death is bad because it deprives us of something, therefore, also founders on Epicurus' Catch. When we exist we cannot be deprived by death (since it has not yet occurred), and when the depriving event occurs, "we" no longer exist.[5] Once again, the fact that the individual and his death cannot be cotemporaneous is decisive.

2. Death As "Mine"

Let us agree with Epicurus that death cannot be a bad thing for the one who dies, since it is not an event in his life. Therefore, no one ought to fear his own death. But what sort of attitude *should* a person take toward his death? It is still important, even if not to be feared. Here, Epicurus is instructive by what he *does:* He *thinks* about death. He thinks about it in terms of value—it is not an evil for the self, and in terms of emotional response—we ought not fear our own death. This suggests that one constructive attitude toward death is the reflective-evaluative one: thinking about it in evaluative, qualitative terms. Epicurus leaves us, however, only with the negative conclusion, not to fear death. In what follows, I suggest a more positive way of evaluatively thinking about one's own demise.

The first aspect of taking up one's own death in a positive or constructive way is accepting it as one's own. This is very difficult so long as people fear death. Fear leads naturally to various avoidance and denial strategies by which we try to keep away the thought of life's ending. One specific strategy is thinking of death in "anonymous" terms, as something that befalls others or man in general, but not "me."

> The syllogism he had learnt from Kiezewetter's Logic: "Caius is a man, men are mortal, thereore Caius is mortal," had always seemed to him correct as applied to Caius, but certainly not as applied to himself. That Caius—man in the abstract—was mortal, was perfectly correct, but he was not Caius, not an abstract man, . . . I and all my friends felt that our case was quite different from that of Caius.[6]

In the phrase "One will die," "one" is no one (in particular) or else the anonymous one. Heidegger makes much of the fact that each person's death is his own, something that no one else can do for him.[7] Viewing one's death as personal makes all the difference between being true to one's human condition and masking it from oneself. Tolstoy and Heidegger both, then, see the importance of facing one's death in a personal, subjective way—not as something that befalls just any (anonymous) one.

Now there is one fairly obvious weakness in what Heidegger says, and Sartre's criticism is worth noting both for what it clearly sees and for what it misses. Sartre points out that death is not so special. The subjective attitude can and should be taken toward many things, such as seeing this tree or writing this letter or loving this person. It is *my* seeing, *my* writing, *my* loving, and no one else can do them for me either; just so, no one else can die in my place. Sartre is correct in that the personalizing or subjective attitude can be taken toward many things in our lives. Death is not unique in this way. "In short, there is no personalizing virtue which is peculiar to *my* death."[8]

But Sartre overlooks something that *is* crucial in death as "mine." *The Death of Ivan Ilych* shows that it is harder to avoid the personalizing view of one's own death, when imminent, than it is to avoid personalizing our own seeing, writing, or loving. Once indisputably upon us, death has an insistent quality. Try as we might, its personal connection with our own particular life cannot be concealed. Now this inescapable quality of our death as "mine" is especially peculiar because *accepting* death as one's *own* is very hard to do. It is much easier to accept this failure or that flaw as mine. Part of this difficulty stems from the fact that we cannot really imagine the world going on without us. We literally have no *image* of ourselves "out of it." We persist in thinking of ourselves as spectators, even of our own deathbed or funeral scenes.[9]

There is a tremendous tension, therefore, between the difficulty of personalizing one's own death and the unavoidability of doing so. When the difficult is unavoidable, a great deal of psychic energy is spent in denying it. I suggest that when the individual finally does personalize his death, taking the subjective attitude toward it, that attitude is *revelatory*. It reveals what Sartre rightly points out, that many (all?) things in our lives *can* be apprehended from the subjective point of view—as our own, not just "anyone's." Psychic energy which had been committed to denying death as personal is freed for the appreciation of everyday experience as personal. But Sartre misses the special role death can play in personalizing the rest of our experience.

It is a catalyst, awaking the individual to the importance of his first-hand experience. His experiences and values are his own—to do what he will with them. Rather than accepting the interpretations others place on his actions, he is opened to giving credence to his own understandings and valuations. Once acknowledging death as his own, his life appears as his own: these are his choices, his desires, his undertakings. In *The Second Coming*, Walker Percy remarks the power of death in snapping us out of fog-bound, fuzzy existence: "Not once had he been present for his life. So his life had passed like a dream. Is it possible for people to miss their lives in the same way one misses a plane? And how is it that death, the nearness of death, can restore a missed life? Why is it that without death one misses his life?"[10] Confronting death personally encourages us to confront living personally, as something about which the individual has something to say and can determine the course. Where Tolstoy treats this as a moral confrontation,[11] I shall pursue it aesthetically. I shall examine how acknowledging death as "mine" is a spur to appreciating everyday features of life in an aesthetically fruitful way.

* * *

When we confront death as "mine" we see ourselves as limited in time. The fact that life ceases indicates life's structure as temporal, in process. We move, act, think, plan, feel in time; most important, we change over time. By seeing ourselves as temporal we grasp a fundamental aesthetic aspect of our lives, because everything about us is conditioned by time. So whatever aesthetic appreciation there is to be had from our lives, it must include the simple fact of temporality, and our time is limited. Our lives are made up of beginnings, transitions, growths, degenerations, and different kinds of endings.

When we confront death as "mine," we accept the irrevocability of endings in everyday life. Perhaps the effect can be greater than mere acceptance, perhaps awareness of the ending of life itself can vivify and intensify all sorts of commonplace endings within it. We are more honest about the fact that this visit or relationship or period in our lives really will come to an end. Instead of something to be ignored or denied, the ending of good times can be appreciated as a culmination or rounding off of the preceding episode. With the ending foreshadowed in them, these experiences then take on a clarified form: The anticipated bask in the sun on hot sand makes the chill of the lake swim invigorating rather than numbing; and a child's interests and talents suggest myriads of future possibilities for him, possibilities which define the end of childhood. Consciousness of endings renews our appreciation for the inherent aesthetic qualities of experience. Events in our lives come to be seen as temporally extended, punctuated by change, heading toward completion. The changes take on meaning because of the direction "endings" provide; reminders and harbingers of *ordinary* living, for instance, give meaning to our holiday's freedom and adventure. The necessity of our own ending enlivens us, then, to the significance of the small, local endings in our lives. With this, the question of completeness is raised.

There is a great difference between mere cessation and culmination.[12] As we saw in Chapter III, an activity or event can be interrupted or "peter out" without reaching a real conclusion. Both sorts of cessation are unsatisfactory; the first because development is broken, the latter because tension and interest is lost. The limitedness of our time can make us sensitive to the precariousness of all of our enterprises. Death as "mine" can add value, piquancy to what an individual manages to accomplish. As mortally limited, projects take on an urgency. The successful completion of a project or course of action is especially valued when death is felt to threaten interruption at any time, heightened by the drama of working in the face of death, perhaps in a *race* with death.[13] The individual does not take his time for granted. This appears rather starkly when acceptance of death as "mine" is contrasted with belief in immortality.

Belief in an endless future (irrespective of any ultimate judgment, reward, or punishment) is another way of denying death. But if we really believed that death were a door, not a wall, then our view of life would alter dramatically. Our lives would lose intensity if death seemed to offer a variation within time rather than its end. Since we would (supposedly) have an endless stream of time in which to act, particular actions and moments would lose weight. I conjecture that a quality of airiness would permeate our experience. No one moment or event would have more importance or solidity than another; they would level out in endless clouds of possibilities.

Accepting death as "mine," on the other hand, sets a boundary to our time. Within its bounds, particular moments are given relative weight and place, and time is understood as opportunity for action and experience. Thus do we identify past and future times with a trip to the shore, the birth of a child, planting or harvesting a crop, and so on. Acceptance of death frames our time so that we fill it with activities and experiences in places, locating ourselves solidly in space because our time is limited. Thinking ourselves immortal, however, conveys a sense of pure space.[14] It is empty, devoid of boundaries or signposts by which to mark our lives. It would seem to lack differentiation, since lacking the tension that threat of death lends to particular moments.

Recognizing death as an irrevocable boundary to our existence includes seeing our power as fundamentally limited. The necessity of death is just the ultimate constraint on what we can and cannot do. So many other things must escape our control; our aging, forces of nature, much of the action and thought of others necessarily lie outside our control. In acknowledging the fundamental limits of our power, however, we implicitly recognize what is within our control. Because limited, what power we do have is that much more valuable.

Choice has a place in our thinking in a way which it could not were we immortal (or thought we were). We take care and deliberate concerning what is in our control precisely because we are finite in time. Choice and action assume an intensity because we do not think that we have "all the time in the world" in which to act. We define ourselves by projecting ourselves toward one future possibility rather than another.[15] But, if we thought ourselves immortal would *any* possibilities be really ruled out? We would have as much time as needed in which to project ourselves again and again into the future. Each time toward a different goal—without limit, without end.

Awareness of what is and what is not within our power is a dimension of self-consciousness. Acceptance of death as "mine" is necessarily consciousness of self as limited. If there were no thought or belief in death, would people *be* self-conscious? Could there be consciousness of self as existing without thought of extinction? I am not sure, but it strikes me as plausible that acceptance of death invites examination of life as a self-consciously chosen whole in a way that seems unlikely without it. Death brings home to us the idea of a *span* of life that is ours to decide. Aware that our powers are limited, giving different weight to different experiences, we are in a position to take up the expanse of our lives self-consciously. Consciousness of self developing in time through actions that are within one's power is the basis for an aesthetic appreciation of one's life as a whole. Acceptance of death as "mine" makes a self-conscious aesthetic perspective on one's own life possible. Without it, our lives would be without the form that awareness of finitude affords.

3. Life As an Aesthetic Whole

The question now is how death specifically provides the kind of limit which makes it possible for life to form an aesthetic whole. To be an aesthetic whole, life requires form and form requires limit. But how exactly does the prospect of death limit in an informing way?

When we think of our lives as a temporal span, we naturally think of goals or projects with which we occupy our time. Through goals, we project ourselves over a period of time, hoping to raise a family, build a business, write a book, change public policy. Death gives us a limited amount of time in which to fulfill our ambitions, but we are unsure of how much time we have since we do not know when we will die. It is what Kierkegaard called the "uncertain certainty." "There is therefore a very slim chance that our death will be presented to us as that of Sophocles was, for example, in the manner of a resolved chord."[16]

Sartre remarks on the chancy nature of our death. We might either outlive the accomplishment of our projects or be interrupted in working toward them. A life that ends like a "resolved chord" therefore is the aesthetic mid-ground between one that is no longer purposeful, prolonged past its consummation and another which is cut short, unfinished. In the former, the "notes" continue past resolution; in the latter, development is truncated before resolution. There is obviously very little chance of death *coinciding* with the "right moment" in our lives; therefore, it would seem highly improbable for anyone's life to form an aesthetic whole since so much seems to depend on the exact moment of closure.

According to Sartre, it is even more difficult than this suggests. The individual must be in *control* of the "resolution" of his life's work in order for his life time to have real aesthetic unity. Otherwise, there is merely the *appearance* of an aesthetic culmination.

> A death like that of Sophocles will therefore *resemble* a resolved chord but will not *be* one, just as the group of letters formed by the falling of alphabet blocks will perhaps resemble a word but will not be one.[17]

What Sartre asserts as a conclusion, however, I propose we take up as a question. Sartre claims that man's life simply cannot be aesthetically formed because completion, so essential to aesthetic unity, is left to the chanciness of death. I suggest, rather, that the chanciness of death poses a question: How can the individual *live* so that the everpresent *chance* of death does *not* preclude the possibility of aesthetic wholeness?

I see some hope of a positive answer to this question because Sartre overlooks much by his narrow emphasis. He puts too much emphasis on "accomplishing purposes" as central to an aesthetically complete life; his thinking is too task-oriented. There is both more and less to aesthetic wholeness and completion than finishing life's projects. However, even within this way of thinking of aesthetic form there is an obvious solution to half the dilemma—the one in which the individual might "outlive" the completion of his life's projects.

Suicide puts control of one's death squarely in one's hands. If the individual has completed his life's work, then by killing himself he not only avoids "hanging on" past its resolution, but he also times death to coincide with its completion. (As an example of a "professional" kind of suicide *within a sphere* of life, consider the athlete who retires before his talents have eroded, thereby authoring his athletic death at an aesthetically opportune moment.) Suicide (either literal and total or "professional' and partial) would seem to take us beneath the "mere appearance" of life as a resolved chord since such resolution is self-determined. More important for us, however, is what the availability of suicide reveals about the possibility of aesthetic form in life.

The moment of contemplated suicide provides us with a *perspective* on our past and future which we can try to maintain whether or not we actually entertain the idea of suicide. The thought of suicide is important because it reveals the prospect of our death as a "pivot"; it impels us to glance back over our past and into future possibilities. The present becomes an occasion for gathering the past toward a particular future. The question of suicide always brings with it death's temporal perspective; however, death can provide such a perspective on the time of our lives independent of considerations of suicide. As awaiting us in an indeterminate future, the prospect of death provides us with a way of looking at the expanse of life, as though on a mountain looking down on plains, hills, valleys, and streams.

The chanciness of death does not foreclose on the possibility of seeing and living life with aesthetic form and wholeness. We can assume the "elevated" perspective on our lives which the prospect of death provides and the idea of suicide strengthens. We can view our lives historically and live our lives as though making history. As a consequence, our lives can take shape so as to be in the *process* of forming a whole. If a life has direction, then whenever it is "cut short" it will possess aesthetic form. It will not be the form of a chord resolved once and for all, this is true. Rather, it will have the form of *developing* toward closure. The concluding resolution will be prefigured *in* the life's shape, the way a plot's dénouement is foreshadowed in its unfolding. This is the sense of aesthetic form and wholeness that a tree possesses even before it is fully matured.

Consider two people, both of whom die before their life's projects are completed—"resolved," in Sartre's sense. The first is merely frustrated. She had given little thought to death; it affected neither the way she thought about living nor the way she lived. The second, however, had purposefully chosen options so as to integrate her activities; each "grew out of" the last. With the prospect of death before her as a temporal limit, she saw the potential for aesthetic unity in her life. Consequently, she organized her energies into *little* "chords" with small resolutions which built upon one another, forming completed episodes that nevertheless connected with one another. The second individual's life had the form of developing-toward-resolution. It had this form, moveover, *because* she aesthetically viewed her life's time as bounded by death. Alisdair MacIntyre suggests that seeing our lives as gathering toward a climax may be a primary psychological need, debilitating when not met.

> When someone complains . . . that his or her life is meaningless, he or she is often and perhaps characteristically complaining that the narrative of their life has become unintelligible to them, that it lacks any point, any movement toward a climax or a telos.[18]

Such a person's unhappiness is self-conscious, unlike the unhappiness of the individual who does not recognize the lack of unity and directionality as the basis for her malaise.

It is important here to distinguish between two related things: an aesthetically formed life, and the individual viewing her life *as* aesthically formed. Each is possible without the other. After all, the tree alluded to a moment ago is not conscious of its life as developing in a particular way. And, conversely, it is possible simply to *see* one's life as aesthetically unified without making self-conscious choices to bring this about; for example, on one's deathbed to see retrospectively an aesthetic pattern to one's previous time. But there is also a causal relationship between viewing and living life. Viewing life as a temporally developing expanse, limited and defined by death, *enables* the individual to act self-consciously so as to form her life aesthetically: The image can prepare for the reality.

The idea is that by seeing one's past and future as forming an aesthetic whole, one is actually able to inform one's living and unify more of life's activities. Because an individual sees his life with a temporal beginning, middle, and end, various episodes may be better appreciated and related to one another. Losses, for example, are put in the larger perspective of what is yet to come . . . and go. What is a very minor "discord" (because of its relative bearing in one's whole life) is in fact grasped as such. A person who lives with his whole life in mind is not disproportionately bothered by what is indeed petty.

More important, such a person *locates* the petty and grand, irritating and awesome, *in* the pattern of a life's time. This is not just intellectual: It is *seeing* something as small or large. Locating significances enables us to enter into rhythms which give contour and definition to life. We prepare well for an important undertaking; take stock after a great disappointment; take big risks for things that open up new and great possibilities. Friendships, for example, develop rhythmically when allowed their own rate of growth. Tentative overtures produce exploration of interests, mutual discoveries and revelations. Even in their full flowering, friendships go through systole and diastole as periods of intense companionship give way to more relaxed communication and the comfort of familiarity is accented by strong feelings and needs.

Perspective on the whole of life, then, helps us give aesthetic shape to it, enabling us to integrate interests and develop in a unified way from one phase to the next. Assuming such a perspective is a bit like looking down on our lives from on high, through God's eye: "One result, possibly, of longevity was divine entertainment. You could appreciate God's entertainment from the formation of patterns which needed time for their proper development."[19] Central in Bellow's (Sammler's) reflection is the idea of *appreciation*, that one's own life be the object of appreciative appraisal as it develops its own distinctive pattern. But here we must not ignore the obvious, for such patterns, however distinctive, develop within the universal form the actual stages or ages of life impose. Like Sammler, we may simply look back on the stages of life once we become elderly, and retrospectively see our lives as an aesthetic whole—a story, as it were. This is fine, but it bestows aesthetic form on life *only* in the imagination. However, by projecting ourselves through life's phases, *before* we actually go through them all, our imaginative synopsis can serve as a dramatic rehearsal which fosters really *living* a life possessed of aesthetic continuity.

Our expectations, plans, and choices should take shape in light of this projected process called aging. If we view our lives as a temporal whole, then we realize that "age" is not simply a' state defined by so much elapsed time, but rather is the result of past living in reference to possible futures. We understand ourselves in a stage of development, essentially connected to preceding and succeeding stages. Unfortunately, this is not easy to effect. The compartmentalization and fragmentation noted in the last chapter also make it difficult to view and live our lives as a developing whole. MacIntyre observes, for example, how ". . . both childhood and old age have been wrenched away from the rest of human life and made over into distinct realms."[20] Each is isolated from the productive life of the community, discontinuous with the middle, adult portion of one's life. Thus we seem to have to leap from childhood into adulthood, only to *stumble* into old age, as if into ignominy. Perhaps this explains the prevailing American reluctance to age at all, at least past the so-called "peak" productive years. Ideally, we grow through our life's stages, looking forward to the virtues and joys proper to each.[21] We do not pine for the irretrievable (and suffer the affliction of nostalgia) nor despair at the inevitable (and suffer premature enervation); consequently, we live so as to give meaning to whatever stage we are in. In this way, each age can build upon what has preceded while laying the groundwork for what is to come. A composer who understands the virtues of and relations among the different movements of a symphony is better able to form them into a whole than one who does not.

Not only does consciousness of ourselves as developing in time enable us to act so as to unify our lives aesthetically, but self-consciousness is itself an aspect of completeness. Unlike trees and other organisms whose growth may possess aesthetic form by developing over time, humans also have an interior dimension. Since consciousness is a basic feature of human life, it plays a part in the wholeness of that life. Self-consciousness is another aspect of wholeness that can be achieved regardless of the chanciness of death. One can be fully conscious of oneself unfolding in time *as* one proceeds with projects and purposes; their interruption by death does not lessen the degree of completeness the self-consciousness has contributed.

Aesthetic wholeness includes the dimension of depth. (Thus do we speak of Shakespeare's *Hamlet* as having more depth than Victorian farce.) Self-consciousness lends depth to life's aesthetic. Paying full attention to whatever is seen, felt, thought, or desired deepens experience. This is what may be called "living in the moment."

4. Living in the Moment

Learning that death is imminent is a momentous event, one which could, maybe *should*, make precious every moment left. So why is it that for so many of us the news is devastating? It seems more than the matter of fear with which we began our discussion of death; it seems to involve *how* we learn this "inevitable" news. In our society at least, most of us are told by a stranger—an anonymous physician. It comes as an authoritative pronouncement, as if we were being sentenced by a judge, and suddenly all our options feel closed off. With the definiteness of a guillotine, we *already* feel beheaded. "When I was told that I was going to die in five months I thought that was the same as telling me that I was going to die that afternoon."[22] We feel powerless, out of control, forgetting (perhaps forever) that there is time left and we *do* have control over how it is spent.

This sense of "being dead" when we are told that our time is up is compounded by physicians and nurses confirming that we are going through a predictable "dying stage":

> All those people who say ... that you will die in the same way that everyone else dies, they are right. ... I resented them saying ... "You're at the angry stage. I understand that. You're depressed. You're lost."[23]

The fact that we follow known patterns, and are reminded of it, seems to deprive us of the dignity that individualized emotion and experience can confer. We are not only already terminated, but our responses are fixed and we can only play out a preordained script.

Yet, the total impact of such verdicts and sentences depends, finally, on the individual and the aesthetic interpretation he gives his life as a result. He *can* feel liberated by his condemnation, free to "shuffle off this mortal coil" in his own way, to the tune he chooses.

> I realized in fact that I felt really good for the first time in my life. Not just a flash of good feeling ..., but a sustained feeling that I had nothing, and having nothing I had nothing to lose, and having nothing to lose I could be anything.[24]

For Ted Rosenthal, the "death sentence" ironically freed him to live in the moment, to see what is—now: a friend's gait; the feel of wind; the smell of fresh sheets; even his own breathing. "And it isn't until you discover that you're going to die that you realize that whatever it is you have, you've already got it. Right there. And it makes that moment an eternity."[25]

The moment stretches out because we attend closely to whatever is going on in or around us, the closeness of death producing a rebirth of awareness. Martha Lear explains how the moment opened up for her as she shares life with her dying husband:

> Now we have all these limits [brought by failing health] and it's as though the sensations have been distilled. It's extract of pleasure. There is more pure sensation in walking ten minutes together on a nice day than there ever was in a ski week.[26]

The habit of attending completely to whatever is experienced is cultivated in Zen meditation.[27] Beginning in quiet sitting, the individual practices "living in the moment," so to speak, so that it eventually becomes his everyday mode of awareness, whether walking or working, talking or playing. Zen tries to accomplish in a tranquil way what belief in the imminence of death jolts us into. The suggestion I offer here is that *anticipating* death imaginatively can also foster this sort of aesthetic attention to the present.

When we really accept death as "mine," we run ahead imaginatively to that time when it *will* be impending. This helps detach us from concerns which clog our attention, concerns which keep us living in the past or future but not in the present. The urgency and "weight" discussed earlier can translate into living "in" the present moment: "Experiencing the present is being emptied and hollowed . . .",[28] not drifting off into what has happened before or may happen in the future.

This would seem less likely were we convinced of our immortality. ". . . A man expecting and believing in eternity will be less concerned with his temporal experiences, will see them in less depth."[29] It is as if the prospect of death is a wall, stopping the flow of water. Contained or retained, the water is under pressure. So can death pressurize our awareness, intensifying it. Without its pressure, our awareness is likely to become flabby: "If death is a wall and not a doorway, . . . every detail of change [in experience] is noted and treasured."[30]

Living *in* the moment is not the same as living *for* the moment. In living for the moment, we cling to the objects of pleasure and look desperately to satisfy our ever-increasing appetites. We live for the moment when we heedlessly abandon ourselves to immediate gratification. It is a natural response to *fearing* death. When we fear death, we panic: Each day could be our last, so we calculate how much we can get out of it. Fear of death promotes a sense of personal constriction. Feeling as though the world is closing in on us, we grab for whatever enjoyments are within reach.[31] When everything is viewed in terms of personal gratification, little is noticed about anything; we are too preoccupied with ourselves.

There is a great difference, therefore, between living for the moment and living in the moment. When living in the moment, there is no desperate grabbing, but a relaxed appreciation for whatever is happening in the present: the sound of the wind, dust motes in the air, the movement of our own breathing. Acknowledging and embracing death as "mine," moreover, facilitates attention to the content of our experience, what is going on in the environment, rather than our own fears and longings. Speaking again of how he felt after "adjusting" to the nearness of his own death, Ted Rosenthal writes: "Because I had nothing, because I had no needs of my own, I wasn't self-preoccupied. ..."[32] Ceasing to worry about ourselves, our attention is freed from the personal attachments which cloud and confuse everyday awareness. Iris Murdoch offers the following explanation of how the acceptance of death works this change: "The acceptance of death is an acceptance of our own nothingness which is an automatic spur to our concern with what is not ourselves."[33] The loss of egocentricity, then, naturally frees attention to take in, clearly and calmly, whatever is going on.

When we live in the moment, the mind is not rushing to see whether or not still more satisfaction could be had later; it is occupied in and with the ongoing experience, filled with the details of the present. They receive our full attention. Then might we notice, as James Agee does, how much is really "there" to be seen or heard in the most commonplace of daily occurrences:

The noise of the locust is dry, and it seems not to be rasped or vibrated but urged from him as if through a small orifice by a breath that can never give out. Also there is never one locust but an illusion of at least a thousand. The noise of each locust is pitched in some classic locust range out of which none of them varies more than two full tones: and yet you seem to hear each locust discrete from all the rest, and there is a long, slow, pulse in their noise, like the scarcely defined arch of a long and high set bridge. They are all around in every tree, so that the noise seems to come from nowhere and everywhere at once.[34]

As they come and go, ebb and flow, the mind's contents are simply noticed—neither clung to nor thrust away. This living in the present moment begets a sense of timelessness. Each moment is "full," a "lifetime" in itself.

Now the idea that a sense of death can free us for timeless absorption in the *moment* certainly seems opposed to the aesthetic function of death as giving structure to the entire *span* of our lives. Timeless attention to present experience appears to be incompatible with awareness of experience temporally unfolding over the course of a life's time. Yet the sense of death as potentially imminent is supposed to reorient us in both ways: toward the immediate present and toward life conceived as an ongoing story. The "easy way out" of this apparent inconsistency is to separate these two functions temporally in our thinking. At one time, we are to think of death as delineating the whole of life, serving a "macro"-function. At another, it is supposed to zero our attention in at the moment, performing a "micro"-function. So long as it determines our attention at *different* times, there is no inconsistency between its two roles. But I would rather look for a more complete, inclusive way of overcoming the opposition between death as structuring the whole of our life's time and death as riveting attention in the moment.[35]

Each can actually be present in or encompass the other. Recall that living in the moment means attending fully to *what*ever is in one's mind, *what*ever is being experienced. No particular content is specified or ruled out. This includes thoughts, thoughts about anything, including thoughts about "my life as a developing whole." Living in the moment simply means paying careful attention to what is going on when such thinking takes place. Thus, the content of the moment in which the individual is "living" *can* very well be "thinking about his life as a temporally limited, developing whole." Indeed, this would be the *best* way to do such thinking, since full attention means full appreciation of aesthetic nuance. In this way, the "whole span" perspective furnished by death can fall *within* "living in the moment."

Conversely, within the "whole span" perspective, each moment can be appreciated for its own sake. The features of each event, their relationships, their development—all can be attended to fully as they occur. Apprehending our lives as a temporal whole certainly can *include* living *in* the moments which comprise that whole as they are experienced.

Thus, the opposition between the two "functions" or roles of death is apparent only. And rather than simply compromising their differences, we can actually see the two fitting together as part of one another. A synthesis in which they join at the same time is possible.

* * *

Of the many things we can attend to "in the moment," time itself has a special place. Corresponding to the macroview of life's time as a developing whole is the immediate awareness of passing time. Living as a self-consciously temporal being means attending not only to big changes such as parenthood or retirement, but also to the immediate flux of experience. Moreover, the continuity of this inner flow of experience is a basis for the continuities we seek to effect within the "whole span" of life. The uninterrupted flow of events in our consciousness provides an intuitive understanding of grosser continuities— between work and play, stages of life, and the like.

This lived time is essentially a continuous flow, uninterrupted movement. The passing of time is experienced as the immediate succession of our mind's content, as the different items in consciousness "continuously prolong themselves into one another."[36] Discontinuity is not therefore the baseline or norm in experience. Even gaps or lacunae are *experienced* as part of the same continuous self. ". . . Even where there is a time-gap, the consciousness after it feels as if it belonged together with the consciousness before it, as another part of the same self . . ."[37] On the level of immediate awareness, at least, continuity is the rule. It is "natural" in psychic life.

> There is a succession of states, each of which announces that which follows and contains that which precedes it. . . . In reality no one of them begins or ends, all extend into each other.[38]

Driving south on a highway, I traverse a long banked curve: I turn the wheel, holding its tension taut; the setting sun washes ice-covered cornstalks gold; the road thumps; air hisses by; my body rolls and weight shifts; cornstalks slide past, turning from gold to silver on the curve; I now see fields of silver spread south before me as the sun's warmth moves from my face to neck. All these events proceed continuously in consciousness, bleeding into one another imperceptibly.

Maintaining continuity in experience, however, becomes difficult for us because we mistake *clock* time for this "lived time," this felt duration. While clock time is eminently useful, it introduces cessation into the fluidity of our inner lives. The time we "tell" by clocks is different from the time we experience as the perpetual flow of consciousness. Clock time is without quality, immobile, and homogeneous. Each unit, obviously, is identical with the next because constructed that way. To be useful, all seconds must be the same, all minutes, all hours, and so on. Clock time thereby facilitates comparison between experiences of time passing, different durations in consciousness.

The goal of clock time is "To measure one flux of duration in relation to another."[39] Thus we can say that *this* immediate experience of music flowing took five minutes and thirty-three seconds. We assign a definite number of homogeneous minutes and seconds to *represent* qualitatively different psychic events.

In so representing experience, moreover, we represent what is in continual movement by what is necessarily static. Each unit of clock time, clicking away, is itself immobile. "Five minutes and thirty-three seconds" is actually therefore a collection of static units as reported by a clock. Clocktime is not itself movement, just as snapshots are not movement but stoppages of it: they freeze parts of movement.[40] This is nicely brought home when we look and listen to the flipping-clicking operation of a digital clock in which one moment-number is clearly unconnected to the next.

Substituting clock time for experienced duration as the accurate reflection of reality reverses the real order by taking *rest* as more basic than movement. Taking the static as more fundamental than uninterrupted movement makes discontinuity primary; continuity must then be *achieved*, reintroduced by effort. This might help explain why people in the Twentieth Century, an age dedicated to quantifying events and objects in measured units of time, find it so difficult to attain continuity in life's larger enterprises.

In the last chapter we saw how this tendency to think in terms of static, quantitative units constitutes the calculative method of decision-making. It is instructive to notice the parallel between clock time and calculation (and the correlative parallel between experienced time and dramatic rehearsal). The counterpart of the homogeneous units of clock time are the quantities of units of pleasure and pain different possible experiences have to offer. Abstracting such units from the relations among activities and experiences results in discontinuous living; different regions of our lives, such as family, work, recreation, and friendship become unrelated from within. They do not flow into one another the way our psychic events naturally tend to do. It is this integrated flow, this continuity, that the integrating procedure of dramatic rehearsal corresponds to. Perhaps attending in the moment to the continuous flow in consciousness can give us an intuitive basis for reestablishing continuity in the larger aspects of our lives—the aesthetic of immediacy facilitating the aesthetic deliberations of dramatic rehearsal. This, then, would be a further contribution that the immediate experience of the moment could make to our perspective on life as an aesthetic whole.

Epicurus can be seen as providing a strong argument against worrying about our own death, but also, more broadly, as offering a model for dealing with death more positively. Reflective evaluation of death reveals its decisive place in the time of our lives, a place which it should occupy in that grandest of decisions—how we should live life as a whole. Within the boundaries death demarcates we can envision for ourselves a "narrative history," as McIntyre puts it. While such a grand rehearsal may not be perfectly realized in fact, thinking in these terms surely makes it more likely that our life will take on the semblance of a work of art. Building toward a climax, each stage preparing the way for the next, it may even be consummated as a resolved chord.

Conclusion

I T SEEMS FITTING that a discussion which opens with a presentation of aesthetic education in the classroom conclude with a proposal for the place of death in the aesthetic of our life's time. For this suggests that the conclusion of life also plays a conclusive role in our overall aesthetic education—the education of our thought and emotion as much as our powers of perception. Aesthetic experience functions pedagogically by shaping and giving direction to our distinctively human endowment. Intellect and affect are drawn out and harmonized in the aesthetically formed classroom; habits of imaginative integration are promoted in aesthetic decision-making; and the dispositions to reciprocate and share in risk are developed in aesthetically complete sexuality. Deprived of the sort of education aesthetic experience provides, the individual lacks habits both of self-expression and social interaction.

Aesthetic experience must inform us physically as well as psychologically if we are to be able to express ourselves and interact fruitfully with others. For we are, quite literally, embodied beings, and our habits, attitudes, and thoughts require physical expression. What I have emphasized is their nonlinguistic expression in sexuality, sport, even violence. Through such activities do we extend ourselves into the public world, the world of social relations and the physical environment. In sport, for example, we are recalled to the way time and space condition our everyday, unathletic lives and we see once again how these universal conditions receive human translation into timing and place. Ignoring our fundamental embodiment not only deprives us of the joys of physical rhythm, grace, power, and coordination, but it also threatens our psychological well-being. Thus, ignoring our relation to the physical environment feeds the psychological distortions manifested in ultraviolence. And overlooking the way deep-seated social habits are formed and expressed in sexual behavior jeopardizes our ability to engage others in harmonious, constructive relationships. Aesthetic qualities and relations, more than any others, address us as whole creatures, which is why their absence shows up in fragmented or distorted patterns of thought and action.

The comprehensive purpose of aesthetic education is to foster aesthetic living: a kind of living that requires not just intellectual but aesthetic apprehension for its realization and understanding. Paraphrasing the beginning of William James' "Conclusion" to *Varieties of Religious Experience*, we may say that whatever conclusions we might come to presuppose aesthetic (instead of "spiritual") judgments, appreciations of the significance for life of its aesthetic dimensions, taken "on the whole." And we have seen how aesthetic judgment ranges from the most personal to the most social of matters, from sexual proclivity to the organization of community. While philosophers have long noted the aesthetic significance of the non-art, everyday environment, aesthetic judgment and appreciation have not been liberated from their peripheral positions; they have not been construed as including in their scope the fundamental features of personhood and society.

What I have tried to show is that basic human goods cannot be fully understood or secured independent of aesthetic considerations, and I have tried to show this in a way that is aesthetically convincing. If my characterization of the aesthetic dimensions of everyday experience has not been aesthetically evocative, then this effort must surely seem pointless. Yet an aesthetic appreciation for violence, classroom dynamics, or dramatic decision-making is not enough by itself, because the book does not aim simply to exhibit the aesthetic harbored in such everyday enterprises. It aims to demonstrate how the aesthetic is instrumental for personal, social, even moral values. Thus, aesthetic appreciation must be linked with a variety of other ends and their evaluative meaning. The varieties of aesthetic experience variously nurture a panoply of human values.

The problems of personal development, the individual's relation to others, and participation in community are not new. But the hypothesis advanced here has been that by looking at them in a new way, from an aesthetic promontory, we can see comprehensive reformulations of experience, reformulations that remain hidden when we think strictly within social, moral, political, or educational categories. The aesthetic runs through all of these domains of life and so seems an especially promising entrance into their interstices, interdependencies, and common problems. Because the aesthetic speaks with a radically different voice to the values cultivated in these various domains, it may uncover radically different approaches to their realization.

"Axiology" is the recently coined name for the philosophical study of these several values. It comprehends what have come to be regarded as such separate "fields" as the moral, social, political, economic, and aesthetic. As in so much else in academic philosophy, once divided, these become disparate subjects, provinces with their own expounders, "schools" of thought, and, of course, journals. As I warned at the outset, this book is not a traditional work in aesthetics; in fact, there is an obvious sense in which it is not "in" aesthetics at all. If anything, it is "in" axiology, with aesthetics providing the point of orientation and departure, using aesthetic categories to critique contemporary culture and suggest meliorating possibilities. So, by reflecting on aesthetic features of experience, we gain a clearer understanding of such normative issues as mental health, community, perversion, and violence. In what has preceded, I have tried to overcome that so anti-aesthetic of contemporary trends—compartmentalization—as it is exhibited in axiology itself. Perhaps taking an aesthetic approach in axiological investigations is most appropriate since most conducive to the continuity and crossover so badly needed in our examination of values.

Just as the events of our daily lives—what happens in classrooms, at work, in bedrooms, or on playing fields—should be integrated, so must philosophy itself reestablish connections among its centrifugally hurtling disciplines. While philosophy needs interdependence among the general disciplines of epistemology, metaphysics, and axiology, I will be satisfied if this work has furthered the effort to bring the variety of subdisciplines swarming within value theory face to face. If successful, this book has managed to disclose fundamental intimacies, under the auspices of an aesthetic purview, among the variety of values which make life good.

Notes

1. Educating Aesthetically

1. *Theatetus:* 150 D

2. As Hume puts it, when necessity obtains, we cannot imagine the situation otherwise; the denial of the relationship said to be necessary results in a contradiction. Although Hume formulates the classical argument showing that we cannot perceive necessity, he subsequently tries to explain the concept of necessity in terms of experience. I believe that this attempt to reduce the concept of necessity to purely sense experience leaves a great deal unexplained.

3. Richard Gotschalk, "Thoughts on Growing Up," in *Essays in Metaphysics* (University Park, Pennsylvania: Pennsylvania State University Press, 1970), Carl Vaught, ed., p. 150.

4. Martin Heidegger, *What is A Thing?* (Chicago: Henry Regnery, 1967), W.B. Barton and Vera Deutsch, trans., p. 73.

5. The *Prime of Miss Jean Brodie,* by Muriel Spark, provides an excellent illustration of students merely taking on the thought of their instructor. The romantic thrill of identifying in thought with an admired, beloved individual, however, is radically different from the aesthetic quality of self-giving. In the former, the student loses herself in the teacher's thought; in the latter, the student experiences her own thoughts growing.

6. Even here questioning is central. Not only do questions embody the duality of irony, but stories, as well, are valuable primarily because they raise questions.

7. The giving to ourselves is also a sharing with others in the midst of their similar self-giving. The dialogical form in which this Platonic view of love emerges precludes seeing its working out apart from social interaction.

8. We enjoy "trivia" games in which our esoteric knowledge of places, people, words, events, and the like is tested. But the term carries an unintentional irony since we value our little stores of "trivia" as real knowledge.

9. John Dewey, *Democracy and Education* (New York: Macmillan, 1916), p. 220.

10. Dewey, pp. 142–143.

11. Dewey, pp. 64–65.

12. Dewey elaborates upon this on p. 155.

13. Dewey, p. 223.

14. Dewey, p. 101.

15. During the nineteen-seventies, the term "dialogue" came into vogue among teachers, educators, and the clergy. Engaging in a dialogue was thought to be, or at least sound, better than simply carrying on a conversation. To get clear on the meaning of this term and give some depth to what is sometimes a "pop" use of it would seem to require looking into its Platonic origins.

16. Friedrich Schleiermacher *(Platon's Werke,* p. 16) quoted by Jacob Klein in *A Commentary on Plato's Meno* (Chapel Hill, North Carolina: University of North Carolina Press), p. 7.

17. John Anderson, "On The Platonic Dialogue," in *Essays in Metaphysics,* Vaught, ed., p. 5.

18. Anderson, p. 15.

19. This entwinement is itself food for thought. The student—of the dialogue or in the classroom—can think and talk about how thinking is enmeshed in the particulars of a lived life.

20. In Plato's *Gorgias,* Socrates leads Gorgias, a teacher of rhetoric, into an indirect self-contradiction. Gorgias claims to be able to make his pupils just after denying responsibility for any wrong-doing they may be guilty of. If he is able to make them just, however, he should take responsibility for their injustices in cases where he fails. Why does Gorgias contradict himself? Because Socrates insinuates a larger perspective into Gorgias' thinking: the perspective of the state as a whole. As a whole, the state is endangered by skilled public speakers who are unjust. Temporarily adopting this larger perspective, Gorgias speaks from its concern and claims to make pupils just. This contradicts his earlier, individual perspective—that of someone who can sharpen a particular skill (like a boxing coach) but who wishes to escape blame or the way that skill is misused by the pupil.

21. Irwin Lieb, "Philosophy as Spiritual Formation," *International Philosophical Quarterly,* No. 3, May 1967, p. 277.

22. Bernard Boxill develops this way of conveying what is owed people who have been discriminated against in his essay, "The Morality of Reparation," in Richard Wasserstrom's *Today's Moral Problems* (New York: Macmillan, 1975). He suggests that we think of Jones stealing a bicycle from Smith. Jones then gives the bicycle to his son, although Smith has willed his now-stolen bicycle to *his* son, Tom. After the deaths of Jones and Smith, Tom (read minority, such as black descendants of slaves) still has a right to what has passed into the hands of the son of Jones.

23. Anderson, p. 16.

24. The teacher's role is to remind the students of the form of aesthetic interaction and to call attention to it when realized in the class. It may also be instructive for the teacher to experiment with the extremes so that the students know experientially when they are departing from the ideal. Since we so easily fall into the extremes, however, this may not be necessary; instead, the teacher can ask why the class departs from the ideal and what seems conducive to its achievement.

25. This Individualist view has been espoused by Libertarians such as Robert Nozick as well as Neo-Kantians such as Robert Paul Wolff. They argue from rather opposite conceptions of freedom. The former are essentially natural rights theorists who see the individual as naturally and unequivocally

free to pursue his desire, whatever they be. The latter conceive of morality such that the individual must be free to legislate moral laws according to the light his own reason provides.

26. This conception of synthesis is obviously descended from Hegel's notion of mediation, in which a third conception mediates the relationship between the two in opposition. By introducing a new way of formulating the issue, the third position makes each of the other two understandable. Their relationship is clarified and brought to wholeness through the thinking involved in the third conception. While restricted in Hegel's theory primarily to philosophical thinking, it has a much wider application in the kind of thinking I here present (for which Hegel is not, of course, to be held accountable).

27. This is clearly a Rousseauian proposal, the details of which can be found in *The Social Contract* and commentary by generations of subsequent philo-sophers. It is helpful to note here, however, that Rousseau's proposal requires that each individual be free when he votes on political matters. Practically, this will limit the amount of private wealth or power that may be accumulated. There must, in addition, be unanimous agreement as to the nature and conditions of such voting; these conditions are spelled out in the details of the Social Contract (as a book, and as a conception of the conditions for legitimate state authority).

28. Earlier in this chapter, I discussed the "synthetic" alternative to two tendencies or modes of classroom life: license and constriction. In the former, the students go their merry ways in a parody of spontaneous discussion. In the latter, students mechanically, passively follow what the teacher says. License and constriction are homologous with the anarchy of the Individualists and the totalitarian potential of the Statists.

29. In the aptly named "Missouri Compromise," an American political response to slavery in the early Nineteenth Century, the opposition reappeared when new states sought admission. Two fundamental dichotomies had not been overcome: the one which involved the federal authority's scope; the other which focused on what it is to be human.

30. No doubt the student learns to cooperate with others in other ways as well, e.g., physical or theatrical activities, but my main concern is with speaking together. This seems most uniquely and most centrally the province of classroom life.

31. "Doing the best one can for the work," is a principle in artistic and philosophic interpretation. It is a principle of generosity, directing the interpreter to develop an interpretation of the work of art or philosophy so as to yield the richest aesthetic object or most insightful position, respectively. This is the sort of principle I see at work in the ideal classroom; each student tries to do the best he can for the thought of the others. In this way, none "lose," all gain.

2. An Aesthetic of Contemporary Violence

1. Taken from police reports of the Parma Police Department, Parma, Ohio.

2. United Press International (U.P.I.) story on violence in Europe, London, June 3, 1981.

3. The Australian film, "The Chant of Jimmie Blacksmith," vividly brings home how an aborigine is "educated" beyond his everyday opportunities and possibilities of self-assertion.

4. Herbert Gold, "Let's Kill the First Red-Haired Man We See...," reprinted from *The Magic Will,* by Gold, in *Someone Like Me,* ed. by Sheena Gillespie and Linda Stanley, 2nd ed. (Cambridge: Winthrop Publishers, 1975), p. 182.

5. George Will, "Onward and Upward," *Newsweek,* June 8, 1982, p. 108.

6. John McDermott, *The Culture of Experience* (New York: New York University Press, 1976), p. 168.

7. McDermott, pp. 84–85.

8. Herbert Marcuse, *An Essay on Liberation* (Boston: Beacon Press, 1969), p. 36.

9. J. B. Jackson, "The Imitation of Nature," in *Landscapes,* (Amherst: University of Massachusetts Press, 1970), Ervin Zube, ed., p. 84. Refusing to yield to despair, Jackson provides a counterpoise, claiming that we can still delight in a "conspicuous example of a rich and almost completely satisfactory sensory exprience" offered by New York City's Grand Central Terminal:

He passes through a marvelous sequence; emerging in a dense, slow-moving crowd from the dark, cool, low-ceilinged platform, he suddenly enters the immense concourse with its variety of heights and levels, its spaciousness, its acoustical properties, its diffused light, and the smooth texture of its floor and walls.... Even posture and gait are momentarily improved." (p. 84)

10. Marcuse, p. 29.

11. Jackson, "The Imitation of Nature," p. 85.

12. McDermott, pp. 166–167.

13. In *Participation and Democratic Theory* (London: Cambridge University Press, 1970), Carole Pateman marshals considerable argument and evidence to the effect that the power structure in the workplace has a distinct and profound effect upon the individual's psychology. In particular, opportunity (or its lack) to make occupational decisions feed "the feelings of personal confidence and efficacy that underlie the sense of political efficacy" (p. 51). Conditions conducive to a sense of political efficacy were found in the printing and chemical industries but were absent from automobile and textile industries. See R. Blaunder's *Freedom and Alienation* (Chicago: University of Chicago Press, 1964).

14. See O. Battalia and J. Tarrant, *The Corporate Eunuch* (New York: Mentor, 1974), Ch. 4.

15. Heywood Hale Broun, *Tumultous Merriment* (New York: Richard Manek, 1979), p. 147.

16. Battalia and Tarrant, p. 28.

17. U.P.I. story on violence in Europe cited in Note 2, above.

18. Marshall Mcluhan sees this in reverse. He sees a public as separate individuals (created by the printed word); the "mass" as "individuals profoundly

involved in one another," *(Esthetics Contemporary* (Buffalo: Prometheus, 1978), Richard Kostelanatz, ed., p. 90). I disagree. The mass of individuals may be aware of situations—earthquakes, strikes, assassinations—and even aware that others are aware. But they are not *involved* in one another's lives the way members of a genuine community are. Mass communication encourages transient interests—in the movie star, the politician, the victim—but not enduring relationships.

19. Gold, p. 186.

20. Anthony Burgess, *A Clockwork Orange* (New York: Ballantine, 1962), p. 28.

21. Burgess, p. 15.

22. Ultraviolence is, ultimately, stylized violence. *A Clockwork Orange* reveals this in a striking way. The characters stylize their violence by costuming themselves in masks, eyelashes, and ritual. But there is more. Alex's self-conscious narration in both the film and novel also makes the violence an artistic genre—commented upon with an art critic's attention to detail and nuance. The greatest stylization occurs in the artfulness of the film version. For example, in the gang fight at the empty theatre, Alex and his "droogs" spring, tumble, and fly through the air with their antagonists. Choreographed to "The Thieving Magpie," this episode has the comic appeal of the Keystone Cops, the timing and tempo of a ballet. Later, when Alex and his gang abuse the writer and his wife, the impression of a vaudeville routine is conveyed by soft-shoe "Singin' in the Rain," which is synchronized so that Alex kicks or snips on the word "love."

23. Burgess, pp. 23-24.

24. Vincent Bugliosi (with Curt Gentry), *Helter Skelter* (New York: W. W. Norton, 1974), p. 85.

25. Bugliosi, p. 95.

26. Marcuse, p. 43.

27. The notion of a sensuous layer is nicely developed in David Prall's *Aesthetic Judgment* (New York: Crowell, 1929), Ch. 5.

28. Marcuse, p. 27, here borrows from Nietzsche.

29. Marcuse, p. 27.

30. Jackson, "To Pity the Plumage and Forget the Dying Bird," in *Landscapes*, p. 141.

31. Bugliosi, p. 297.

32. The film version of *A Clockwork Orange* portrays Alex as a lover of Beethoven's more energetic symphonies which feature increasing volumes of sound (with insistent percussion and brass) and crescendoes which build to an intensely overblown climax. This seems to mirror the intensity and scope of the ultraviolent individual's aesthetic desire and behavior. Beethoven fashioned "ultra" symphonies, bringing to a conclusion and going beyond the controlled classical form begun by Haydn and clarified by Mozart.

Their magnitude suggests that Beethoven's symphonies and the sensational payoff of ultraviolence share greater aesthetic affinity with sublimity than with beauty. However, the sublime includes cognitive and self-conscious components lacking in ultraviolence. In experiencing the sublime we are awed by a natural magnitude or force before which we feel insignificant or helpless. Not only is the force the ultraviolent individual experiences his own, but he is not intimidated (as perhaps he should be) by it—as alien and beyond his control.

33. McDermott, p. 135.

34. In the language of "Modern" political philosophers such as Hobbes and especially Rousseau, the ultraviolent society has a government but no sovereign. A sovereign is the effective will wherein the particular wills of all the people are united. Unless the wills of the individuals are united as one, the society has no legitimate political rule; the members of government are simply acting as private parties and have no rights over those they rule. We might put this succinctly by saying that in the ultraviolent society there is social force but no political power.

35. Violence *can* be a public, political response to the destructive use of force. It can be an expression of power. Ultraviolence, however, is a private answer to the force of *devastation* which Heidegger describes in this way: "Destruction only sweeps aside all that has grown up or been built up so far; but devastation blocks all future growth and prevents all building." *What is Called Thinking,* (New York: Harper and Row, 1968) Wieck and Gray, trans., p. 29. A completely "devastated" society in my understanding, would be beyond even violence as a remedy.

36. Marcuse, p. 35.

37. Other indications of cultural loss are the ascendancy of "cheap" art (see the next chapter for a detailed discussion of this) and the degeneration of art into propaganda.

38. See D. R. Grey's article, "Art in the Republic," *Philosophy,* Vol. 27 (1952).

39. This goes beyond the mere negative stipulation which holds that none shall obstruct or interfere with another's pursuit. It extends to the positive "sharing in and furthering of ends." Goals are held in common and each contributes to others' satisfactions.

The difference between merely not interfering with another's interest and positively furthering it reflects Kant's distinction between perfect and imperfect duties toward others. Perfect duties are prohibitions, forbidding harm or interference. Imperfect duties are prescriptions, requiring the performance of actions that do good for others or self). While it is always incumbent upon us to satisfy the demands of perfect duties without exception, imperfect duties require only that we *sometimes* further the ends of other people. This notion of furthering others' interests is also part of Kant's understanding of treating others with respect. Kant calls this treating people as "ends-in-themselves." It means that we regard people as originators of ends and goals, and not merely as instruments to be used to satisfy our ends. See Kant's *Foundations of a Metaphysics of Morals,* or his *Critique of Practical Reason,* for his more complete discussion.

40. Yet the reverse also holds: The aesthetics of the environment can determine the degree to which a people have the opportunity to engage in political life in the first place. As J. B. Jackson notes, "An environment is impoverished when its inhabitants cannot come together easily and agreeably, and when there are no suitable places of public assembly." ("To Pity the Plumage . . .", p. 142). Thus, the anti-aesthetic strucure of the roads, land use,

and town centers can "handicap" the very political processes through which agency is achieved.

3. Aesthetic Experience As Moral Education

1. My indebtedness to the thought of Kant and Dewey is too pervasive to specify at every turn.

2. In a certain sense, aesthetic experience *is* necessary for moral education. We must become habituated in the *formal relations* (which define the aesthetic object and our relation to it) in *some* way in order to develop morally.

3. The extremes of petering out and premature constriction occur, respectively, as events in the licentious and in the constricted classroom, discussed in Chapter I, Section 3.B.

4. This is Kant's insight. See Chapter V, on Sport, Section 3, for a more extended treatment, in particular as it is connected with the notion of purpose and the purposelessness of aesthetic objects.

5. John Dewey, *Art as Experience* (New York: Capricorn, 1934), p. 18. The union of past and future in the present is addressed on the larger scale of our whole lives in the concluding chapter on "Death and the Time of Our Lives."

6. Dewey, *Art as Experience,* p. 310.

7. Dewey, *Art as Experience,* p. 314.

8. Dewey, *Art as Experience,* p. 42.

9. John Dewey, *Democracy and Education* (New York: Free Press Macmillan, 1966), p. 15.

10. This claim will be developed and extended in the next chapter to include other dispositions, when we consider the far-reaching effects of sexual conduct on habit formation.

11. Iris Murdoch, *The Sovereignty of Good* (New York: Schocken, 1971), p. 65.

12. Murdoch, p. 31.

13. Murdoch, p. 41.

14. Marcia Cavell, "Taste and Moral Sense," *Journal of Aesthetics and Art Criticism,* Vol. 34, No. 1 (Fall 1975), p. 30.

15. Arnold Isenberg discusses the concept of critic as teacher with insight and sensitivity in "Critical Communication," *The Philosophical Review,* Vol. 58, (July 1949), pp. 330–344.

16. Paul Ziff, "Reasons in Art Criticism," in *Philosophy and Education* (Boston: Allyn and Bacon, 1958), Israel Scheffler, ed., pp. 219–236.

17. Abraham Kaplan, "The Aesthetics of the Popular Arts," in *Modern Culture and the Arts* (New York: McGraw-Hill, 1967), James Hall and Barry Ulanov, eds., p. 67, reprinted from *Journal of Aesthetics* (Spring 1966).

18. Kaplan, p. 68.

19. Kaplan, p. 72.

20. Murdoch, p. 86.

21. Murdoch, p. 85.

22. R. G. Collingwood, *The Principles of Art* (London: Oxford University Press, 1938), p. 95; see also sections of Chapter V. Kaplan has similar things to say with regard to boredom.

4. Sexuality: Good, Deficient, and Perverse

1. As if to emphasize how "kinky" sex has come aboveground, *Newsweek* (March 2, 1981) ran a story on these "erotica" parties, and Phil Donahue hosted sex sales personnel as well as male striptease artists in the spring of 1981.

2. Gagnon and Simon, *Sexual Conduct: The Social Sources of Human Sexuality* (Chicago: Aldine, 1973), p. 6.

3. Daniel Day Williams, *The Spirit and the Forms of Love* (New York: Harper and Row, 1968), p. 220.

4. Thomas Nagel, "Sexual Perversion," in *Moral Problems,* 1st ed. (New York: Harper and Row, 1971), Jame Rachels, ed., p. 77.

5. By the same token, masturbation is perverse but is not usually or generally perverting. It is perverse in the way voyeurism is, viz. it isolates the individual from others and in *itself* is a force for withdrawal and solitary sexuality. Its danger eclipses the jeopardizing of the particular social habits we are considering (responsivity, risk-taking, and reciprocity). It segregates the individual from others in general, negatively encompassing these particular habits by excluding others from one's sexual activity.

Yet masturbation is not usually perverting, and for the same reason that casual voyeurism also is not: It is but a component in a larger sexual life. Often it runs parallel to a more or less healthy social sexuality. As one man puts it, he has two sex lives, one with his wife and one with himself (Nancy Friday's *Men in Love* (N.Y.: Dell, 1980). It seems fair to say, however, that sex in which masturbation is exclusive or predominant should turn out to be perverting.

6. Isadore Rubin, "What Should Parents Do About Pornography?" in *Sex in the Adolescent Years* (New York: Association Press, 1968), Isadore Rubin and Lester Kirkendall, eds. p. 202.

7. G. L. Simons, "Is Pornography Beneficial?", in *Social Ethics* (New York: McGraw-Hill, 1977), Thomas A. Mappes and Jane S. Zembaty, eds., p. 246.

8. Nagel, pp. 79–80 (my italics).

9. Erich Goode and Richard Troiden, eds., *Sexual Deviance and Sexual Deviants* (New York: William Morrow, 1974), p. 1 (my italics).

10. C. S. Lewis, *The Four Loves* (New York: Harvest, 1960), p. 139.

11. C. S. Lewis, p. 143.

12. Eustace Chesser, *The Human Aspects of Social Deviation* (London: Jarrolds, 1971), p. 236.

13. Quoted in John M. MacDonald, *Indecent Exposure* (Springfield, Ill.: Thomas, 1973), p. 108.

14. MacDonald, p. 154.

15. Chesser, p. 236.

16. W. Stekel, *Patterns of Psychosexual Infantilism* (New York: Liveright, 1957), quoted in MacDonald, p. 93.

17. Goode and Troiden, p. 158.

18. Sara Ruddick, "On Sexual Morality," in Rachels's *Moral Problems,* pp. 84–105.

19. Nagel provides a recursively complex illustration of what he means, with his Romeo and Juliet sexual scenario.

So Romeo senses Juliet, rather than merely noticing her [that is, he regards her with sexual desire]. . . . Let us suppose, however, that Juliet now senses Romeo . . . [and] he notices, and moreover senses, Juliet sensing him. . . . But there is a further step. Let us suppose that Juliet, who is a little slower than Romeo, now senses that he senses her. This puts Romeo in a position to notice, and be aroused by, her arousal at being sensed by him. *He senses that she senses that he senses her* (pp. 76–77).

20. See Robert Solomon, "Sexual Paradigms," *Journal of Philosophy* (June 13, 1974), for a vigorous articulation of the communication view of healthy versus perverse sexuality.

21. Solomon, p. 526. If Solomon means that all excessive expression as such is perverse, then he is surely given difficulty by such benign but strong emotions as tenderness and trust. On the other hand, if he means that excessive expression of dominance and submission are, in particular, perverse, then he must provide a more extensive account. My suggestion, of course, is that what is perverse about their expression is the "excessiveness" of the behavior, the expression, rather than the emotion itself.

22. C. I. Lewis, *Analysis of Knowledge and Valuation* (LaSalle, Ill.: Open Court, 1946), p. 453.

23. Chesser (p. 120) offers an example of a fetish developing out of a creative response to a repressive society and a stifling situation. He quotes the Chevalier d'Eon de Beaumont speaking of the Countess of Rochefort: "'The very thought of putting on the Countess' dress, of feeling on my skin a garment that had covered the bosom of this adorable woman, and whose material had touched her beautiful body, filled me with indescribable happiness. . . . It was going to intoxicate me. . . !'"

24. John McDermott, *The Culture of Experience* (New York: New York University Press, 1976), p. 27.

25. See Gabrielle Brown's *The New Celibacy* (New York: McGraw-Hill, 1980).

26. McDermott, p. 110.

27. John Dewey, *Art as Experience* (New York: Capricorn, 1934), p. 10.

28. Chesser, p. 41.

29. Chesser, p. 69.

30. Chesser, p. 51 (my italics).

31. Goode and Troiden, p. 360.

5. Sport—The Body Electric

1. *New York Times*, March 8, 1981.

2. Ron Powers, *Toot-Toot-Tootsie, Good-Bye* (New York: Delacorte Press, 1981), p. 112.

3. Frederick Exley, *A Fan's Notes* (New York: Simon and Shuster, 1977), p. 231.

4. Heywood Hale Broun, *Tumultuous Merriment* (New York: Richard Manek, 1979), p. 20.

5. This is, of course, subject to a mild qualification. Variations in conditions such as a "following wind" in track do make a difference to performance and are taken into account.

6. A boyhood friend of mine actually gave up watching sports in favor of poring over their epiphenomena—statistics. The numerical results became

more fascinating than the events which produced them.

7. David Best, *Philosophy and Human Movement* (London: Allen and Unwin, 1978), p. 110.

8. Broun, p. 80.

9. John McDermott, *The Culture of Experience* (New York: New York University Press, 1976), pp. 166–167.

10. Although games, golf and bowling are really individual sports, since no opponent is necessary for their play; where present, the opponent plays *beside* rather than against or with another. They also seem to be more emphatically numerical than competitive game sports, counting the number of strokes or pins being more essential to the play of the game.

11. My thanks for this go to Professor Melvin Rader, who was kind enough to comment on an earlier draft of this chapter.

12. David Best, "The Aesthetic in Sport," *British Journal of Aesthetics*, Vol. 14, No. 3 (Summer 1976), p. 199.

13. The question of purposefulness is clarified by the Kantian distinction between purpose and purposivity. Art is purposive but not purposeful. This means that it displays those properties such as we find in objects which exist in order to serve an external purpose, but it does not in fact serve any such purpose. The unity of art works does not derive from something external to themselves, i.e., a function, as does, say, a telephone or car. Although a work of art does not exist in order to serve some external end, it may contain within itself aims or purposes, as for example literary works in which the narrator or characters act or speak in order to attain some end. The purely purposive then may include purposes within it without as a whole being subservient to an extrinsic purpose or end. Sport is like art in being purposive but without external purpose. We engage in the activity or its viewing for its own sake.

14. Paul Ziff, "A Fine Forehand," *Journal of the Philosophy of Sport*, Vol. 1 (September 1974). Ziff seems to view performance in some sports, including the competitive, as "counting," i.e., important only with regard to scoring. He maintains that form matters (as a "grading factor") *only* in the qualitative, formal sports. He writes that ". . . if one manages somehow to sink the ball expeditiously enough one may end up a champion" (p. 101). He is obviously viewing sporting events only with a concern for their outcome, with a "professional" attitude, for he continues: "It is not looks but points that win a tennis match" (p. 104). My question for Ziff is: But is it points that make a tennis match good or worth watching?

15. Bill Russell (with Taylor Branch), *Second Wind: The Memoirs of an Opinionated Man* (New York: Random House, 1979), p. 157.

16. John Dewey, *Experience and Nature* (New York: Dover, 1958), p. 370.

17. Dewey, p. 397.

18. What counts as a particular stingy or luxurious game is, of course, relative to the nature of the sport; thus, an 8–6 score in professional hockey is heavy with scoring, while a 75–70 score in professional basketball is a very tight contest.

19. A. J. Liebling, *The Sweet Science* (New York: Viking Press, 1956), p. 97.

20. Russell, pp. 155–156.

21. Russell, p. 156. Note here how scoring contributes yet is subordinated to the game's *aesthetic* qualities.

22. For a more detailed account of cooperation inherent in competition and the role of suspense in sports, see Warren Fraleigh's "On Weiss on Records and on the Significance of Athletic Records," *Philosophic Exchange*, Vol. 1, No. 3, (Summer, 1972), pp. 105–111, and E. F. Kaelin's "The Well-Played Game: Notes toward an Aesthetics of Sport," *Quest*, No. 10 (May 1968), pp. 16–28.

23. Broun, p. 155.

24. Powers, p. 224.

25. New York Times News Service, May 21, 1981.

26. Powers, p. 224.

27. Exley, pp. 348–349.

28. Broun, pp. 118–119.

29. Jerome Stolnitz, "The Aesthetic Attitude," *Introductory Readings in Aesthetics* (New York: Free Press, 1969), John Hospers, ed., p. 20.

30. Paul Ziff, "Reasons in Art Criticism," *Philosophy Looks at the Arts* (New York: Scribner's 1962), Joseph Margolis, ed., p. 176.

31. See Roger Angell's *The Summer Game* (New York: Popular Library, (1978). Powers suggests, in *Toot-Toot-Tootsie, Good-Bye*, that there are also aesthetic aspects of a ballpark's relation to its urban context:

He'd come up in the days of the great old upright neighborhood ballparks—Ebbets Field, the Polo Grounds, old Sportsman's Park, Crosley Field—the old square-bottom parks that were ... fitted like tiles into the existing mosaic of the city ... and settling, over the decades, into the stew of summer urban life. . . . (p. 7).

32. Defending baseball's pace, Broun remarks:

That very slowness of which some fans complain is twisting the nerves of players [and fans] as they seem endlessly to contemplate the possibilities of triumph, defeat, or disgrace that are possible with every pitch. . . . The beautiful balances of the game produce a sawtooth of success and failure. (p. 77)

33. This must, of course, be qualified, since a sport *could* be rejected totally as too meager in aesthetic dividends. But we must be especially wary of implying in such wholesale dismissal that it is the structure of the sporting activity that is responsible for our aesthetic dissatisfaction. As with the rejection of a kind of music or style of painting, the fault may lie more with the audience than the object of apprehension.

34. John McPhee quoting Bill Bradley (former star player for Princeton and the New York Knickerbockers) in *A Sense of Where You Are* (New York: Farrar, Strauss, and Giroux, 1965), p. 75.

35. The closing of his career intensified the competitive horizon Bill Russell felt in playing against Wilt Chamberlain.

. . . I was acutely aware that my career was ending, and I wanted to leave on a high. . . . I was offended the instant Wilt left the game. I didn't think he'd been hurt that badly, and even if he was, I wanted him in there. We were close—so close—to finishing with a great game . . . I thought to myself. "This is my last game. Make me earn it. Come on out here."

36. *Black Music* (New York: Morrow, 1968), pp. 58–59.
37. Russell, p. 156.

6. The Drama of Decision Making

1. While this whole book is animated by Dewey's conception of the vocation of philosophy and draws upon various of his views, this chapter is more directly an explication of one of them. The contrast between dramatic rehearsal and calculation is Dewey's. Aside from elaborating and clarifying the difference between these two ways of arriving at decisions, my contribution lies in seeing aesthetic experience as the ideal standard by which to evaluate our dramatic rehearsals. Seeing aesthetic experience as providing the form by which to decide *about* our decision-making itself completes the discussion begun by Dewey.

2. The problems would be comparable, if not identical, for any other interpretation or translation of plus/minus, cost/benefit, credit/debit.

3. The difficulties become still more interesting when the situation involves someone who has had little or no pleasure for a rather long time. Such a person might very well be willing to pay the price of *great* pain for a sizable portion of pleasure rather than settle for *less* pleasure on the basis of *either* net gain *or* proportional gain. The individual's past and present *circumstances* call both the simple subtraction and the ratio criteria into question.

4. Alasdair MacIntyre, *After Virtue* (Notre Dame, Indiana: University of Notre Dame Press, 1981), p. 62.

5. John Dewey, *Human Nature and Conduct* (New York: Modern Library, 1957), p. 190.

6. John Dewey, *Democracy and Education* (New York: The Free Press, 1916), p. 245.

7. Dewey, *Democracy and Education*, p. 247.

8. See Section 1.A., above, for why the appearance of providing a common denominator is misleading.

9. MacIntyre, p. 190. MacIntyre deals incisively with the unity of human life from an ethical viewpoint, in particular, with regard to the role the virtues play in constituting such a life. It is important to notice in his account, however, the aesthetic form such unity takes: It is the unity found in a "narrative history"—whether of a real or a fictional or a quasi-fictional *character*. See especially Chapters 10 and 15 for his creative integration of the aesthetic and the ethical, the narrative form of life and the role of the virtues.

10. This seems to me to be a legacy of DesCartes' philosophy. He transferred his mathematical method of knowing to his metaphysics with the result that what could not be quantified simply was not "real" or objective. These "leftovers" (such as color, odor, emotion) were then relegated to the perceiving subject and labelled "subjective" in contrast to the "objective" quantities (such as length, weight, and the like).

11. *The Writings of William James* (New York: Random House, 1968), John McDermott, ed., p. 10.

12. James, p. 17.

13. James characterizes the neurological process of habituation in this way: "...a new pathway of discharge formed in the brain, by which certain incoming currents ever after tend to escape." (p. 9)

14. James, p. 20.

15. Dewey notes that, "We judge present desires and habits by their tendency to produce certain consequences. . . . And so we know what is the tendency of malice, charity, conceit, patience." *Human Nature and Conduct*, p. 206. He might have gone on to list less morally loaded habits such as neatness, assertiveness, or joviality. But whatever the kind of habit, we *learn* of its tendencies by observing ourselves and others. Intelligent decision-making draws upon these observations, and post-decision observations should help us understand the adequacies and deficiencies of the decision.

16. John Dewey, *Human Nature and Conduct*, p. 208.

17. John Dewey, *Human Nature and Conduct*, p. 207.

18. Works of art that appear simple, such as Blues music, often turn out to be complex. Their complexity may lie in the range of emotions at work, the depth of meaning, or the connections among lyrics, music, and thought. The point is that there are any number of ways in which an art work may be complex, some of which are not readily noticed in our appreciation.

19. For a more complete discussion of the nonpractical nature of aesthetic experience, see Chapter III on Moral Education, especially Section 2. In addition, the "object" formed as a result of the individual's activity is not brought under a concept; it is not a "thing" like a tree, car, or hammer. This notion of a formed whole without a definite concept also bears on the question of "purpose" and is discussed in Chapter V, on Sport, Section 3.

20. The way in which art short-circuits our freedom by telling rather than showing, by reliance on formula rather than invention is discussed at length in Chapter III, on Moral Education, Section 5 (Cheap Art).

21. This notion of integrating diverse, even opposing, habits is elaborated upon below in connection with freedom.

22. Otherwise, one would choose poorly in the future and be stultified—unless, of course, luck came to one's aid. Since the purpose of deliberation, however, is to do the best we can by our own lights, luck as such can never be a relevant consideration in making decisions; we can *always* say, "Well, maybe we'll get lucky!"

23. "Habits reduce themselves to routine ways of acting, or degenerate into ways of action to which we are enslaved just in the degree in which intelligence is disconnected from them. Routine habits are unthinking habits . . . which put an end to plasticity." *Democracy and Education*, p. 49, and elsewhere in Chapter 4.

24. John Dewey, *Democracy and Education*, p. 45.

25. John Dewey, *Democracy and Education*, p. 45. For a discussion of when and why this transference of learning from one situation to another does *not* occur, see Section 2 in Chapter I on Educating Aesthetically. In discussing the teaching of technical skills, the point is made that the skill can remain bound to the "situation of acquisition." This means that the skill has not been connected with other habits and knowledge, and is good only for a specialized, narrow set of tasks.

26. Our future will be filled with particular events, objects, problems, and demands on us which are all but impossible to foresee in detail. We cannot, therefore, very well prepare for them by laying a myriad of specific contingency plans. Rather, we best prepare for the uncertainties of the future by developing habits varied and numerous enough to allow us to respond to a wide range of contingencies. An especially important subset of such habits are those which enable intelligent decision-making. For when the future materializes in its particularity, we then *will* be faced with particular choices.

27. It can, of course, be applied exclusively to others: will sending my child to boarding school tend to satisfy the criteria which compose the aesthetic ideal? But here I prefer to consider the decision-maker as part of the interpersonal relationship.

7. Death and the Time of Our Lives

1. Epicurus, "Letter to Menoeceus" (125), in *Letters, Principal Doctrines, and Vatican Sayings* (Indianapolis: Bobbs-Merrill, 1964), Russell Geer, ed., p. 54.

2. I have named Epicurus' Catch after the "Catch" in Joseph Heller's novel, *Catch-22*. Like it, Epicurus' Catch concerning death exposes as something illusory what is commonly taken for granted. Heller's Catch in one (or part) of its protean forms, goes something like this: (a) one can obtain a discharge from the United States Air Force if certified as insane; (b) one can be certified as insane *only if* one requests an examination; but (c) requesting an examination is conclusive evidence that one is not insane. The result is that it is not practically possible to obtain a discharge from the Air Force on the basis of being certified as insane. The Air Force regulations provide the illusion that such a discharge is possible, an illusion which disappears once the complete nature of the regulations is grasped. Similarly, ordinary language fosters the illusion that death is bad for the one who dies—an illusion that is dispelled once the temporal nature of existence is noticed.

3. This is a "de-hedonized" version of Epicurus' argument, i.e., it abstracts from Epicurus' hedonistic claim that the good is pleasure and evil is pain. Including his hedonism would add premise (1'): The only evil is pain; and conclusion (4'): When dead, one experiences no pain. I have de-hedonized the argument by leaving "evil" or "bad" uninterpreted. For if Epicurus' argument holds for any interpretation of "evil," then it is stronger than as a strictly hedonistic formulation; it becomes a formal argument, independent of the specific content we give to "evil."

4. Epicurus (125), p. 54.

5. While the force of the Catch by now should be apparent to readers, contemporary philosophers have nevertheless been caught on the Catch. Two recent articles on the subject of death in *Moral Problems* (New York: Harper and Row, 1971), edited by James Rachels, unsuccessfully try to evade the implication of Epicurus' Catch. Thomas Nagel attempts to do so without mention of Epicurus, while Mary Mothersill does so with explicit discussion of his argument. Both endeavors are seriously flawed, although for different reasons. Nagel attempts to reason from the analogy between Jones' death and Jones'

regression to the mentality of a three-month-old baby following a head injury. This approach fails because "Jones" has ceased to exist, has lost his personal identity, once reduced to the state of a three-month-old baby (Nagel himself admits as much, p. 366). Mothersill fails by committing a *petitio*—the fallacy of begging the question. She *assumes* that death is "injurious" and therefore that it is rational to fear it, but in no way demonstrates how to overcome the obstacle posed by Epicurus' Catch.

6. Leo Tolsty, *The Death of Ivan Ilych* (New York: Signet, 1960), pp. 131–132.

7. Martin Heidegger, *Being and Time* (New York: Harper and Row, 1962), John Macquarrie and Edward Robinson, trans., p. 240.

8. Jean-Paul Sartre, *Being and Nothingness* (New York: Philosophical Library, 1956), Hazel Barne, trans., p. 535.

9. The persistence of this "spectator imaging" is cited by Walter Kaufmann, "Existentialism and Death," in *The Meaning of Death* (New York: McGraw-Hill, 1959), Herman Feifel, ed., p. 48.

10. Walker Percy, *The Second Coming* (New York: Farrar, Straus, and Giroux, 1980), p. 124.

11. In *The Death of Ivan Ilych,* Ivan's confrontation with his death forces him to face the moral question: "Have I lived as I should have?" The quick and easy answer—"But of course, since I have always lived 'properly'"—cannot stop his torment, evidence of the inadequacy of the first response. The imminence of death forces the moral question to resurface, until Ivan sees that conforming to conventional expectations, living decorously, with propriety, is not equivalent to living as one ought.

12. See John Dewey's *Art as Experience* (New York: Capricorn, 1934), Chapters 3 and 4.

13. Kaufmann, p. 59.

14. See Frederick Hoffman's "Mortality and Modern Literature," in Feifel's *The Meaning of Death,* for an insightful discussion of space and light as symbols of immortality in modern literature.

15. Sartre, p. 545.

16. Sartre, p. 537.

17. Sartre, p. 537.

18. Alisdair MacIntyre, *After Virtue* (Notre Dame, Indiana: Notre Dame University Press, 1981), p. 202.

19. Saul Bellow, *Mr. Sammler's Planet* (Greenwich, Conn.: Fawcett Crest, 1969), p. 69.

20. MacIntyre, p. 190.

21. Bernard Lonergan has a rather unproblematic view of old age: "…old age, when perforce the self becomes selfless as the field of enjoyment contracts to joy in the enjoyment of others, in the romping vitality of grandchildren." *Collection: Papers by Bernard Lonergan* (New York: Herder and Herder, 1967), p. 37. What Lonergan sees as "perforce," a natural occurrence, by no means seems to be the case in the real world. Many older people, feeling their time running short, become more and more self-centered and selfish, while others justifiably remain professionally or avocationally active. In both sorts of case, the field of enjoyment has not become vicarious.

22. Ted Rosenthal, *How Could I Not Be Among You?* (New York: George

Braziller, 1973), p. 44. This is the personal as well as poetic account of the experience of a 30-year-old leukemia patient. With lyrical detail and philosophical insight, it describes his responses to death during the course of his fatal disease.

23. Rosenthal, p. 24.

24. Rosenthal, p. 77.

25. Rosenthal, p. 46.

26. Martha W. Lear, Heartsounds (New York: Simon and Schuster, 1980), p. 289.

27. Sitting Zen (Zazen) aims to calm and simplify the mind. The resulting "stillness" is nothing more than attention to present experience. "The way to practice without having any goal is . . . to be concentrated on what you are doing in this moment . . ., then you can express fully your true nature. . . ." (Shunryu Suzuki, Zen Mind, Beginners Mind (New York: Walker-Weatherhill, 1970), p. 71) "Emptied" of preconceptions or anything else that will get in the way of noticing whatever is before it, the mind can clearly pay attention. Zen practice aims at attending to everything, equally. When that attention includes the events we take for the self, the ego, we are freed of the illusion or attachments of selfishness. For then these events have but the status of all other passing events—still worthy of attention but not special. Since not special, we are freed of clinging and repelling, desire and fear.

Conceptual-linguistic frameworks easily obstruct us from simply seeing, feeling, hearing whatever we come into contact with. With enough practice at fully attending, we are able to notice our use of concepts itself. Thus, it would be a mistake to say that Zen is opposed to the use of concepts. They are useful and necessary in daily pursuits. But being aware of how we are employing concepts is one thing, and being trapped in them so that we fail to attend to their employment is quite another.

28. Annie Dillard, Pilgrim at Tinker Creek (New York: Bantam, 1974), p. 82.

29. Hoffman, p. 136.

30. Hoffman, p. 137.

31. Note how this contrasts with its opposite-belief in uninterrupted, infinite life. There, a sense of airy lightness leaves the individual with no sense of urgency, much less desperation. In between fear and denial (by means of belief in immortality) lies acceptance of death as "mine." Consequently, it yields a mean position between the extremes of constriction and airy boundlessness, viz. structure, order, and form.

32. Rosenthal, p. 47. The experiential "proof" that the pronouncement of the nearness of death is of singular importance in this liberation from self-absorption is found in the "loss" felt when Ted Rosenthal learns that it may be postponed—the pain of the reprieve: "And as soon as I was told that I had a chance of surviving, this [freedom] just went crashing to the ground" (p. 52).

33. Iris Murdoch, The Sovereignty of Good (London: Routledge and Kegan Paul, 1970), p. 103.

34. James Agee, A Death in the Family (New York: Avon, 1959), pp. 12–13.

35. See the discussion of compromise and synthesis (Section 3.C) in the opening chapter on Educating Aesthetically for an examination of the superiority of synthesis over compromise.

36. Henri Bergson, An Introduction to Metaphysics (New York: Liberal Arts Press, 1949), T. E. Hulme, trans., p. 30.

37. *The Writings of William James* (New York: Random House, 1968), John McDermott, ed., p. 31.

38. Bergson, p. 25. Bergson observes that "without this survival of the past into the present there would be no duration, but only instantaneity" (p. 40).

39. Bergson, p. 41.

40. This is so, of course, no matter how finely we subdivide our units of clock time; microseconds, milli-microseconds, etc. We are still subdividing unmoving quantities.

Index

Abstraction, 49, 112; and death, 173; and intellectual principles, 12; quantification, 48, 115, 118, 122-23, 145, 167; and sexuality, 92; and time, 188; and value, 148-49

Aesthetic: appreciation, 37, 52-54, 58, 78-79, 83, 112-38 passim, 175-92 passim, 205 n. 31, n. 32; attention, 170, 182-84; completeness, 68, 169, 177-80; deprivation, 2, 5, 55-56; enhancement of the everyday, 86, 112-13, 127-32, 175-76, 183-85; extremes in departures from, 29-31, 44, 49, 69, 83, 94-105 passim, 127, 201 n. 3, 210 n. 31; ideal form of, 157-67; judgment, 117-18; need(s), 56, 61, 68-71, 75-85 passim, 99; richness, 16, 81, 95, 125, 127; unity, 169-70, 177-82, 186; unity of life, 29

Agee, James, 185

Agency, 44-45, 48-52, 198 n.13, 200 n.34, n.39, n.40; and aesthetic experience, 76; and death, 182; development of, 161-63; and environment, 57, 62; force as content of, 59; in learning, 19, 25-26, 29; and powerlessness, 43, 54, 59; and reason, 28; in sexual behavior, 97-100, 107; situation of, 27; society's, 60; in sports, 137; and violence, 42. *See also* Self

Aisthesis: as a quality of experience, 7; isolation of, 57; in learning, 13, 18, 25; and limits, 59; in violence, 52, 55; of wonder, 14

Aristotle: on habituation, 91

Art, 1, 2, 100, 204 n.13; composition of, 159; criticism, 78, 80; and emotion, 83-86; form in, 82, 139, 157; and human development, 82; and improvisation, 127; instrumental value of, 83; integration of, 159; life as, 178-79, 189; meaning in, 148; modern, 108; and politics, 60-62; work(s) of, 68-72, 79, 167, 207 n.18

Bellow, Saul, 181

Bergson, Henri, 187, 211 n.38

Broun, Heywood Hale, 48, 127, 133, 205

Burgess, Anthony, 52-53, 199 n.22, n.32

Capacities of interaction, 88

Cavell, Marcia, 78-79

Chesser, Eustace, 100-101, 109, 203 n.23

Climax. *See* Consummation

Clockwork Orange, A, 52-53, 199 n.22, n.32

Collingwood, R. G., 85

Community, 4-5, 45; structure of aesthetic object, 70-73, 77-78; habits of, 81; of inquiry, 32, 37; and meaning, 75; and private ends, 64; social, 74-75

Completeness: of aesthetic object, 70; of community, 74; in social relations, 91

Comprehensive: development of aesthetic object, 69; thinking, 5, 32-36

Conflict in learning, 33

Consummation, 6, 19, 90, 127; in aesthetic object, 69; in community relations, 74; in everyday experiences, 175; in learning, 18, 23-24; of life as a whole, 169, 177-78, 189; and play, 123, 139; in sports, 131

Continuity: 6, 142; in action, 161; in aesthetic object, 68; in decision-making, 150; in everyday life, 181, 186-88; generational, 63; in philosophy, 193; in physical movement, 138

WESTMAR COLLEGE LIBRARY